The Baby and the Cc

The Baby and the Couple provides an insider's view on how infant communication develops in the context of the family and how parents either work together as a team or struggle in the process. The authors present vignettes from everyday life as well as case studies from a longitudinal research project of infants and their parents interacting together in the Lausanne Trilogue Play (LTP), an assessment tool for very young families.

Divided into three sections, the book focuses not only on the parents but also on the infant's contribution to the family. Section I presents a case study of Lucas and his family, from infancy to age 5. With each chapter we see how, in the context of their families, infants learn to communicate with more than one person at a time. Section II explores how infants cope when their parents struggle to work together – excluding, competing, or only connecting through their child. The authors follow several case examples from infancy through to early childhood to illustrate various forms of problematic coparenting, along with the infant's derailed trajectory at different ages and stages. In Section III, prevention and intervention models based on the LTP are presented. In addition to an overview of these programs, chapters are devoted to the Developmental Systems Consultation, which combines use of the LTP and video feedback, and a new model, Reflective Family Play, which allows whole families to engage in treatment.

The Baby and the Couple is a vital resource for professionals working in the fields of infant and preschool mental health, including psychiatrists, psychologists, social workers, family therapists, and educators, as well as researchers.

Elisabeth Fivaz-Depeursinge is a former professor of clinical ethology at the University of Lausanne School of Medicine, where she was president of the Centre for Family Studies and head of its research department. She was a practicing child analyst and family therapist before moving into clinical research.

Diane A. Philipp is an assistant professor in the Department of Psychiatry at the University of Toronto Medical School and a member of the faculty at the Hincks-Dellcrest Centre, where she is part of the infant and preschool assessment and treatment team.

The Baby and the Couple

Understanding and treating young families

Elisabeth Fivaz-Depeursinge
and Diane A. Philipp

Routledge
Taylor & Francis Group

LONDON AND NEW YORK

First published 2014
by Routledge
27 Church Road, Hove, East Sussex, BN3 2FA

and by Routledge
711 Third Avenue, New York, NY 10017

*Routledge is an imprint of the Taylor & Francis Group,
an informa business*

British Library Cataloguing in Publication Data

A catalogue record for this book is available from the British
Library

Library of Congress Cataloging-in-Publication Data

Fivaz-Depeursinge, Elisabeth.
The baby and the couple : understanding and treating young
 families / Elisabeth Fivaz-Depeursinge and Diane Philipp.
  pages cm
 1. Parent and infant. 2. Infants. 3. Infant psychology.
I. Philipp, Diane. II. Title.
 BF720.P37.F58 2014
 155.42'2—dc23
 2013047752

ISBN: 978-0-415-84495-6 (hbk)
ISBN: 978-0-415-84496-3 (pbk)
ISBN: 978-1-315-77977-5 (ebk)

Typeset in Times New Roman
by Apex CoVantage, LLC

MIX
Paper from
responsible sources
FSC   FSC® C013056
www.fsc.org

Printed and bound in Great Britain by
TJ International Ltd, Padstow, Cornwall

To Alexiane and Zoélie, who joined us at the outset of this writing
To the memory of Daniel Stern, who left us by the end of this writing
– E.F-D.

To the family of my childhood – Rudy, Eva, and Ronnie
To the family of my motherhood – Rob, Aviva, Aaron, and Noah
– D.A.P.

Contents

Contributors

Sarah Cairo, Department of Psychology, Faculty of Psychology and Educational Sciences, University of Geneva

Antoinette Corboz-Warnery, Research Unit of the Centre for Family Studies (UR-CEF), University Institute of Psychotherapy (IUP), DP-CHUV, Lausanne University, Switzerland

Joëlle Darwiche, Institute of Psychology, Faculty of Social and Political Sciences, University of Lausanne, Switzerland

Nicolas Favez, Department of Psychology, Faculty of Psychology and Educational Sciences, University of Geneva and Research Unit of the Centre for Family Studies (UR-CEF), University Institute of Psychotherapy (IUP), DP-CHUV, Lausanne University, Switzerland

Elisabeth Fivaz-Depeursinge, Research Unit of the Centre for Family Studies (UR-CEF), University Institute of Psychotherapy (IUP), DP-CHUV, Lausanne University, Switzerland

France Frascarolo-Moutinot, Research Unit of the Centre for Family Studies (UR-CEF), University Institute of Psychotherapy (IUP), DP-CHUV, Lausanne University, Switzerland

Christie Hayos, Hincks-Dellcrest Centre & University of Toronto, Canada

Miri Keren, Geha Mental Health Center, Tel-Aviv University, Israel

Chloé Lavanchy Scaiola, Research Unit of the Centre for Family Studies (UR-CEF), University Institute of Psychotherapy (IUP), DP-CHUV, Lausanne University, Switzerland

Francesco Lopes, Research Unit of the Centre for Family Studies (UR-CEF), University Institute of Psychotherapy (IUP), DP-CHUV, Lausanne University, Switzerland

Diane A. Philipp, Hincks-Dellcrest Centre & University of Toronto, Canada

Hervé Tissot, Department of Psychology, Faculty of Psychology and Educational Sciences, University of Geneva and Research Unit of the Centre for Family Studies (UR-CEF), University Institute of Psychotherapy (IUP), DP-CHUV, Lausanne University, Switzerland

Foreword

Understanding triadic and family-level dynamics is not work that comes effortlessly. Yet somehow, almost magically, Fivaz-Depeursinge and Philipp make the work seem effortless and bring the process of understanding and helping families into the clear light of day in this compelling book. Laying a foundation in the careful science of reading and interpreting the affective and behavioral signals of triadic interactions, Fivaz-Depeursinge and Philipp first guide the reader through their process of understanding the normal development of three-way intersubjective and multiperson communication in infants. With this foundation of what cooperative coparenting and family alliances can look like, they move on to illustrate families that struggle with exclusion, misattunement, competitiveness, triangulation, and difficulty sustaining a shared focus. Family patterns and dynamics come to life in the stories of Lucas, Gabriella, Miles, Myriam, and the other children featured in this book, and make the kinds of interventions Fivaz-Depeursinge and Philipp bring into the consulting room seem intuitively obvious.

One of the more creative elements of Fivaz-Depeursinge and colleagues' work has always been the attention given to the infant's contribution to the family dynamic and to coparenting, from the outset. In structural family theory, there is an emphasis on hierarchy – the clear delineation of lines of authority, with the coparents in the family collaborating effectively as the architects and heads of the family system. The capacity of adults to work as a team is what initially captivated me in my own work on coparenting, and many of the ideas and tenets that followed from this focus privilege the adults' propensities during family interactions. The parallel attention given to the infant or child, and how he or she affects the family process both in the moment, and later, as an integral player in a crystallized family pattern, adds a missing and in some ways indispensable layer of meaning to the process of interpreting the family's story. This book provides many vivid examples of child contributions and the role they play in contributing to and maintaining the choreography of the family's dance.

Though their focus is largely on behavior, Fivaz-Depeursinge and Philipp do not minimize the importance of individual family histories and representations. Their detective work begins during the pregnancy, when they establish how the parents are already showing signature leanings towards meshing or failing to mesh as coparenting partners. They then follow their families longitudinally, illustrating through individual case studies how prenatal "hints" gleaned from their innovative assessments later take root in triadic patterns after the baby arrives. A particularly effective feature of this book is the authors' explication of how they use the Lausanne Trilogue Play paradigm, both across cases and repeatedly, within families. The reader is left with a convincing sense of how standard observational methods can be brought to bear in both clinical research and clinical practice to better assess and treat the whole family. Chapter 11's careful rendering of how video-feedback can be used in clinical applications was especially appreciated; the authors provide an extended and measured discussion of principles of video-feedback, how footage can be identified and used therapeutically with families, and what the aims of such video-feedback are for helping families gain insight and make positive adjustments to their well-established patterns.

Though their focus in this book is on two-parent nuclear families with young children, the potential of expanding the use of observational methods to understand the coparenting and triadic patterns of non-traditional families and coparenting teams, both within and beyond western culture, is limitless. My associates and I have actually already begun such work in studying the triangular patterns of kinship families (mother-grandmother coparenting teams) and of "fragile families" – unmarried parents who have had a first baby together but who are frequently not living together or in a committed, ongoing relationship. There are both direct parallels between the kinds of family dynamics outlined in this book and kindred dynamics observable in non-nuclear family systems, and also some distinctive and unique features that demand a culturally informed and emic approach to understanding the family processes and dynamics. But the LTP and its related variants that accommodate older children and siblings stand as a paradigm well poised to enable such work, and the careful analyses of families undertaken in this book provide an aspirational model for disentangling and understanding how diverse families come together to coparent and create functional family systems.

In reflecting on this important contribution to the family literature, it would be remiss not to comment on the creative partnership and alliance of these two fine clinicians in the co-creation of this book. I have long been a follower of both women's work, respectful of the individual traditions that have guided their work and fascinated by the innovative contributions of each scholar individually. Even more intriguing, though, are the results of their having thought and written together. Their dialogues are evident not only in the excellent chapters on clinical consultations and on Reflective Family Play, the latter bringing together some of the powerful and transformative elements of the LTP and of the Watch, Wait, and Wonder paradigm, but also in their deliberations and interpretations of the individual families they write about. This book is an emergent product, in the best sense, bringing together two complementary but distinctive perspectives to generate a product that captures the best of both, and offers something beyond each. Readers will find not a blueprint but a framework for approaching and engaging families from a systemic orientation. So doing offers the promise of intervening in a manner that both respects what the family is already doing well and provides them with new avenues for reaching their fondest aims.

James P. McHale
St. Petersburg, FL
November 6, 2013

Acknowledgments

This project and prior investigations on which it was based received funding support from the Swiss National Science Foundation, grant No 32–52508.97. This foundation has our gratitude for its long-term support of a not quite conventional program of research since 1977. This study would not have been possible without the support of the Institute of Psychotherapy, and of the director, Jean-Nicolas Despland, as well as of the Lausanne University Psychiatry Department and its director at the time, Patrice Guex.

The Baby and the Couple is a sequel to *The Primary Triangle: A Developmental Systems View of Fathers, Mothers and Infants* (1999), co-authored by the senior author, Elisabeth Fivaz-Depeursinge, and Antoinette Corboz-Warnery. The bulk of the research on infants' triangular communication was done at the Centre d'Etude de la Famille, as reflected in the references to the research papers.

In 2003, the second author, Diane A. Philipp, joined the Centre for a sabbatical year and worked with the team on clinical data of high-risk infants and their families. As she developed a clinical application combining the LTP and Watch, Wait, and Wonder, our further collaboration over the last 10 years grew into an idea for writing a book intended for a wider, clinical audience than the first one. The focus was to be on longitudinal case studies and the infant's contribution to the family alliance and its clinical implications and applications. Several chapters of this book bear the names of co-authors who contributed substantively to the research presented in those chapters. We have also taken the pains to acknowledge throughout the text the intellectual contributions of many other colleagues. Here, though, we want to formally thank all those colleagues without whose collaboration the longitudinal study would not have been realized: Antoinette Corboz-Warnery and the present heads of the Centre research, France Frascarolo-Moutinot and Nicolas Favez. Our close collaborators since 1999 are Claudio Carneiro, Sarah Cairo, Joëlle Darwiche, Florence Donzé, Chloé Lavanchy Scaiola, Francesco Lopes, Véronique Montfort, and Hervé Tissot, all of whom contributed in various ways to the data collection and analysis.

In terms of the clinical component of this book, many of the aforementioned also figured significantly in shaping our thinking and technique in the interventions presented here. Once again we include Antoinette Corboz-Warnery and

Daniel Stern in this group, but also Christie Hayos, Roy Muir, Elizabeth Muir, Nancy Cohen, Mirek Lojkasek, and all the trainees along the way who brought fresh ideas and enthusiasm, and asked the right questions at the right moments.

We had the privilege of lively exchanges and debates with experts on early infant development and the family. Besides our primary mentors and colleagues, Daniel Stern and James McHale, who made invaluable contributions to our understanding, many other colleagues and experts are present in the landscape of our thinking. In alphabetical order they are: Beatrice Beebe, Dieter Bürgin, John Byng-Hall, Bertrand Cramer, Bob Emde, Graziella Fava, Roland Fivaz, Hiram Fitzgerald, Bernard Golse, John Gottman, Antoine Guédeney, Sybil Hart, Monica Hedenbro, Marie-Joelle Hervé, Evan Imber-Black, Miri Keren, Frank Lachmann, Martine Lamour, Serge Lebovici, Maria Legerstee, Joe Lichtenberg, Karlen Lyons-Ruth, Marisa Malagoli Togliatti, Silvia Mazzoni, Salvador and Patricia Minuchin, Jeremy Nahum, Luigi Onnis, David Oppenheim, Kaija Puura, Bruce Reis, Elida Romano, Sandra Rusconi-Serpa, Alessandra Simonelli, Hélène Tremblay, Edward Tronick, Tuula Tuminen, and Kai von Klitzing.

We are also grateful to our colleagues Robert Muller and Christie Hayos, who painstakingly and graciously read through the manuscript for this book, making invaluable recommendations on how we could make the concepts clearer for all.

We would also like to express our gratitude to Mirvana Kimball, who provided administrative support in the final details of preparing this manuscript. Joanne Forshaw, senior editor at Routledge, took a leap in faith and accepted our manuscript and, along with Susannah Frearson, editorial assistant, trusted us to write this book to be able to share it with you, our readers.

To our husbands, Roland Fivaz and Robert Muller, we are especially grateful for supporting, sustaining, and soothing us throughout the process of writing this book.

Finally, we are most indebted to the families who agreed to collaborate with us. They gave us their time, their attention, their understanding, and their trust. They let us into their family life and have taught us what we know about family triangular communication and its challenges.

Introduction

Imagine a typical family scene. It's just before dinner and the family is in the kitchen. The parents are busy preparing the meal, and their 9 month-old, Olivia, is seated nearby with her toys on the floor. The parents talk with each other as they move about the kitchen, taking turns checking in with Olivia, who is playing happily. With dinner now ready, the parents transfer Olivia to the table, chatting with her as she smiles, looking back and forth at the two of them. Now imagine the same couple in the car, having an argument about who does more around the house. Baby Olivia watches from her car seat, her head moving back and forth observing each of her parents in this heated discussion. Distracted for a moment, she looks out the window. Then, perhaps resonating with the tension, Olivia starts to cry, and her mother turns to the father and says, "Now look, you've upset the baby!" They pull over and her mother lifts Olivia out of her car seat, while the father glares angrily out the window.

These real-life situations will be quite familiar to most of us. Intuitively we sense that how couples manage – how they coparent when things are going well and when there is conflict – will have an influence on their children, even their infants. Olivia certainly seems aware of both of her parents. She looks back and forth at them when they speak. In the second situation she even becomes distressed and the parents stop arguing. What we all sense on an intuitive level about families has only recently been explored systematically. Historically the focus was on understanding the mother-baby dyad, and more recently the father-baby dyad.

Whether an infant is raised in a traditional family with a mother and father, or in any number of other configurations, the vast majority of children under age 5 continue to be raised in households with more than one adult parenting ("Family Structure," 2012; Children in Families OECD Family Database, 2012). The focus of this book is to understand the impact of coparenting on the infant, the role the infant plays in shaping the family moving forward, and ways we can intervene with the whole family at such an early stage.

Real-life scenarios, however, are a difficult place to start when first trying to understand families, and so it was necessary to create a more controlled way to observe interactions between infants and their two caregivers from early infancy onward. In 1999, a new model for observing interactions between mothers, fathers, and their babies was presented in *The Primary Triangle: A Developmental Systems View of Mothers, Fathers, and Infants* (Fivaz-Depeursinge & Corboz-Warnery, 1999). The Primary Triangle outlined a systematic approach to observe interactions in families with infants, already at this preverbal stage, and to analyze their family alliances. Central to the model was the Lausanne Trilogue Play paradigm (LTP), developed at the Centre for Studies of the Family (Centre d'Etude de la Famille – CEF), part of the University of Lausanne Institute for Psychotherapy. Families were brought into the CEF to play together in this semi-structured task that asked each family member to interact with one another while all seated together in the same room.[1] The LTP allows us to observe, from very early on, how infants develop three-person or "triangular" communication. Later it was also used to look at multiperson communication in very young children with siblings. Finally, with this tool we were able to begin recognizing and describing problematic patterns and trajectories for these infants and their families.

More recently investigators have looked at the infant's participation in internal family dynamics. The idea that an infant could exert influence on family dynamics may seem surprising to some. Once again, until the infant was actually observed within the context of the family, rather than exclusively in dyadic settings, we could not begin to explore this question. Too often in both research and clinical assessment of infants and very young children, we still do not observe whole families interacting with one another. We rely instead on what we see in the dyads, and verbal reports about how the family is doing. So it is necessary to adopt a new lens, without this dyadic bias.

From the outset the LTP was also used as an assessment tool to help clinicians understand and develop appropriate interventions for referred families. Several treatment strategies have now been developed at the CEF to work with very young families. In the last decade a number of models have also emerged at other settings where coparenting and the whole family are considered part of the intervention.

In this book we use case studies to provide researchers and clinicians with a foundation for understanding the development of infants in the context of their two-parent families. In the first two sections the cases are drawn from a longitudinal study of non-clinical, volunteer families who were seen at the CEF. The last section of the book explores clinical applications of the LTP, and the cases are drawn from our own practices. Consent was graciously given by all of these families to present the material. In order to protect the confidentiality of the families, any identifying information has been altered, as have the transcripts we present.

A note on culture and diversity: In this book we primarily discuss traditional families – mothers, fathers, and babies. In fact a number of centers, including each of our own, have looked at diverse populations and family configurations. Where possible we have presented this information, particularly in chapter 13. At times, for simplicity, we have used the shorthand of "husband" and "wife"; however, in a number of the families the partners were common-law. Finally, the two authors themselves come from two different cultures and cohorts, which has provided for enriching and lively debate and points of communality in the process of writing this book.

Map of this book

Section I

While the aim is to use cases to illustrate concepts, in chapter 1 we provide some of the theory and research results that laid the foundation for our understanding of families. The remaining chapters in section I follow the development of Lucas, a typical baby with parents who cooperate well with one another in what is called cohesive coparenting (McHale, 2007). Lucas and his family were part of the longitudinal study of non-clinical families. By following the assessments when Lucas was 3, 9, and 18 months as well as at 5 years of age, we see how a cooperative family evolves, including the addition of a sibling. The various adaptations of the LTP that were created to capture functioning at these different developmental stages are discussed in several of the chapters in this section. We also present the family's prenatal LTP, a tool that can be used to screen families even before the couple has their first child. In addition to the case of Lucas, other case examples are used to further illustrate elements of family communication.

Section II

In certain families the development of the infant's triangular communication can become derailed. Some couples struggle to coparent and are not cohesive. When this happens, the infant's triangular communication suffers, as does the family alliance. A number of the volunteer families from the longitudinal study did have problematic trajectories. In this section a different chapter is dedicated to each style of problematic communication, using representative cases from the study sample.

Section III

At the CEF, the seed for starting the longitudinal study was that families were being clinically referred for consultations and treatment. The LTP was developed and then used in these cases, as part of an assessment protocol and later treatment. Video footage was shared with families as a form of intervention known as video-feedback. In the last two decades a variety of sites throughout the world have incorporated this type of LTP with video-feedback in their work with clinical families. These centers have also developed further applications from the LTP. Cases from the CEF, as well as work at some of these other centers, are presented in section III.

The last section of the book brings us full circle back to the origins of this work, exploring ways to understand and help young families, as they are just beginning their journey.

Note

1 The LTP will be described in detail in subsequent chapters.

References

Children in Families OECD Family Database. (2012). OECD – Social Policy Division – Directorate of Employment, Labour and Social Affairs. www.oecd.org/els/soc/41919533.pdf

Family structure and children's living arrangements. (2012). Forum on child & family statistics. www.childstats.gov/americaschildren/famsoc1.asp

Fivaz-Depeursinge, E., & Corboz-Warnery, A. (1999). *The primary triangle: A developmental systems view of fathers, mothers and infants.* New York: Basic Books.

McHale, J. (2007). When infants grow up in multiperson relationship systems. *Infant-Mental Health Journal, 28*, 370–392.

Section I

Growing up with cohesive coparenting

Optimizing triangular communication

In section I we present the case of Lucas, a child, and his parents from our community sample, whom we followed from the prenatal stage until he was 5 years old. Each chapter captures Lucas and his family at a different stage of Lucas' development, allowing us to follow the natural trajectory of infant triangular or multiperson communication. We also present examples of other children from the sample, in order to elaborate further on certain key concepts.

Chapter 1

The baby and the couple

Some theory and research foundations

In this book we use case examples and vignettes to illustrate the development of infants within the context of the family. In particular, we are interested in how parents coordinate their efforts as coparents and then how babies manage and adapt to different coparenting styles. We felt it was important, however, to begin with some of the background thinking and research that laid the groundwork for the material we will be presenting later in the book.

The decision to study infants within the context of the family involved something of a paradigm shift. Historically our understanding of infants was based on studies of mothers and their babies or what we refer to as dyads. More recently there has also been interest in the father-baby dyad, but the bulk of our current understanding of infant communication and social skills is based on the research from mother-baby dyads. Despite this bias, several investigators began suggesting that infants are actually more often in multiperson contexts than they are in dyadic ones (Dunn, 1991; Schaffer, 1984). Infants are often cared for by more than one person and from the outset they often interact in a group (Tronick, Morelli, & Ivey, 1992). In other words, infants need and appear to have an innate ability to deal with a variety of caretaking contexts (Stern, 2004). This ability may in fact be evolutionarily advantageous. If part of our survival depends on group cooperation, then it would be critical to be able to read social situations in order to communicate and coordinate with more than one person at a time. The first and most basic group unit that most of us will encounter is the family, with our parents providing the conditions for us to develop the skills we need to manage.

Lausanne Trilogue Play

The Lausanne Trilogue Play paradigm (LTP) was the first model that allowed researchers to begin exploring the infant in the context of the family (Corboz-Warnery, Fivaz-Depeursinge, Guertsch-Bettens, & Favez, 1993; Fivaz-Depeursinge & Corboz-Warnery, 1999). We briefly describe the basic format of an LTP next. There are now a number of variants of the model, depending on the age and stage of the child. We will describe these variants in the relevant chapters as we explore normative and maladaptive development of family communication.

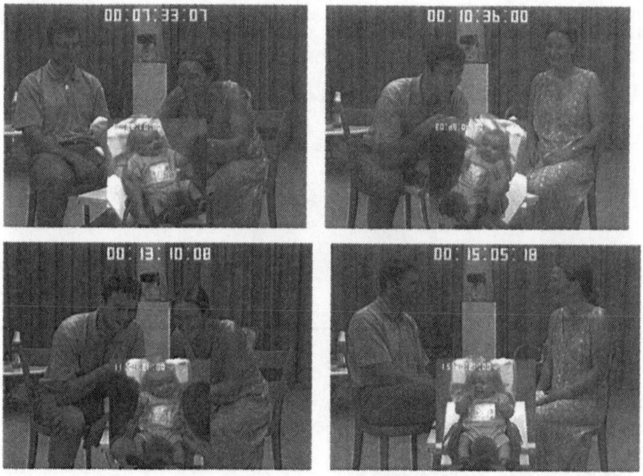

Figure 1.1 The four parts to the Lausanne Trilogue Play situation (LTP):
 I   A "2 + 1," where one parent is actively playing with the infant while the other parent is the observer, in a third-party position.
 II The parents reverse roles.
 III "3-together," where the two parents play with the infant.
 IV Both parents directly interact with each other while the infant is the third party. This format is applicable to any age, providing the task is adjusted to the child's developmental stage.

During an LTP, families are asked to play together in four different configurations corresponding to the four possible combinations in a triad (see Figure 1.1).

When the child is an infant, the parents are seated in chairs angled to form a triangle, allowing them to face the infant. The distances between all three of them encourage dialogue, as well as allowing them to keep each other in their peripheral vision. The infant is seated in a chair that can be inclined according to the baby's motor development, as well as oriented toward either of the parents or between them. The following instructions are given:

> *We ask you to play together as a family, following the directions for the four separate parts of the exercise. In the first part, one of you plays with your child, while the other is simply present. In the second part, your roles are reversed. In the third part, you both play with your child together. In the last part you will talk with each other for a bit; and it will be your child's turn to be simply present. It is up to you to decide the inclination of the seat, in which direction to orient it, and how long each part is to last. Generally, at this age, it takes about 8–12 minutes. Please signal when you are done.*

Once the child is older, the family sits at a small round table, with the child in a high chair, and a small number of toys are provided. The instructions remain the same, except the direction the high chair is facing remains fixed, and the time range is slightly longer – generally around 12–15 minutes.

When asked to interact with their young baby in an LTP, most parents intuitively behave in ways that help the infant understand what is expected. In parts I or II, when playing actively with their infants, parents turn the infant's seat to face them and lean forward at dialogue distance from the baby. When parents are in the third-party role, they sit back, resonating with the play, but giving a clear nonverbal message that they are not involved. Similarly, when playing as a threesome, parents orient the baby's seat midway between themselves and align their bodies at dialogue distance. Finally, during their own dialogue, parents typically leave the infant's seat at the midway point. They sit back in their chairs, away from the baby, and face one another. Even very young infants are quite sensitive to these nonverbal signals of orientation and distance between people.

The family alliance

The family alliance is in the fabric of daily life. It is how the mother, father, and infant work together toward a common goal. Consider a couple getting their infant, Olivia, into the car.

> *The mother is carrying Olivia, and the father has brought the diaper bag and the car seat. The mother talks to Olivia about their plans for the afternoon while the father quietly puts the diaper bag on the back seat. As the father now leans over to install the car seat, he talks with his wife about how they need to first stop to fill up the car. The mother listens and Olivia alternates between playing with a button on her mother's coat, and looking at each of her parents. With the car seat now strapped in, the father turns to take Olivia. Her mother lets her know, "Daddy's going to put you in your car seat now." Olivia initially protests, burying her head in her mother's coat, but with some coaxing by both parents, she eventually reaches her arms out to her father and her mother passes her to him. As he buckles Olivia into her seat, the mother waits, holding a bottle to give to the baby once he's done. In the meantime Olivia tries to pull off her father's glasses, and he smiles and tells her, "I need those to drive!"*

While not in the order prescribed by the LTP and with some adjustments along the way, the family has passed through all four parts of an LTP. Each of the parents interacted directly with Olivia while the other was simply present. The parents worked together to coordinate the transfer of Olivia from her mother to her father, and Olivia complied. Finally, while the father was installing the car seat, he and the mother had their own discussion, while Olivia distracted herself or watched them. Families may not always do every single part of an LTP in their daily lives, but these configurations of family interaction are something they will do in many contexts through the course of development. Sometimes it will go smoothly, and at other points they will encounter bumps along the way.

Since real-life situations pose all kinds of unexpected variations, the simple structure of the LTP allowed for a standardized way to observe families in these configurations. It was then possible to develop a number of coding schemes to look at the family alliance, the coparenting, and the infant's capacity to participate in three-person or triangular communication and later multiperson communication. The cases we present in sections I and II are drawn from a longitudinal sample of 38 non-referred volunteer families who came in periodically to do LTPs at various stages of their children's development. They were seen at the Centre for Studies of the Family (Centre d'Etude de la Famille – CEF), part of the University of Lausanne Institute for Psychotherapy.

Historically, the first question explored in this data was the family alliance. In a well-coordinated alliance there seemed to be four components to consider when evaluating a family's LTP:

1   Participation – Is everyone included, even if each person's role is different at any given moment?
2   Organization – Is there a division of roles, and a respect for each person's role in the interaction?
3   Focalization – Is everyone sharing a common focus?
4   Sharing of affects – Are similar or complementary feelings experienced and shared by the family members?

These four functions are hierarchically embedded. If the family struggles with the very first function, participation, and instead excludes one or more partners, then by definition they are not able to play as a family. Moving up the hierarchy, even if everyone is included, if individuals do not keep to their roles, once again the goal of play in each part may not be reached. For example, if the third-party parent keeps commenting on what the active parent and infant are doing, then she has violated the goal of that part; that her partner and infant are supposed to be playing actively while she remains simply present. The same applies to focus and sharing of affects; each of these is a necessary ingredient in the LTP in order for the task to be experienced as the shared pleasure of playing together. With this system it was now possible to compare families that were able to coordinate this task well in a functional alliance to those families who struggled (Frascarolo, Favez, Carneiro, & Fivaz-Depeursinge, 2004).

The use of the term "alliance" is a reference to the work of Salvador Minuchin (1974) and Structural Family Therapy. According to Minuchin, family alliances occur when intergenerational boundaries in a family are clear and flexible. More specifically, he considered the coparents as a "subsystem" within the family. The parents are in charge and make decisions together for the family, but they are also responsive and can occasionally break the "rules" of the boundary. In contrast, Family Coalitions, another Minuchin term, is used to describe certain families presenting with difficulties. The parents are unable to cooperate and struggle with creating that clear and flexible boundary. They implicate their children in some way in order to avoid dealing with the distance or frank conflict between them, so that the intergenerational boundaries are distorted (see chapters 7–9). As we will see at the end of this chapter and in sections I and II of this book, these same family alliances and coalitions are linked to findings from families doing the LTP.

The infant's triangular communication and the triangular bid

The term triangular communication refers to the ability to interact with two partners at the same time, including any of the configurations possible in the LTP. In addition to assessing alliances, the LTP was developed to ask the following question: when an infant is in a group of three, does he exclusively use a dyadic template and interact with one person at a time, or does he also have a triangular template of communication?

Let's take a hypothetical situation with baby Jesse in part I of an LTP. His father has turned his seat to face him and is playing with him while his mother sits back, simply watching and resonating with what is happening. If Jesse exclusively engages with his father and ignores his mother, then he would only need to activate a dyadic template. But suppose Jesse briefly shifts his gaze towards his mother a few times, as if to share with his mother the delight he is experiencing playing with his father. In that case some sort of triangular template would be required.

Now suppose they are in part III of the LTP and the parents invite Jesse to play all three together. Perhaps this is a bit unusual for Jesse, but for many families play can happen spontaneously, like on Sunday mornings in the parents' bed, or at the kitchen table during family meals. Note that this three-together play condition may be more challenging for Jesse than dyadic play. All of a sudden he has to coordinate with two parents at the same time rather than just one. Within this three-together situation, a dyadic program could work, if Jesse were to simply alternate playing with each of his parents for brief episodes. But suppose all three were to play a game together? Then he would have to have a triangular program. Jesse would most likely have to shift his gaze rapidly back and forth between his parents to gauge and react to each of their responses in close succession in order to successfully participate.

With his gaze moving so quickly from one parent to the other, we consider Jesse's experience as a single unit of sharing with both parents and no longer alternately playing with one or the other. We see this kind of shifting back and forth in older individuals as well (Kendon, 1990), but this was a first for our understanding of infant behavior. Tremblay, Lemonnier, Sorin, and Rovira (submitted) have recently demonstrated shifting gaze and affect in newborns that were on average 59 hours old. We have called this back and forth "triangular bids" (Fivaz-Depeursinge, Favez, Lavanchy, de Noni, & Frascarolo, 2005). We have come to recognize the presence of triangular bids as an important early indicator of emerging triangular communication in children. Depending on Jesse's affect and expression as he makes his triangular bids, he can signal interest, pleasure, uncertainty, or discomfort to his two parents.

Back in Jesse's LTP, the parents have moved on to part IV and sit back to talk on their own. This configuration is a very common "2 + 1" situation, with Jesse now in the third-party role. In the normal day-to-day parents often consult with each other. Olivia's parents discussing the car is an example. Just as in real life, in the LTP, babies readily recognize this change of context. In an LTP they can notice: my parents are sitting further from me, they are facing each other and using adult talk.

When Jesse's parents talk with one another, he loses their direct attention, which can be frustrating. On the other hand, it does allow him to observe how his parents relate with one another. Observing relationships is another way babies learn to understand social interactions. When Jesse notices that his parents are talking on their own he is surprised and frustrated, especially since he just had their full attention during part III. To manage, he may cycle through a series of behaviors: protesting, distracting himself, observing his parents, laughing along with them, and most importantly trying to regain their attention.

Returning to the question of dyadic versus triangular programs, the data suggest that infants use a triangular program to communicate in a group of three (Fivaz-Depeursinge et al., 2005; McHale, Fivaz-Depeursinge, Dickstein, Robertson, & Daley, 2008). From as early as 3 months, they engage in triadic play by orienting their faces and dividing their attention differently depending on their roles. For instance, when an infant is supposed to be playing with his mother, he looks at her more than at his father. At the same time, he still seems aware of his father, glancing over at him periodically, perhaps to check in on his response. The baby divides his attention more evenly between his parents when he plays with them both in part III and also when he is in the role of third party during his parents' dialogue. He also uses other tools at his disposal, such as the triangular bids described earlier.

From dyadic to multiperson intersubjective communication

Intersubjectivity is the ability to share other people's feelings or mind states (Stern, 2004). Beginning in early infancy, and proceeding through early childhood, intersubjectivity matures in the context of children's relationships with more or less attuned social partners. Others have discussed similar concepts such as mentalization and reflective function, but these are typically referring to a parent's ability to imagine or hold in mind her child's experience (Fonagy, Steele, Steele, Moran, & Higitt, 1991). In the case of intersubjectivity, we are speaking about a bidirectional relationship where ideally both parties have a mutual sense of the other's experience.

The development of intersubjectivity has been traditionally understood only in dyadic terms with the mother-baby dyad as the prototype studied most. We propose that there is a parallel in triangular interactions – a multiperson form of intersubjective communication in the early family. Infants share their internal states and begin to read them in others as they interact with both of their parents at the same time. For children exposed to adequate coparenting, the parent's relationship may act as a catalyst to the development of their intersubjective capacity. For example, as the child sees how his mother reacts to his father, he gains insight into the meaning of his father's behavior, and what his father's intention might be (Stern, 2004). Furthermore, by definition, multiperson intersubjectivity includes our understanding of the relationships between others. As the infant observes his parents' relationship, he increasingly understands the ways they feel and think about one another, and his role in their relationship.

Infant styles of engagement

The infant's style of engagement (Fivaz-Depeursinge, Lopes, Python, & Favez, 2009) is actually a combination of a number of variables or dimensions that are observable in family interactions during the LTP and that tell us even more about how the infant communicates in a multiperson context. These dimensions are as follows:

- *Form* – Does the infant mainly use triangular or dyadic bids, or is she simply withdrawn?
- *Degree* – Is the infant appropriately engaged, or is she disengaged, responding but, for example, looking away? Alternatively is the infant over-engaged, always attuned and never taking a natural break from her social partners?
- *Affective balance* – On average is the infant's affect most often positive or negative during the interaction?
- *Frequency of triangular bids* – Is the frequency within age norms, lower, or perhaps above average?

Together these dimensions allow us to classify infants into one of four infant engagement styles. Triangular Engagement occurs in the context of cohesive coparents and is described in chapters 2–6. The remaining three styles of infant engagement emerge in the context of non-cohesive coparenting: Split Engagement (see chapter 7), Go-between/Withdrawal (see chapter 8), and Role Reversed Engagement (see chapter 9). All four styles can appear early in infancy, solidify by toddlerhood, and may continue into the preschool years.

Coparenting styles in the LTP

As noted these infant styles of engagement are believed to be responses to corresponding coparenting styles. McHale observed that in two-parent households, families establish a "signature coparenting relationship" into which infants are socialized (McHale, 2007b). The nature of the coparenting relationship leaves an indelible "imprint" on the socio-emotional development of children (McHale, 2007a). Just as work at the CEF focused on infant variables that combine to form the four styles of infant engagement, McHale found four coparenting variables:

- *Affective Connection*, or the warmth between the parents
- *Mutual Involvement* between the parents
- *Degree of Cooperation* between the parents
- *Adult- versus Child-Centered Behavior* – whether the family interaction was led more by the adults or by the child

These coparenting variables yielded four different coparenting styles:

- *Cohesive Coparenting*: High degree of warmth, mutual involvement, cooperation, and moderate Child-Centeredness
- *Excluding Coparenting*: Large imbalance in the parents' levels of engagement, as well as a lack of warmth, poor cooperation, and yet not a great deal of antagonism
- *Child-at-Center Coparenting*: Parents affectively disconnected from each other (low warmth and mutual involvement); they cooperate in so much as they are focused exclusively on the infant (high Child-Centeredness).
- *Competitive Coparenting*: Parents affectively disconnected (low warmth and mutual involvement), competing for the child's attention (low cooperation).

Making connections: Infant styles of engagement, coparenting styles, and family alliances

In the CEF longitudinal study, families were categorized into the four coparenting styles and their corresponding infant engagement styles. When the family alliances for these same subjects were assessed, their coparenting styles and infant engagement styles also corresponded with Minuchin's (1974) structural categories of alliances and coalitions.

Table 1.1 is meant as a quick reference that shows each coparenting style and its corresponding infant engagement style as well as the family alliance or coalition all in the same row. We will refer to this table particularly in section II of the book, when we are discussing maladaptive family trajectories.

Table 1.1 Associations between infant engagement styles, coparenting styles, and resulting family structure

Infant engagement style	Coparenting style	Family structure
Triangular engagement	Cohesive	Alliance
Split engagement	Excluding	Binding coalition
Role reversed	Child-at-center	Detouring coalition
Go-between/withdrawal	Competitive	Triangulation coalition

Clinical comment

It is important to note that early coparenting and infant engagement styles were correlated with the child's later social and emotional development at age 5 (Favez et al., 2012). This correlation to later functioning was there even when looking only at the precursors to coparenting in couples still just expecting their first child who did a prenatal LTP with a rag doll (chapter 6). In addition, categories remained stable from infancy into the preschool years. While still quite preliminary, what these two findings may suggest in practical terms is that without intervention problems in coparenting and family structure may remain problematic up to the follow-up at age 5. On the other hand, this also means that at various points in infancy, and even during the pregnancy, concerns can be identified and potentially set on a different trajectory.

The goal of this chapter was to lay the groundwork for the rest of this book. By providing some of the theoretical background and results we can proceed to the heart of the matter – namely, the case studies which illustrate our main findings on the baby and the couple. We begin with cohesive coparenting and the development of infant triangular communication.

References

Corboz-Warnery, A., Fivaz-Depeursinge, E., Guertsch-Bettens, C., & Favez, N. (1993). Systemic analysis of father mother baby interactions: The Lausanne Triadic Play. *Infant Mental Health Journal, 14*(4), 298–316.

Dunn, J. (1991). Young children's understanding of other people: Evidence from observations within the family. In D. Frye & C. Moore (Eds.), *Children's theories of mind* (pp. 97–114). Hillsdale, NJ: Erlbaum.

Favez, N., Lopes, F., Bernard, M., Frascarolo, F., Lavanchy Scaiola, C., Corboz-Warnery, A., & Fivaz-Depeursinge, E. (2012). The development of family alliance from pregnancy to toddlerhood and child outcomes at 5 years. *Family Process, 51*, 542–556.

Fivaz-Depeursinge, E., & Corboz-Warnery, A. (1999). *The primary triangle: A developmental systems view of fathers, mothers and infants.* New York: Basic Books.

Fivaz-Depeursinge, E., Favez, N., Lavanchy, C., de Noni, S., & Frascarolo, F. (2005). Four-month-olds make triangular bids to father and mother during trilogue play with still-face. *Social Development, 14*(2), 361–378.

Fivaz-Depeursinge, E., Lopes, F., Python, M., & Favez, N. (2009). The toddler's role in family coalitions. *Family Process, 48*, 500–516.

Fonagy, P., Steele, M., Steele, H., Moran, G., & Higitt, A. (1991). The capacity for understanding mental states: The reflective self in parent and child and its significance for security of attachment. *Infant Mental Health Journal, 12*, 201–217.

Frascarolo, F., Favez, N., Carneiro, C., & Fivaz-Depeursinge, E. (2004). Hierarchy of interactive functions in father-mother-baby three-way games. *Infant and Child Development, 13*(4), 301–322. doi:10.1002/icd.361

Kendon, A. (1990). *Conducting interaction: Patterns of behavior in focused encounters.* Cambridge: Cambridge University Press.

McHale, J. (2007a). *Charting the bumpy road of coparenthood.* Washington, DC: Zero to Three Press.

McHale, J. (2007b). When infants grow up in multiperson relationship systems. *Infant-Mental Health Journal, 28*, 370–392.

McHale, J., Fivaz-Depeursinge, E., Dickstein, S., Robertson, J., & Daley, M. (2008). New evidence for the social embeddedness of infant's early triangular capacities. *Family Process, 47*, 445–463.

Minuchin, S. (1974). *Families & family therapy.* Boston: Harvard University Press.

Schaffer, H. R. (1984). *The child's entry into a social world.* London: Academic Press.

Stern, D. (2004). *The present moment in psychotherapy and everyday life.* New York: W.W. Norton.

Tremblay, H., Lemonnier, L., Sorin, A-L., & Rovira, K. (submitted). Neonates' triangular communication abilities.

Tronick, E. Z., Morelli, G. A., & Ivey, P. K. (1992). The Efe forager infant and toddler's pattern of social relationships: Multiple and simultaneous. *Developmental Psychology, 28*, 568–577.

Chapter 2

Early infancy
Primary triangular communication

With Chloé Lavanchy Scaiola

We begin this chapter by meeting Lucas.[1] He and his parents were part of a longitudinal study of infant communication in the context of the family, and we will be following his development over the next several chapters. Just 3 months old, this is the first time that Lucas has come in for an assessment at the Centre for Studies of the Family (Centre d'Etude de la Famille – CEF), part of the University of Lausanne Institute for Psychotherapy.

> *The family members are seated. Lucas' parents are listening to the facilitator explain the Lausanne Trilogue Play task (LTP). She has just told them that in parts I and II of the LTP, each of them will take a turn playing with Lucas, while the other will be "simply present." At this point, the father interrupts, "Am I allowed to laugh? Because it makes a difference . . ." Immediately everyone laughs, including Lucas, who looks at his father and then his mother. He continues smiling at his mother as she looks at the facilitator and then he finally looks at the facilitator too.*

Before the task has even started, Lucas has already engaged in a number of behaviors that tell us a lot about his ability to manage a multiperson interaction. While we are not suggesting that Lucas understands the humor shared between his parents and the facilitator, like many infants, he smiles along with the feeling in the room. He looks at both of his parents in the process. Finally, on seeing that his mother is looking at the facilitator, he looks at her too. Lucas has already developed a rich set of skills to manage this social situation and these skills, as well as the things his parents intuitively do to support his development, are the focus of this chapter.

Developmental context

To understand multi-person communication at this very early stage, we need to have a quick background discussion of what was already known in the literature on dyadic interactions. Bretherton (1992) characterized dyadic infant communication as progressing through stages. Initially infants engage in what she termed "primary communication," which is interactions that have no topic other than the interaction itself – for example, a mother and her infant exchanging coos as they gaze at one another in a face-to-face interaction. There is neither language involved nor any pretend play. There is not even any purpose to the communication beyond this moment of play. It is simply a "sense of shared experience" – something even very young infants have the capacity to resonate with in social interactions (Rochat & Striano, 1999).

The question now is, can we extrapolate that there might be a triangular version of this type of exchange? What would the infant need to do in order to convince us that she is also capable of primary communication at the triangular level? What signs would there be that she is aware she is interacting with two people, not just one? By observing many infants we have come to recognize that, like adults, infants shift their gaze, looking back and forth at both of their partners, in order to check in with each of them. We have called this "shifting gaze" and its associated affect in infants "triangular bids" (Fivaz-Depeursinge & Corboz-Warnery, 1999). Even at this early stage babies engage in this behavior and in fact use several types of triangular bids, depending on the type of affect they are experiencing. Positive bids of interest or delight would signal to parents that the infant wants the activity to continue. Negative bids of tension or protest would signal to them that she wishes the interaction to change. Social referencing in the 8 month-old can then be seen as a more sophisticated form of such bids. Lying somewhere between positive and negative bids, social references signal that the infant is uncertain about the meaning of an event, and wants to refer to the parents' affective expressions to guide her behavior. But it is the precursors in younger infants, triangular bids, to which we now turn.

Lucas at 3 months

LTP parts I and II

Since our focus is on the infant's ability to handle interactions with two people at the same time, we often will fast forward to the second half of the LTPs, as it is here that the infant is most pressed to manage. But first we should at least note that during parts I and II, things went relatively smoothly for this family.

> *The mother-infant play is fairly long with lots of positive affect and vocal dialogue or cooing back and forth. Towards the end, Lucas tires and begins to fuss a little. In part II, the father seems a bit tentative, but he warms up and works hard to get Lucas to perk up. Finally, we should note that during both of these first two parts, the non-active parent sits back quietly, but "simply present," clearly resonating with and enjoying the action between Lucas and the other parent, but not interfering.*

LTP part III

When the time comes to proceed to the 3-together play, Lucas is whining. As the parents adjust the seat to the middle, the mother tries to distract Lucas, leaning over towards the father's side and removing the baby's sock. She kisses Lucas' foot and then turns to her husband and, handing him the sock says, "Here, I'll give you this one and I'll take the other one." The father takes the sock in his hands and the two proceed to play with Lucas' feet. They remain mostly aligned, shoulder-to-shoulder, ready to respond to Lucas' bids. We have divided this foot game into five segments:

1 ***Lucas settles and engages with his mother.*** *Talking softly, Lucas' mother begins to kiss his foot and bit-by-bit he shows signs of warming up again. His father looks as though he is going to kiss the other foot, but then seems to change his mind. During a pause in the mother-baby exchange, when the mother briefly sits up, the father finally kisses Lucas' foot, and the mother exclaims, "Look at Daddy, he's kissing your foot!" Lucas turns towards his father, but then reorients to his mother and they laugh together.*

2 ***Lucas engages with his father.*** *The father caresses Lucas' cheek asking, "And me, are you going to look at me too?" Finally, the baby looks up at his father, who smiles back with the typical exaggerated-type of greeting response that adults give to babies. Lucas watches his father closely and perks up even more as his father resumes kissing his foot. Meanwhile, his mother adds commentary, asking the father "Are you going to eat it all?" To which the father replies, "I am!"*

3 ***Lucas reengages with his mother.*** *Now Lucas' mother actively reengages in the game, kissing Lucas' other foot. Lucas becomes increasingly vocal, responding with gurgles and coos as she talks to him, "You did this yesterday too . . ."*

4 ***Lucas engages with the couple.*** *As Lucas "converses," he looks back-and-forth three times between his two parents; in other words, he makes three consecutive bids between them, as if to also share with his father the fun he is having with his mother. Finally, the father actively reengages, tickling Lucas' foot, but Lucas looks sternly back at his father, his hand in his mouth. Not put off by Lucas' stern look, his father asks, "Does that hand taste good?" He strokes Lucas' neck and talks softly to him. Lucas responds with slightly plaintive vocalizations, looking intently at his father, then at his mother, all the while sucking hard on his fist. Finally, he looks away.*

5 ***Pause.*** *30 seconds later, Lucas appears tired again. He looks up at the ceiling and the parents follow him, looking up as well. He yawns, and turns up the volume of his complaining. The parents try again, each taking a foot, but Lucas only looks at them more intently, and continues whining.*

Comment

Initially, we have the impression that perhaps Lucas is able to engage with only one parent at a time, as he shifts from looking at his mother and interacting with her for a stretch, and then does the same with his father. But to his parents' credit, they work hard at engaging him together, and Lucas eventually initiates positive triangular bids to them and they quickly respond. When his interest fades the parents move on to part IV.

LTP part IV

Leaning over, the mother kisses Lucas softly, and gently tells him, "OK, now we're going to leave you . . . and talk together. Let's see what you'll say to that!" She sits up and the father follows her.

The parents sit back and turn to face one another, leaving the infant seat oriented in the middle. The next part may be divided in two segments:

1   ***Lucas requests attention.*** *Facing one another, the mother leads the discussion with a series of comments and observations about Lucas. The father nods or responds softly to her questions and comments. In the meantime, Lucas begins whining softly and then gets progressively louder, looking intently back and forth at his parents. About a minute into the parents' discussion, he screeches loudly, looking sternly at his father. Both parents look at him, father smiling and mother chuckling. The parents turn back to each other, while Lucas continues to look intently at his father.*

2   ***Lucas self-soothes and monitors his parents' dialogue.*** *The parents continue to talk as the mother says to the father, "He's clearly interested in you the most . . . It's probably not very fun for him to be just sitting there watching two people talking and not paying attention to him." The father responds with, "Maybe he's learning how people talk with each other?" Lucas is now actively watching or monitoring his two parents. He makes a half smile and gets animated as he flaps his arms and vocalizes. After another triangular bid to his parents, Lucas is rewarded; they turn to him looking amused. The mother concludes, "I think we're OK," and the father replies, "I guess so . . ." They look at the window to signal that they are done and laugh as the mother tells the research team, "We're done!" Precisely at this moment, Lucas squeals with delight.*

Comment

At the outset of this interchange Lucas gave off signals that he was not happy, yet he quickly calmed down and began to monitor his parents' conversation. Something about briefly getting their positive attention after screeching, and then witnessing their peaceful, playful dialogue helped him make this switch. In fact in contrast with other infants, Lucas showed a remarkable ability to soothe himself or regulate his emotions. Taking all four parts of the LTP into consideration, Lucas' style of engagement fulfills all the criteria of triangular engagement: it is often triangular and age-appropriate, his affect is predominantly positive, and he makes an average number of predominantly positive triangular bids.

Variant 1: Zoe's triangular imitation

The story of Zoe offers us a quasi-natural experiment of infant imitation in a triangular setting.[2] Meltzoff has described "invisible imitation," where even newborn infants are able to imitate facial expressions such as smiling, surprise, and even sadness. The invisible aspect of this behavior is that the infant does not see himself imitating the adult, but rather is able to do so on a proprioceptive basis – in other words, somehow taking what he sees on the adult's face and copying it. While the function or meaning of this behavior may still be open to interpretation, there are now numerous studies demonstrating this phenomenon (Meltzoff & Moore, 1997).

Zoe is an energetic 3 month-old girl. Her parents interact with her in a lively and fast-paced manner, and seem relatively sensitive to her, even if Zoe sometimes has to signal a few times before they lower their level of activity. She maintains a high level of attention throughout the interaction, clearly enjoying the attention. All told, it is once again a very pleasant interaction for the observer to witness.

For this case we start the story in the first parts of the LTP, as an example of triangular capacity in the infant, even in this "2 + 1" configuration (one parent active with Zoe while the other is simply present). In other words, it would be easy to assume that in parts I and II, such a young infant might "forget" about the third-party parent, perhaps too young to manage in this more subtle situation. However, we have in fact seen many infants turn to the third-party parent in what appears to be a clear bid to share the affect they are experiencing with the active parent.

LTP part I

Zoe plays with her mother first, while her father is "simply present." However, on a number of occasions, Zoe turns to look at her father, sharing with him the same affective signal of interest, pleasure, or frustration that she has just addressed to her mother.

> *The bulk of the mother-daughter play is a game of sticking out tongues. First the mother sticks out her tongue. Zoe looks at her mother quite attentively, and perhaps to process the information further, she looks away, waves her arms about, and looks at her mother a second time. At this point her mother sticks her tongue out again. Now Zoe imitates her mother, initially with a very concentrated look on her face and then with enthusiasm two more times within a few seconds. Her mother laughs, "Good job, Zoe!" The mother then sticks out her tongue a third time. Zoe finally sticks out her tongue more boldly; delighted, she does it two more times over the next five seconds.*

Comment

These observations fit a model of imitation as an active process that is presumably innate. Through a series of sophisticated studies, Meltzoff and Moore (1995) suggest that imitation in early infancy serves as a form of identification and communication with others. In the same way a baby looks at her hand and moves it in order to explore it, or manipulates a toy in order to know it, the infant imitates her partner to get to know her.

LTP part II

Zoe and her father also have fun. But let's see what happens when the infant is interacting with another adult, who may not be behaving in the same way.

He alternately takes her hands and her feet and pedals them, while responding to her facial expressions by exaggerating them, the way adults do when playing with babies. As father and daughter reach a delightful level of animation, Zoe initiates the sticking-out-the-tongue game. The father acknowledges her invitation with a smile, but then refuses to take up that game. Instead, he makes a mock expression of disgust and explains with a smile, "Daddies don't teach you how to stick out your tongue; mommies do that!" Zoe gives him a half-smile and looks away. She sucks on her fist, and then reorients her gaze towards her father. They return to the pedaling game.

Comment

For Zoe, this puzzling experience presumably stands in contrast to the reciprocity she has experienced playing with her father at other times. What's more, Zoe, like most infants, likes her behavior to be matched. In the lab, infants have been shown to not only recognize when they are being matched but also increase their behavior precisely when they are matched (Meltzoff & Moore, 1997). Assuming Zoe is able to differentiate between her two parents, will we be able to see some sign of this differentiation during the next part of the LTP, when she plays with both parents?

LTP part III

From the outset of the 3-together Zoe recognizes that she now has two equal partners, in large part thanks to the coordination of her two parents. She makes a number of triangular bids, signaling interest, pleasure, or frustration. We find them next as Zoe tries to play the same game.

Suddenly, as the parents are puffing out their cheeks in unison, Zoe reintroduces something from before as her turn comes to "reply" to the cheek puffing. She first looks at her father very carefully, then gives him the same half-smile she gave him in part II when he refused to play the sticking-out-the-tongue game. Then she turns, looks her mother straight in the eye and sticks out her tongue at her. The mother immediately sticks out her tongue, and it looks like Zoe is getting ready to do it again when her mother suddenly leans to the father and with an adult tone of voice says to him, "This is too complicated." The parents laugh softly, and Zoe turns towards her father with interest. He starts making exaggerated faces, shutting his mouth tightly, pretending he is working hard to keep from sticking out his tongue. While Zoe is still looking at her father, her mother laughs, asking Zoe, "What is Daddy doing . . . ?" and Zoe, having given a second half-smile to her father, turns towards her mother and sticks her tongue out at her again. The mother exclaims, "Right!" The little girl is tired and the parents soon decide to move on to the last part.

Comment

This baby girl seems able to selectively play the sticking-out-the-tongue game with her mother, while refraining from it with her father, all within the same triangular context. The parents themselves show that they too have the same game in mind, where the mother plays the sticking-out-the-tongue game and the father does not.

Reading these vignettes, it is important to bear in mind that it was only through microanalysis (Tronick, Als, & Brazelton, 1980) of the videotaped moment-to-moment interchanges in these families that we have come to recognize these patterns (see Appendix 2.1 for an overview of this process). On first viewing these interactions, the patterns can often appear quite subtle to the uninitiated. By slowing the interactions down we were able to fine-tune our understanding of the families as well as the patterns across families and through different developmental stages.

Let's move on to see how Zoe manages as third party to her parents' interaction.

LTP part IV

The parents engage in an animated conversation while Zoe looks attentively back and forth, visibly interested by what is going on between them. At one point, she even laughs along with them, like Lucas did earlier when the facilitator was still in the room. At other points she appears tired or even in some mild distress. At these times her parents briefly interrupt their discussion to acknowledge her discomfort with an empathic face or vocalization, and then they return to their discussion.

Comment

Zoe is also able to adopt the third-party position and be interested in her parents' interaction. Of course she does have the occasional moment of distress or fatigue, but her parents' brief empathic acknowledgments are enough to tide her over and she is able to resume monitoring their conversation with interest.

Variant 2: Primary triangular communication put to experimental test

Through these microanalyses of the LTPs, it was certainly looking like very young infants did indeed have the capacity to manage a three-way interaction; however, could the situation be manipulated to further test this question? We decided to adapt the "still face" paradigm to further test our hypotheses. In the "still face" paradigm (Tronick, Als, Adamson, Wise, & Brazelton, 1978) a baby is seated in an infant chair and plays with one parent. At a certain point the parent is asked to pose a still face for the infant – in other words, to stop playing and simply look blankly at the baby. The young infant's reactions to this still face have now been well documented. It begins with initial surprise and confusion, followed by looking away. The baby will then make various attempts to alter the situation, in particular by protesting or trying to charm his parent.

The still face condition is quite challenging for the infant. She has to manage this highly unusual behavior in her still face parent all on her own (Fivaz-Depeursinge, Favez, Lavanchy, de Noni, & Frascarolo, 2005; Tronick et al., 1978). It includes contradictory messages: the parent is facing the infant at dialogue distance, thus giving the message, "I'm ready to interact with you." At the same time that parent is maintaining an expressionless, silent stance, not responding to the infant's signals and thus giving the message, "I'm not ready to interact with you."

The idea was to incorporate the still face into the LTP. Families were brought into the lab when the infants were 4 months old. They were instructed to play together in four parts, each lasting 2 minutes, but different from the standard LTP instructions:

I   All three are asked to play together.
II One of the parents is invited to play with the infant while the other is "simply present."
III The active parent is asked to pose a still face to the child for a period of 2 minutes. The non–still face parent is asked to remain "simply present," empathic to the infant's bids, but to visually redirect the infant to the still face parent. Note the parents are free to stop the situation if they find it too disturbing.
IV The family is asked to play all three together again.

The question put to the baby was: confronted with this unusual behavior, will you turn to the simply present parent, clearly showing us you are aware that this is still a triangular relationship? We have already described this kind of behavior in the standard LTP. For example, in the case of Zoe, at peak moments of shared affect, she spontaneously turned to her father, as if to also share her delight with him about her mother sticking out her tongue or perhaps to see his response to it. In a sense the LTP with still face pushes the baby further, confronting her with clearly unusual behavior in the active parent. This then allowed us to observe the infant's response in a more controlled manner in the lab. Seeing the parent's still face, most 4 month-old babies did in fact turn towards the third-party parent, showing a whole array of often mixed expressions: sometimes distress or protest, more often confusion, surprise, and, for some, interest or even attempts to charm the third-party parent (Fivaz-Depeursinge, Favez, Lavanchy, de Noni, & Frascarolo, 2005). Below we describe Lola's experience in more detail.

Lola in the LTP still face

During the initial 3-together play, 18 week-old Lola has some delightful threesome sharing.

> *Her parents sing to her and she looks back and forth at them. She shares her joy with them throughout the 2 minutes with numerous triangular bids. The sharing of dyadic as well as three-way delight continues as she next plays with her mother, while her father remains simply present. She seems keenly aware of her father's presence, and actively seeks out his participation even though he clearly follows "the rules" of a non-active parent. He sits back in his seat, acknowledging Lola only when she turns to him and then guides her back to her mother by pointedly turning his gaze and his head towards the mother to reorient Lola's gaze in that direction.*

Next comes the still face, lasting 2 minutes, during which the mother remains impassive and silent. We have divided Lola's still face experience into five segments:

1 *Lola immediately reacts to her mother's still face. Having seen her mother's face, Lola immediately looks down at her feet, and then cycles through either looking down again or sitting back in her chair, avoiding looking at her mother. After 16 seconds she slowly raises her eyes again to stare at her mother with a stern expression on her face. This look at her mother is actually the beginning of a triangular bid.*

2 *Lola looks at her father. The next thing Lola does is to look sideways with a pout. She is not yet looking at her father, but within two seconds she seems to do a double take, glancing briefly at him, only to look down again, but then she slowly raises her eyes and looks at him with a stern expression on her face. She remains there long enough to see him acknowledge her, and then she rapidly shifts her gaze to look at her mother again.*

3 *Lola attempts to change the context. Lola spends the next ten seconds focused on her feet, then protests with a grimace. She next uses a well-known strategy seen in the original still face research: charm. She looks up and smiles at her still face mother – granted, it is a half-hearted smile.*

4   *Lola turns to her father again.* *Lola now repeats her earlier triangular bid: a stern look at her mother, shifting to her father with a frown, and then looking down.*

5   *Return to normal.* *When the parents stop the still face and transition back to 3-together play, Lola immediately responds by turning to her father and mother with a smile – and then suddenly sobering. Bit by bit she cheers up and eventually fully reengages in three-way sharing with numerous triangular bids, just as she had done at the beginning.*

Comment

In the traditional still face with just one parent, infants typically work hard to regulate their affect when confronted with this contradictory situation. They engage in self-soothing and distraction strategies, on the one hand, and on the other hand, they try to change the situation by protesting or trying to charm the still face parent. These two actions are related but distinctly separate ways of managing. The self-soothing and distraction serve to regulate the infant, whereas the protesting and charming are ways to engage the parent in an interaction.

In the LTP with still face, the infant adds triangular strategies to the repertoire. She can now make direct bids to the third-party parent, but also triangular bids including both parents. The affective tones of her bids – charming, protesting, or vigilant – all communicate her discomfort with the situation and her wish to change it. Once again, in the context of this confusing situation of the still face, we can clearly see the precursors to social referencing which will not fully appear until near the end of the first year.

Conclusion

The example of Lucas was chosen as representative of normative families in the sample. He manages the 3-together play with his parents using a number of typical strategies for infants of this age, in particular triangular bids. He is also able to signal clearly to his parents when the level of activity needs to be toned down. In turn, while not perfectly attuned, his parents are sensitive enough to his cues and able to modify their play in a coordinated way, responding to their infant's signals. As an onlooker to his parents' dialogue in part IV, Lucas uses strategies typical of 3 month-olds managing this role. He finds a number of ways to regulate his frustration, such as distraction and self-soothing. At other points he just watches his parents' interaction. Of course, he also makes a variety of attempts to try to change the situation.

We included Zoe's LTP here because of her ability to differentiate between her two parents in three-way imitation games. The sticking-out-the-tongue game is certainly something we saw in other families at 3 months. But in addition, Zoe is able to learn quite quickly that her father is not going to play this game with her. She continues to play it with her mother, while still engaging with her father in other ways. In the still face protocol at 4 months, infants like Lola typically turn towards the third-party parent, as if to ask for help, in what we presume to be a precursor of social referencing.

Together these cases illustrate the capacity of young infants to handle primary triangular communication. In the standard LTP situation, we saw the infants in all four of the possible configurations of a triad. Each dyad had the chance to interact in parts I, II, and IV, and the families played all together in part III.

More recent studies have replicated some of this work and developed it further. In one study families were assessed in their homes, using a mirror to capture the parents' faces, while the infant's face was directed at a single camera (tradition- ally the LTP uses two cameras). The LTP with still face was then further modi- fied, as the parents were asked to pose the still face together before returning to 3-together play. Once again the infants used shifting gaze and the other strate- gies noted earlier to manage the challenges posed (McHale, Fivaz-Depeursinge, Dickstein, Robertson, & Daley, 2008). The study also looked at coparenting beyond the LTP situation, through observational measures and semi-structured interviews with the parents. They concluded that "advanced triangular capacities may best be cultivated in families where there is better-developed coordination between the child's coparents" (McHale et al., 2008, p. 458). We will return to these important findings in section II, where the coordination between coparents is less than optimal.

Notes

1 Names and identifying data have been altered to protect confidentiality.
2 This case has been previously described in Fivaz-Depeursinge (2002).

References

Bretherton, I. (1992). Social referencing, intentional communication, and the interfacing of minds in infancy. In S. Feinman (Ed.), *Social referencing and the social construction of reality in infancy* (pp. 55–77). New York: Plenum Press.

Fivaz-Depeursinge, E., & Corboz-Warnery, A. (1999). *The primary triangle: A develop- mental systems view of fathers, mothers and infants.* New York: Basic Books.

Fivaz-Depeursinge, E., Favez, N., Lavanchy, C., de Noni, S., & Frascarolo, F. (2005). Four-month-olds make triangular bids to father and mother during trilogue play with still face. *Social Development, 14*(2), 361–378.

McHale, J., Fivaz-Depeursinge, E., Dickstein, S., Robertson, J., & Daley, M. (2008). New evidence for the social embeddedness of infant's early triangular capacities. *Family Pro- cess, 47*, 445–463.

Meltzoff, A., & Moore, M. K. (1995). A theory of the role of imitation in the emergence of self. In P. Rochat (Ed.), *The self in infancy: Theory and research* (pp. 73–93). Amster- dam: Elsevier.

Meltzoff, A., & Moore, M. (1997). Explaining facial imitation: A theoretical model. *Early Development and Parenting, 6,* 179–192.

Rochat, P., & Striano, T. (1999). Social-cognitive development in the first year. In P. Rochat (Ed.), *Early social cognition: Understanding others in the first months of life* (pp. 3–34). Mahwah, NJ: Erlbaum.

Tronick, E., Als, H., Adamson, L., Wise, S., & Brazelton, T. B. (1978). The infant's response to entrapment between contradictory messages in face-to-face interaction. *Journal of the American Academy of Child & Adolescent Psychiatry, 17*(1), 1.

Tronick, E. Z., Als, H., & Brazelton, T. B. (1980). Monadic phases: A structural description analysis of infant-mother face-to-face interaction. *Merril Palmer Quarterly, 26,* 3–24.

Appendix 2.1

Microanalytic method of infant's engagement

In order to study the development of the infant's engagement, we needed to be able to see moment to moment how the infant communicated when faced with her two parents at the same time. We proceeded in three steps (for details, see Fivaz-Depeursinge, Favez, Lavanchy, de Noni, and Frascarolo [2005]).

First step

Microanalytic coding of the infant's gaze and affect was done using an adaptation of Tronick's monadic phases (Tronick, Als, & Brazelton, 1980). Coding was done at half-second intervals whether the infant is looking at her mother's face, at her father's face, or elsewhere and the affect she is displaying. Note that in monadic phases, all modes of expression (vocal, facial, gestural) are integrated into a global category, with five "phases" in which the infant interacts with her social partners.

Summary description of monadic phases codes:

- Social engagement: infant bids parent with facial and vocal expressions of joy (smiles, coos, positive vocalizing, laughing).
- Social monitoring: infant bids parent with a neutral or interested facial expression; may vocalize.
- Tense monitoring: infant bids parent with attention colored by weariness or fear, yet not distress or protest.
- Active protest: infant bids parent with facial expressions of anger, grimaces, and/or with crying, and/or with negative moves such as pick me up, arching the back.
- Non-engagement: infant addresses neither parent.

Second step

The second step involved detecting and categorizing triangular bids, where the infant rapidly shifts his gaze back and forth between his two parents within

5-second intervals (at 3 months) and 3-second intervals (9 and 18 months) and addresses them with the same affective signal.

- Triangular engagement (social engagement directed at both parents)
- Triangular monitoring (social monitoring directed at both parents)
- Triangular tension (tense monitoring directed at both parents)
- Triangular protest (protest directed at both parents)

Third step

The third step consisted of the characterization of the infant's "style of engagement."

- The form: mainly dyadic or mainly triangular
- The intensity: appropriate or either over-engaged or disengaged
- The affective balance: predominance of positive or negative affects
- The frequency and the affective balance of the triangular bids

The analysis of these variables yielded four infant engagement styles:

- Triangular engagement
- Split engagement
- Go-between/withdrawal
- Role reversal

While the latter three styles are problematic, triangular engagement is the typical pattern, the one we are concerned with in section I.

References

Fivaz-Depeursinge, E., Favez, N., Lavanchy, C., de Noni, S., & Frascarolo, F. (2005). Four-month-olds make triangular bids to father and mother during trilogue play with still face. *Social Development, 14*(2), 361–378.

Tronick, E. Z., Als, H., & Brazelton, T. B. (1980). Monadic phases: A structural description analysis of infant-mother face-to-face interaction. *Merril Palmer Quarterly, 26,* 3–24.

Chapter 3

Late infancy

Secondary triangular communication

With Sarah Cairo

Olivia is 9 months old and at a routine check-up with her mother. The two wait in the exam room together, when suddenly the nurse arrives. Olivia startles as the door opens and she sees this unfamiliar person. She looks to her mother, who is smiling at the nurse and starts talking with her. Seeing her mother is comfortable with the nurse, Olivia settles back into playing with her toy.

Many of us are familiar with the interchange above as an example of social referencing; when an infant feels uncertain about the meaning of an event he turns towards his caregiver to check on her facial expression as a way to clarify how to react. Until recently social referencing was not necessarily understood in the context of triangular communication per se, but for many it might have been considered the first marker of the infant's ability to manage an interaction with more than one other person. Our work with young families, however, suggests that the trajectory that brought Olivia to this new skill likely began months earlier.

In the previous chapter we discussed how 3 month-olds manage three-way interactions using both examples from everyday life and data from a longitudinal study of volunteer families at the Centre for Studies of the Family (Centre d'Etude de la Famille – CEF), part of the University of Lausanne Institute for Psychotherapy. By 9 months infants are capable of participating in much more complex interactions with their two parents, as well as better able to manage being a third party when their parents are interacting among themselves.

Developmental context

As discussed in chapter 2, the development of early communication can be broken down into primary and secondary communication (Bretherton, 1992). Primary communication occurs in the early months of development, and is characterized by interactions that have no topic other than the interaction itself – for example, a father and baby at the change table exchanging gurgles and coos. By 9 months babies are now capable of what is also referred to as "intentional communication." This secondary communication involves an "intentional stance" (Bates, 1979) or what we might consider a precursor to "theory of mind" (Baron-Cohen, 1991). They are developing a sense of the intentions or what is in the minds of others. With this added understanding of relationships, messages can now be exchanged about a common topic; parents and infants can now talk about "something." For example, an infant points to a balloon and his mother responds, "Yes, a balloon." Later a dog approaches quite abruptly in the park, frightening the infant, who turns to his mother in distress. The mother crouches down and pets the dog, while reassuring the infant, "The dog's just excited to see you." In both instances, the infant seems to some extent aware that he is sharing his experience with his mother, and in turn she is able to appropriately respond. Now what would happen to this secondary, intentional communication if there were three or more people?

In triangular and multiperson interactions the baby must coordinate his attention with two partners or even more. At 3 months the infant is able to share basic positive or negative affects with both parents. Through triangular bids, rapidly looking back and forth between the parents, the infant conveys to them a number of affects: pleasure, distress, uncertainty, and so on (see chapter 2). By the end of the first year that same infant is also able to share his feelings about an object or an event. In addition, when frustrated, these older infants use a number of complex strategies to communicate with both parents to try to change the interaction. They may even be starting to play one parent against the other. Consider Olivia, protesting as her father wipes off her face after a meal. She turns to her mother and even calls out "Ma!" but to no avail, as the face wiping continues. It is as if she is thinking, "I don't like what Daddy is doing. Maybe I can get Mommy to do something about it." Her mother might even respond empathically, "You don't like that one bit, but Daddy needs to clean your face." The mother resonates with Olivia's overture but without undermining her partner.

Let's come back to the question of social referencing. In chapter 2, we proposed that this phenomenon does not appear out of nowhere, but may have its precursors in the triangular bids seen in 3 month-olds. In classic developmental theory, however, social referencing in its full form emerges only towards the end of the first year.

Because we have broadened our focus to include both parents and not simply the mother-baby dyad, our task once again is to explore the possibility of three-way or even multiperson social referencing. What would this look like?

> *Olivia is at her cousin's house with her two parents. Her mother picks up a tambourine; something she has never seen before. She begins to tap on it. Surprised by the novelty and sound, Olivia gives her mother a questioning look. Her mother encourages her, "Try tapping on it too." Olivia looks at the tambourine, and then turns to her father. Her father nods and smiles, encouraging Olivia further. Eventually she starts to tap on the tambourine too.*

In this example one has the sense of Olivia wondering, "That's weird – Mommy wants to tap on that strange thing." And then after looking at her father it is as if she thinks, "Daddy seems to think it's a good idea too, I guess I'll do it then." In this three-way communication the baby checks in with her two parents, who are able to accurately read her confusion and encourage her.

We also see the intentional stance when the infant finds herself in the third-party position, observing her two parents interacting. Wanting to be included, she draws on her new capacities to attract her parents' attention. For instance, discovering that she is no longer the center of attention, the infant might cycle through a set of maneuvers such as whimpering, imitating her parents' tones, calling out to one or both of them, laughing along with her parents (although not necessarily understanding why they are laughing). While the 3 month-old might do some of the same things one does not have the same sense of the baby's intentions at that earlier stage. Now the infant can set a goal, use different means to attain it, and sometimes even succeed (Bates, 1979).

As in the previous chapter, we return to Lucas and his parents, a typical family from the longitudinal study at the CEF. We present details of their Lausanne Trilogue Play (LTP; Fivaz-Depeursinge & Corboz-Warnery, 1999) at 9 months to better illustrate the concepts presented here.

Lucas at 9 months

The family is seated in a triangle formation, facing one another. Lucas is in an infant seat and the parents in chairs. The researcher has just given them the instructions for the LTP – first the mother will play with Lucas as this has been randomly assigned for the study. The father is to be "simply present." In part II he will become active while she is in the role of third party. In part III they will play all together, and then in part IV the parents will talk with one another while Lucas is the third party.

> *The play between Lucas and his mother is quite joyful and lovely. She sings a nursery rhyme using her hands as the puppets. Lucas imitates his mother's "puppet" gestures. At several high points, he looks at his father with delight, as if to share his pleasure with him too. In part II, the father tries similar games, with somewhat less success, but all-in-all, their play generally works well too.*

After a fussy moment for Lucas, the parents decide to proceed to part III and they move his seat to position it so he is angled between them.

LTP part III

What follows is a more detailed description of this third part. We have divided this part into four segments. Pay attention to the moment when the family finally engages in 3-together play well into what we have called the "sneezing game." Remember, when Lucas rapidly shifts his gaze between his two parents, that is the hallmark of infant triangular communication. Also watch for how the parents work together to coordinate with one another to reach their goal, in what McHale has referred to as a "cohesive coparenting alliance" (2007).

1   ***Lucas warms up.*** *It takes about 40 seconds for the family to fully transition to 3-together play. There are a number of false starts and Lucas becomes a bit fussy. The mother tries a few different games.*

2   ***Lucas fully engages in twosome and threesome games.*** *Lucas' mother now introduces one more game that will last a full 90 seconds, relatively long for this age. She makes a small pretend sneeze and then, pointing towards her husband, exclaims, "Daddy can do it too!" This seems to be a familiar game, as Lucas looks at her, and immediately brightens up in anticipation. The father now "sneezes" as the mother exclaims, "This time it was Daddy!" Excited, Lucas looks only at his mother and then quickly looks down at his seatbelt. Still looking down he laughs as his father "sneezes" once more. The parents laugh too. Next the mother brings her head in close to Lucas and he laughs without looking up from the seatbelt. She straightens up and playfully says, "You're being difficult!" Lucas coos happily. He finally looks up at her in anticipation of the next sneeze, and she exclaims, "Wait for it!" Both parents sneeze at the same time. Laughing, Lucas quickly looks from his mother, to the ceiling, and back at her. She points at his father. "Daddy can do it too, you know." Lucas looks at her with a surprised expression and then finally turns to his father, for the first time. His father sneezes once again. Lucas looks away; flapping his arms and then rapidly alternates his gaze, back and forth between his parents. He keeps laughing as his parents continue sneezing separately and together. Throughout this segment it is clear all three are sharing in this joyful moment together. Eventually Lucas gets the hiccups and he comes down from the high of the sneezing game for a brief pause (8 seconds in total). His mother tries starting a new game of making faces.*

3   ***Lucas moderates his level of engagement.*** *The father joins the mother in the face-making game and the next segment lasts about 30 seconds. Lucas looks back and forth at his two parents, with a serious expression on his face. Then he reaches out to each of his parents, trying to touch their mouths. As he alternates between exploring each of their faces, Lucas remains calm and focused.*

4   ***Lucas signals the end.*** *Lucas holds out both arms to his mother and then to his father, in a pick-me-up gesture and then he yawns. This is the signal the parents choose to terminate the 3-together play.*

Comment

It is important to note that we chose Lucas' family not because they illustrate a perfect LTP but rather because, despite some minor glitches along the way, they successfully complete the task as a "good enough" interaction. While the mother seems to mostly take the lead, the father is a willing follower, and so they end up highly coordinated with one another. As for Lucas, he manages how excited he gets by looking down, even at times when he is laughing and vocalizing excitedly.

Where the infant looks, at his parents or elsewhere, is referred to as "gaze orientation." Lucas' gaze orientation is directed away from his parents to such an extent that he ends up scoring below average for his age. We might interpret this as a lower threshold for arousal in Lucas, or perhaps his parents are a little overstimulating with their son. In the end, however, the overall feeling in the room is positive, and this is what makes their interaction "good enough."

In terms of his triangular communication, the sneezing game was the first time Lucas engaged in triangular bids during this part. At the height of it, he makes ten of them, looking back and forth from one parent to the other and showing interest and pleasure. Lucas expresses much more positive affect than negative affect, both overall and if we were to look at just his triangular bids. We will see in Part II of this book, where we discuss problematic interactions, that this ratio, during triangular bids too, is a key indicator of success or difficulty for families.

We also see evidence of Lucas' intentional stance. During his play with his mother in part I, Lucas imitates how she makes her hands into "puppets." Imitation is seen as a precursor to the intentional stance (Meltzoff, 1999), but by 9 months it is more elaborate than it was at 3 months. At 3 months, Lucas simply imitated the facial expressions he saw, whereas now his imitation is about "something."

Another example of the intentional stance comes when Lucas' mother points to her husband and exclaims, "Daddy can do it too, you know!" Lucas follows her pointing and looks to his father, who goes along with the game and sneezes. All three laugh together. Through his mother's words, gaze, or pointing, Lucas has understood that he should look at his father too. This is another example of intentional stance in that the family is communicating about "something."

Let's move on to see how Lucas manages part IV of the LTP, where he will need to call on many more skills to manage his parents talking with one another, while he is in the third-party position.

LTP part IV

After establishing that they need to move on to the next part, the parents simply turn to face one another, and while initially a little self-conscious, they engage in a playful, animated discussion. Throughout this next part, Lucas will resort to a variety of behaviors to manage on his own or try to regain their attention. What follows is a detailed description of this part, divided into five segments:

1   ***Lucas protests.*** *For the first half minute of part IV, Lucas protests, looking back and forth at both of his parents and screeching a couple of times. Both his face and his vocal expressions convey whining.*

2   ***Lucas monitors his parents.*** *Still in the first minute of part IV, Lucas now starts to follow his mother's hand gestures. He focuses on her hands, looks up at her with what seems like a mixture of surprise and interest, and then focuses on his father's hands. He also looks up at his father's face.*

3   ***Lucas tries to get his parents' attention.*** *Now Lucas sets out to actively get his parents' attention. He will try a number of strategies: quietly protesting, calling out, clapping his hands, becoming more animated, making some of the same noises he made with his parents earlier, and even making faces.*

4   ***Lucas distracts himself.*** *For the next 40 seconds, Lucas focuses his interest on the seatbelt, grabbing at it and pulling it. This behavior is interspersed with a few brief "withdrawals" where he looks off to the side.*

5   ***Lucas tries to get his parents' attention again, using "approaches."*** *Finally, during the last minute, Lucas once again tries to get his parents attention, making all kinds of overtures, including new ones. He looks intently at his father and calls to him softly. He whimpers quietly, and finally looks pointedly at both parents and makes the puppet gestures from the game played earlier in parts I and II. At the end of all this effort, he finally wins his parents over. "Okay, that's enough sweetie. We'll stop here so you're not too tired for the next part."*

Comment

We have introduced the concept of "approaches" in this section – those behaviors with which Lucas is trying to capture his parents' attention. Approaches are like bids, in that they involve this meaning or intention we have been discussing. As with bids, they can also be dyadic or triangular. In other words, they can be directed simply at one parent at a time, or to the coparenting unit, but do not always include shifts of gaze between them (Fivaz-Depeursinge, Favez, Lavanchy Scaiola, & Lopes, 2010).

Lucas' behavior in this part is quite typical. He tries a series of strategies to manage, including approaches. He cycles through the strategies until he finally succeeds in getting his parents' attention back. Clearly the order and nature of the repertoire will vary from one infant to the next, but we see nice examples of the intentional stance. Lucas has set himself a goal – winning back his parents' attention – and creatively employs different strategies to reach it. We also see the hand "puppet" game. Now Lucas is not simply imitating the game, he is recalling it and using it as a strategy to win his parents over, and he succeeds.

The moments where Lucas appears to be following his parents' conversation reflect how interested infants are not only in their parents but also in the relationships they have with each other. We see this in the various monitoring bids where he attends with interest to either or both parents.

As for the parents, although they are somewhat shy talking in front of the research team, their relationship appears playful and reciprocal. The fact that

Lucas is successful in regaining their attention through his approaches speaks to their "benevolent inattention" towards him. Benevolent inattention occurs in families with a good-enough coparenting alliance. The parents follow two agendas in parallel – as they often do in real life. They engage with one another, and may even be quite absorbed by their own dialogue, but they almost continuously monitor the state of their child, in their periphery, even if they do not directly focus on him. Others might refer to this as a clear boundary around the parents as a couple (Minuchin, 1974), while at the same time the boundary is flexible enough for the parents to meet the child's needs when appropriate. The parents remain especially sensitive to the infant's capacity to manage his frustration and reward him with success when enough time has passed to fulfill the fourth part of the LTP, or maybe if he does something particularly brilliant to win them over.

Variant: The 9 month-old faced with the parents displaying affection

In the next section we return to Lola, who we also met in chapter 2. We chose her to further show how infants at this age manage as third parties, particularly when the parents' behavior makes it even more challenging.

Lola at 9 months

We join Lola and her parents just as the parents are transitioning into part IV. They both sit back in their chairs and focus on each other. Neither turns to look at Lola, even when after about a minute, she manages to push the seatbelt a bit too far into her mouth and startles a little. While part IV for this family is a bit short in duration, the parents' dialogue is playful and loving, reflecting a deep connection between them. In fact at one point the father affectionately takes the mother's hand, to help her hold back from intervening with Lola shortly after the startle from the seatbelt. Lola had already recovered, and it was clear that she was managing just fine without help.

Let us now go over this sequence, divided into four segments. Watch for Lola's changing strategies:

1 *Lola discovers her parents in dialogue – monitoring, distraction, and approaches. Lola is looking down at the belt in her chair when her parents shift to face one another for part IV. She now straightens up, still holding the belt, and catches sight of her mother. Lola's expression switches to one of surprise but she immediately looks back down. She spends much of the next 40 seconds exploring the belt with her hands and her mouth, but also looks up at her parents' gestures, extends one foot towards her father and at times calls out to each parent enthusiastically.*
2 *Lola manages on her own. Lola refocuses her attention on the seatbelt, vocalizing with enthusiasm. It is here that she pushes the belt somewhat*

too far into her mouth and ends up grimacing with disgust. She looks at her mother, fussing slightly. She quickly recovers and resumes observing her parents and resonating with their animation.

3   **Lola finds her parents holding hands – monitoring and sadness.** As her father takes her mother's hand, Lola looks at her parents' hands and her expression shifts from serious to sad, ending in a full pout. This transition in expression is punctuated by a few social references directed at her mother. As her parents release their clasp, Lola continues to look at her mother's hands, then her own, which are still clutching the belt.

4   **Lola reanimates and shifts to protest.** Lola settles back into exploring the belt, but a moment later becomes agitated, shifting her attention to various things in and around her seat. She seems unable to maintain focus. Without actually looking at her parents, she starts to raise her arms in what looks like a pick-me-up gesture, but then stops midway through it. She keeps her eyes averted from her parents until they finally end the fourth part. They call to her and she responds immediately by looking up at both of them.

Comment

Lola appears to have two agendas in parallel. She focuses on the objects around her, and in so doing distracts herself and remains relatively calm in the first part of this segment. At the same time she monitors her parents' interaction: observing it, resonating with their animation, and making numerous approaches to regain their attention. This is all typical and what we saw with Lucas. We draw your attention to this normal variant because of Lola's reaction when her parents held hands. While we cannot know for sure what Lola is thinking or feeling as she starts to pout, it certainly suggests she is feeling distressed in the context of seeing her parents' closeness as she is left to fend for herself. It is only after she gets agitated about the seatbelt, and then notices the physical closeness of her parents, that she shows any sign of distress. It is here that she loses her ability to self-regulate. She tries out typical strategies: protest and distraction, but without much success. It is not until her parents end part IV that she finally and quite easily settles.

Given the LTP is a play context where the goal is to share delight, the typical infant at this stage might experience the inattention of part IV as a threat. As they develop, infants increasingly develop intersubjective communication or the ability to share other people's feelings or mind states (Stern, 2004). Intersubjectivity is thought to be a motivational system in humans, not unlike other motivational systems such as feeding, attachment, reproduction, and so on (Trevarthen & Hubley, 1978). Intersubjective communication is linked to the other emerging capacities we have been discussing in this chapter – namely, the intentional stance and theory of mind. In order to experience intersubjectivity, one must also have a sense of what one wants and how others understand that.

In addition to the rupture in intersubjective communication, part IV challenges infants and their parents with a mild separation. The parents do not actually leave the room, but they are no longer attending to the infant. In the case of Lola, this separation is exaggerated when her parents hold hands. It opens the question of Lola's attachment to them and the parents' response to her need for security. When infants feel threatened in some way the attachment system is activated and the infant will then seek security from her caregivers. In this book we are interested in what all of these motivational systems might look like on a family level. Just before her parents were holding hands, Lola was in mild distress from gagging on the seatbelt. She addressed a bid to her mother at that time, but her mother did not respond, and shortly after that she was holding hands with the father. Initially the parents maintain the boundary around their couple, but then they show the flexibility to stop their discussion and attend to Lola's needs. This example highlights the interplay between the need for clear but flexible intergenerational boundaries, where in this case the flexibility may be about meeting the child's attachment needs.

We cannot exclude the possibility of jealousy also being triggered in part IV of the LTP. For example, faced with the inattention of her two parents, the infant might feel jealous of one of the parents and try to reengage her and relegate the other back to the third-party position. This is not a typical reaction, but one we have observed in a minority of cases.

Finally, the infant might simply be motivated by a feeling of jealousy about the relationship between her two parents (Fivaz-Depeursinge et al., 2010). In most families, infants distributed their attention between both parents in part IV, making multiple triangular bids and approaches in an attempt to regain the relationship with both parents.

More on 9 month-old approaches

Compared to 3 month-olds, the motor development of 9 month-olds allows them to move about more. Their cognitive, social, and emotional development means they can follow more of their parents' interaction, and also that they can use a wider variety of strategies and more deliberate ways to get their parents' attention. In practice, some infants try to physically connect, leaning over and touching a parent or making a pick-me-up gesture. Others vocalize, and this can vary from semi-playful to fussy and all the way up to loud, imperative yells. Each infant might cycle through a number of physical and vocal maneuvers several times, leaning over towards a parent, whining, and then laughing along with the parents.

We have also seen infants making approaches at key moments during the parents' exchange. For instance, in one family with some tension in the parents' marriage, at the outset of part IV the mother says, "We don't even know what to say to each other . . ." The father replies, "It's difficult . . ." At this very moment the infant breaks the tension with a burst of animation. He looks at his mother with a huge smile, vocalizing with enthusiasm, and his arms and legs wriggling about, as if to draw their attention to himself. This has occurred in a regular way in the lab, such that we cannot consider it mere coincidence. We will encounter more examples like this in chapter 8 when we discuss "Child-at-Center" coparenting.

With their emerging intentional stance, many babies at this age make reference to games they played earlier in the LTP in the hopes of regaining their parents' attention. We saw this with Lucas, and the "puppet" game hand gestures. Similarly, in another family, one infant held out a toy to his father, as they had just played a game of giving and taking the toy in the 3-together. A third infant scratched the headrest, looking at her mother and father, apparently hoping to draw their attention with this interesting noise as she had so successfully done before during play. In contrast, a more provocative child from yet another triad gleefully and noisily sucked on the seatbelt, looking wide-eyed up at his father. His parents had repeatedly stopped him from playing with the seatbelt during the 3-together play and so this was perhaps a way to engage them once again.

Comment

Nine month-olds have a variety of ingenious approach strategies to attract their parents' attention and to try to change the course of events. On the other hand, these same infants do attend to their parents' dialogue, despite the frustration generated by the inattention. They appear to monitor the discussion, perhaps trying to understand what is being said, and they also try to actively participate in it. Finally, they now have the resources to find other things to do, such as focus on objects, and as a result regulate their emotional states.

Conclusion

We have now explored the expanding intersubjective repertoire of infants towards the end of their first year of life. As they grow, infants become more active and differentiated in their communication with their parents, as well as more sensitive to their parents' relationship, particularly as third parties. They are also beginning to find ways to manage even minor tensions between their parents. In the next chapter we will see how the introduction of symbols, such as pretend play and language, changes the scene once again.

References

Baron-Cohen, S. (1991). Precursors to a theory of mind: Understanding attention in others. In A. Whiten (Ed.), *Natural theories of mind: Evolution, development and simulation of everyday mindreading* (pp. 233–251). Oxford: Basil Blackwell.

Bates, E. (1979). *The emergence of symbols.* New York: Academic Press.

Bretherton, I. (1992). Social referencing, intentional communication, and the interfacing of minds in infancy. In S. Feinman (Ed.), *Social referencing and the social construction of reality in infancy* (pp. 55–77). New York: Plenum Press.

Fivaz-Depeursinge, E., & Corboz-Warnery, A. (1999). *The primary triangle: A developmental systems view of fathers, mothers and infants.* New York: Basic Books.

Fivaz-Depeursinge, E., Favez, N., Lavanchy Scaiola, C., & Lopes, F. (2010). Family triangular interactions in infancy: A context for the development of jealousy? In S. Hart &

M. Legerstee (Eds.), *Handbook of jealousy: Theories, principles and multidisciplinary approaches* (pp. 445–476). New York: Wiley-Blackwell.

McHale, J. (2007). *Charting the bumpy road of coparenthood.* Washington, DC: Zero to Three Press.

Meltzoff, A. (1999). Origins of theory of mind, cognition and communication. *Journal of Communication Disorders, 32,* 251–299.

Minuchin, S. (1974). *Families & family therapy.* Boston: Harvard University Press.

Stern, D. (2004). *The present moment in psychotherapy and everyday life.* New York: W.W. Norton.

Trevarthen, C., & Hubley, P. (1978). Secondary intersubjectivity: Confidence, confiding and acts of meaning in the first year. In A. Lock (Ed.), *Action, gesture and symbol: The emergence of language* (pp. 183–229). New York: Academic Press.

Chapter 4

Toddlerhood

Symbolic and moral triangular communication

With Francesco Lopes

Toddlerhood is a time of tremendous developmental strides, and this includes how children manage three-way interactions. In this chapter we return to Lucas and his family, in order to get a better understanding of some of these new skills. The family was part of the longitudinal study where volunteer families came to the Centre for Studies of the Family (Centre d'Etude de la Famille – CEF), part of the University of Lausanne Institute for Psychotherapy. Before we get to Lucas, let's go straight to some of the developmental context.

Developmental context

In the previous chapters we discussed infant communication at 3 and 9 months. At this stage the toddler is now capable of even higher-order communication or "symbolic communication." Since these stages were all first described in mothers and babies, or dyads, part of the goal is to elaborate on and provide examples of symbolic communication at the triangular level (mother-father-baby). Here, "symbol" is referring not only to newly acquired language and gestures but also to more sophisticated symbols, such as miming out actions in pretend play.

In chapter 3 we discussed the intentional stance (Bates, 1979) – how near the end of the first year infants use various communication strategies to reach an intended goal, whether on a dyadic level, or in a triangular or multiperson setting. In the toddler years with symbolic communication there comes a deepening awareness of self and other. In addition children now seem to have rudimentary ideas of what might or might not be going on in the mind of the other – in other words, theory of mind (Meltzoff & Gopnick, 1993). This capacity appears both in games of pretending and in words. In the following example we see our prototype baby, Olivia, now 20 months old, putting a number of new skills into action.

> *Olivia is seated at the table waiting for her parents to let her out at the end of a meal. She bangs her spoon loudly on her tray and is making quite a racket singing. Suddenly her father grabs a banana from the fruit bowl and says, "Hello? Yes? Oh it's for you, Olivia!" He holds out the banana to her, but she looks perplexed for a moment. She turns to her mother, who is chuckling*

as she watches them. Olivia returns her gaze to her father, and very seriously reaches for the banana. She holds the banana to her ear and babbles into it, still looking at her father. Improvising, he takes his phone out of his pocket and says, "Yes, Miss?" and they continue in this way, Olivia babbling into her "phone" and her father responding. Olivia's mother looks on, smiling, and Olivia's enthusiasm grows as she looks back and forth between her two parents and babbles into the banana-phone.

In this example the family is truly sharing this exchange between all three of them, even if the mother is more of a bystander. In addition Olivia uses social referencing. She looks to her mother to help her understand her father's strange offer of a banana for a phone. What is new is that much of this interchange involves symbolic play at the triangular level.

At the same time as symbolic communication is developing, emotions based on social or parental expectations are beginning to emerge as well. The toddler experiences the pleasures and pains of emotions such as pride, enthusiasm, embarrassment, guilt, and shame. These emotions have been referred to as moral emotions (Emde, Biringen, Clyman, & Oppenheim, 1991). The infant is torn between two contradictory forces: the wish to comply with the social rules that his parents try to instill in him and feel that sense of pride, versus the wish to assert his autonomy and risk embarrassment or shame. He uses elaborate and deliberate triangular strategies with his parents – not only to share his emotions with them but also to test the limits his parents are by now playfully, but sometimes also harshly, negotiating with him. Needless to say, these new developments can challenge the parents' solidarity.

The classic game of a family tea party recruits each of these new capacities. We very frequently see this at 18 months during the third part of the Lausanne Trilogue Play (Fivaz-Depeursinge & Corboz-Warnery, 1999), when parents play together with their child. At this stage the family is seated at a round table at equal distances from each other. They are provided with a small selection of toys. Parents often initiate a tea party, but frequently toddlers start by saying, "No!" This opposition is often immediately followed by the toddler cooperating. The family then joyfully toasts their teacups, all three parties sharing a sense of joy and pride.

This example mainly taps into the moral emotion of pride; however, what happens when there is more conflict between the toddler and his parents? For instance, one 18 month-old boy is playing with his mother while his father is "simply present" in part II of an LTP.

The boy starts out by following his mother's suggestion to use the toy brush on his hair. Next he brings it to his mouth, looking her straight in the eyes, with a challenging expression on his face. His mother, remaining playful, responds, "You're teasing me!" At this point the little boy throws the brush down on the floor, and then asks her to pick it up. She playfully says, "Bye-bye brush!" As the baby protests, he looks to his father, sitting back in his chair. The father makes an empathic face but then visually redirects the boy to his mother by quietly looking at her himself. She adds a bit more firmly, "I'm not going to get it," and then immediately distracts the toddler with a new game.

Note, how parents respond to these provocations as a pair is part of what we refer to as coparenting (McHale, 2007). It tells us a lot about how these family situations are regulated – towards growth or towards conflict escalation. In the example above, humor and playfulness along with firmness seem to be the best bet, together with the support of the coparent.

We did not observe intense negative moral emotions very often in the interactions of families with good-enough coparenting. Rather, the emphasis seemed to be placed on positive moral emotions, such as pride, humor, or empathy. Had we observed the toddlers in situations requiring more compliance to rules, necessitating more discipline or obedience, we might have seen more negative moral emotions. Certainly in the case studies presented in part II of this book we will have the opportunity to see examples where the more negative moral emotions predominated even in this play situation.

We did expect the toddlers to experience several emotions when placed in the third-party position during part IV of the LTP – for example, interest and frustration. We will see in the following examples that the responses were similar to those of previous ages, yet again more differentiated.

Lucas at 18 months

LTP parts I and II

Once again, we begin with a quick overview of the first half of the family's LTP, and then fast-forward to parts III and IV, where we go into greater detail.

In part I Lucas and his mother engage in mainly symbolic games, like drinking from the teacups or brushing their hair. Lucas keeps trying to include his father in the games, despite his mother explaining, "Daddy will play with you later." When the mother signals the father that it is his turn, Lucas applauds, showing his pleasure. As his mother sits back in her seat, the father does not immediately take over. It is only when Lucas begins to excitedly throw toys down that his father finally takes charge, saying, "No, Lucas, you're throwing everything onto the floor . . . That's not nice!" He then redirects Lucas with a game toasting the teacups and saying, "Cheers!" Lucas enthusiastically participates, looking up at his father with delight, and then towards his mother too. Interestingly he does not try to entice her out of her role as the third party, as he had tried with his father. At the end, Lucas throws down his cup, and now his father responds in a more playful way with, "Again?" Next they move on to part III.

LTP part III

We have divided this part into four segments. Pay attention to how Lucas challenges his parents' authority. In response they will have to cooperate to make this whole thing work. Our expectation is not that they always experience 3-together sharing, but rather that they reach these moments some of the time.

1 ***Lucas shifts from opposition to cooperation with his mother.*** *Part II of the LTP ends with Lucas throwing his cup to the floor. This same theme continues into the beginning of part III, with Lucas' level of excitement and agitation increasing somewhat. The mother tries to start a game with the animals, but Lucas starts wildly mixing up all the toys on the table, sending some to the floor. His mother protests, "Lucas, don't do that!" and successfully distracts him with the Legos. Note that up to this point, despite this being part III, the father has remained in the background.*

2 ***Lucas engages in play with his parents.*** *Finally the mother finds an entrée into 3-together play. Peering through a hole in one of the Lego pieces she exclaims, "Oh look, there's a hole!" Delighted, Lucas watches as she offers his father a turn, and then Lucas finally takes a turn as well. As the three share this experience, Lucas looks proud and his parents resonate with him and with one another. Not surprisingly, this moment of togetherness is immediately followed by a moment of gleeful excitement, where Lucas throws everything down on the floor again. The pattern for Lucas is clear; moments of togetherness are to be followed by excitement and throwing.*

3 ***Lucas faces divergence between his parents.*** *The mother starts building a tower with the Lego and the father alternates between helping or staying in the background. It is at this point that the parents diverge, creating a moment of confusion for Lucas. As the tower comes to its completion, Lucas' father proposes they place a hen on top, but his mother, presumably absorbed in her own plan, proposes a pig instead. Lucas suddenly grabs hold of the mat on the table, about to pull it out, and thereby topple everything down. Instead, he seems to change his mind and makes the sound of the hen – his father's choice of animals. The parents do not respond to any of this, but rather work together and distract him with a car game.*

4 ***Lucas cooperates with father.*** *The family ends part III after Lucas gives a broken car to his father to fix. The mother checks on the time and says, "Shall we leave him on his own?" The father repairs the car, hands it back to Lucas, and then sits back in his chair, away from his son.*

Comment

The 3-together begins as it has in previous LTPs with this family: the mother leads and the father follows. With some effort, the mother is able to find a way to engage her husband and son in a creative game that results in that 3-together moment where they all share in looking through the Lego piece. As noted, this moment of togetherness is followed by Lucas throwing down some of the toys in his excitement.

The parents regroup to start the tower, but then the mother proposes a different animal than the father, presumably inadvertently. As soon as the parents are not coordinated, Lucas gets agitated and is about to throw everything down again when he suddenly opts for the animal his father suggested. If we were to see more of this pattern you could speculate that this is a sort of "siding" with his father. Alternatively we wondered whether Lucas is trying to draw his father out given that he is always following the mother. While we are not suggesting that his intentions are so calculated, recall that in part I, Lucas keeps trying to involve his father when he is supposed to be playing with his mother. He does not try to include his mother when the roles are reversed. On the other hand, Lucas' choice could have more to do with other factors, such as a discomfort with any conflict between his parents.

To their credit, the parents quickly repair the lapse in their coordination, joining together to distract him with the car. This vignette, of the parents having different agendas for the play, is important to underscore for two reasons. First, it is exactly these kinds of scenarios that we see in much greater frequency in families with more problematic interactions. Second, it also underscores that these kinds of miscoordinations happen even with "good enough" coparenting and, more importantly, that they can be successfully repaired.

LTP part IV

In this next part Lucas must manage on his own while his parents have their own discussion but are still seated with him at the same table. The part is divided into four segments, according to Lucas' communication strategies, which we have labeled at the top of each segment.

1   *Lucas plays and provokes.* The mother starts the conversation with her husband by commenting on how hard it is to leave Lucas on his own and then asks the father, "Don't you want to jump in when I'm playing with him?" The father answers, "No, not at all." The mother goes on, "It's really hard for me not to. I have to hold back all the time." She later notes, "Did you notice, he's not upset by us not paying attention to him?" Lucas has been busy crashing cars, throwing toys quite happily (unimpeded by his parents now), as well as playing quietly with the ones he has not thrown yet.

2   *Lucas requests help.* Lucas tries, without success, to force an animal into the truck. He holds it out to his father, then to his mother, looking up at them and calling out to them. The father looks at the mother, smiling. The mother playfully announces to her husband, "More things are going to fall down soon!" Instead, Lucas keeps playing with the truck.

3   *Monitoring the parents and making approaches.* The parents discuss plans for the next day. Lucas pays attention to them for an entire minute, while also trying out a number of "approaches" (see below), without success. He looks at each of them several times with a surprised expression. He holds out his hand to his mother, starts to stand in his seat, sits back down, and hits the table, glancing at his father. In between, when he is not doing these things to attract attention, he amuses himself by looking around the room, or playing with the car. Finally he returns to watching his mother. Looking puzzled, he switches to his father and then says to him, "Not nice not nice." He starts to hum, still looking at his father.

4   *Lucas throws down toys.* Humming, Lucas begins to take the Lego car apart. Systematically he shoves each of the pieces off the table. The mother looks to the father as if to say, "Should we quit now?" The father smiles approvingly. She turns towards the facilitator behind the window: "I think we're through!"

Comment

Faced with his parents attending to one another and not to him, Lucas' ability to self-regulate is remarkable. At no time does he appear to be overwhelmed. Rather, he manages his frustration by means of a number of strategies. He distracts himself by focusing on objects. He reenacts activities from earlier, including the words "not nice." He regulates himself by observing or monitoring his parents' dialogue. Finally, Lucas makes repeated approaches – goal-directed behaviors aimed at regaining the parents' attention (see chapter 3). Overall, his engagement is triangular in that it is directed to both parents. All told, Lucas' behavior is typical of what we observe when the coparenting is cooperative or what McHale has referred to as cohesive (2007).

The parents maintain a balance between having their own exchange while keeping track of Lucas. In contrast, in non-cohesive coparenting, couples struggle with striking this balance. If they are too rigid, and do not attend to the child even when he truly needs them, then they have not been sufficiently sensitive to his needs. If they fail to create any boundary around their interaction (Minuchin, 1974), and simply respond to his every approach, then there is no space for them to have a relationship that is separate from their child. Furthermore, the child misses the chance to exercise his new skills, in particular his ability to manage on his own.

More on approaches

In the group with cohesive coparenting, the toddler's approaches are by now mostly symbolic. They are more numerous and varied than at the earlier ages and all of these toddlers made approaches. They varied only in the number and types of strategies used, and in the proportion of time spent playing versus making approaches. In this context of cohesive coparenting, the children all succeeded in maintaining balanced emotional regulation as well. None of them showed excessive distress or withdrawal. Again, this is in contrast to the cases we will discuss later in section II of this book.

Interestingly, there was a gender difference at this age in the sample. Boys tended to use more provocation (throwing down toys, hitting the table with their hands, or kicking the underside with their feet), while girls tended to use more relational strategies.

To be sure, there was overlap between genders, and the general sequence was fairly consistent for all toddlers. First, the child registers that a change has occurred and that the parents are no longer playing with him. This recognition is evident to the observer as a look of surprise along with social referencing to one or both parents. Most boys sooner or later throw down some toys. They may sweep them all away in one go, or throw them one by one, looking down at each toy as it drops and then often checking if the parents noticed. If not, the next step is to ask the parents to pick up the toys. Certainly at this age children are fascinated with throwing down objects and this may account for some of their motivation. However, given how universal throwing toys is at this particular point in the LTP, it is likely intended to provoke the parents and regain their attention. Many toddlers will give up trying to regain their parents' attention for a while and just play, but then they start up again.

In the midrange of approaches, girls as well as boys use symbolic play, not only as a distraction to help them manage but also as an approach to regain their parents' attention. They will often repeat their favorite games from earlier in the LTP. They then show off the game or present the more interesting toys to their parents to attract their interest. We already saw this strategy in Lucas and the other babies at 9 months, but here it is more sophisticated, even more intentional, and involves symbolic elements.

The more subtle strategies are mostly, but certainly not exclusively, used by girls. The toddler tries out a range of deliberate signals addressed to her parents, such as staring, grimacing, smiling, protesting, pleading, verbalizing, and shouting. She also uses gestures such as pointing, holding her arms out in the pick-me-up gesture or waving bye-bye. All of these approaches occur at strategic points – for example, at a pause in their discussion, or when one of the parents glances at her. Her timing makes her goal, to capture her parents' attention, all the more clear.

Conclusion

Toddlers have come a long way across the first 18 months. They move independently, can engage in rudimentary pretend play, use words, and are motivated by moral emotions to share in their parents' culture, and to affirm their own will. Their initial triangular strategies of sharing their experiences with their parents have reached the symbolic-moral stage, in parallel with their dyadic communication. They have at their disposal multiple tools for handling their parents and their parents' relationship. They not only read their parents' affects and intentions, alternating between confrontation and cooperation, but also are very sensitive to their coparenting, always ready to challenge them if they sense the slightest crack in the foundation. At this age, most of these first-born children still do not have siblings, so they experience their parents' cohesive coparenting on their own. In the next chapter we meet the cohort at age 5. Many of them will now have siblings, giving us the opportunity to discuss multiperson interactions in addition to thinking about where all these skills have led to in the preschooler.

References

Bates, E. (1979). *The emergence of symbols.* New York: Academic Press.

Emde, R., Biringen, Z., Clyman, R., & Oppenheim, D. (1991). The moral self of infancy: Affective core and procedural knowledge. *Developmental Review, 11,* 251–270.

Fivaz-Depeursinge, E., & Corboz-Warnery, A. (1999). *The primary triangle: A developmental systems view of fathers, mothers and infants.* New York: Basic Books.

McHale, J. (2007). When infants grow up in multiperson relationship systems. *Infant-Mental Health Journal, 28,* 370–392.

Meltzoff, A., & Gopnick, A. (1993). The role of imitation in understanding persons and developing a theory of mind. In S. Baron-Cohen, H. Tagerflusberg, & D. J. Cohen (Eds.), *Understanding other minds: Perspectives from autism* (pp. 335–366). New York: Oxford University Press.

Minuchin, S. (1974). *Families & family therapy.* Boston: Harvard University Press.

Chapter 5

From triangular to multiperson communication

With Nicolas Favez

By the time a child reaches age 5 a lot has changed since infancy. Chances are he has now had opportunities to venture beyond the family unit, entering into a variety of social contexts – play groups, day care, and school. In addition to learning to socialize with same-age peers, he must now conform to more rules and expectations set by adults other than his own parents. Many children are now siblings as well, with the pleasures and challenges those relationships hold, including the need to share the parents' attention. In other words, increasingly the child is a partner in multiperson communication beyond the primary triangle.

Developmental context

Narratives

With the gains made in their language and cognitive development, 5 year-olds are able to participate almost fully in "narrative communication." Narratives allow us to convey not simply stories but also our internal states, the thoughts and feelings attached to the experience or event (Favez et al., 2012). Families share and co-construct such narratives with one another organically (Fiese et al., 1999), passing on the family's cultural values from one generation to the next (Bruner, 1990). Narratives reflect how the family gives meaning to their social world, but also help to develop a sense of cohesion by reinforcing expectations and emotions in the family (Favez, Frascarolo, & Lavanchy, 2006).

Even before the arrival of language, infants begin to participate in family narratives, constructed during their earliest interactions with their parents. Once language emerges, even in its earliest stages, children increasingly take on a more active role. By age 5, they not only are able to describe an event factually, but also are starting to convey meaning to the story. For example, they may recount a story about a dog they met in the park, inserting elements about how they felt (happy, excited, or scared) and how others around them may have also reacted. This narrative capacity, while still developing at age 5, significantly shifts how we look at and understand families at this stage.

Siblings

Another shift for first-borns is the arrival of siblings and a move from mother-father-baby communication in the family to interactions involving siblings. In order to accommodate the new family member the distribution of roles between the parents may also change, and the child's relationship with each of them. Of course siblings themselves present a mixed experience for the first-born. There is the potential for rich relationships with siblings, including love and an enduring bond, as well as the natural, inevitable jealousy and rivalry triggered by the division of the parents' attention between the children. The child may also discover the strength of an alliance with his siblings in relation to his parents as he finds he is no longer alone in facing them. Taking these changes into consideration, let's return to our example of Olivia and her family.

> *Olivia's mother is giving her strained peas for the first time. The 7 month-old looks at the spoon and then looks to her father, seated beside them. He smiles encouragingly and so Olivia takes a spoonful in her mouth. Suddenly she spits it out with a look of disgust and refuses any further attempts to try the peas. Her parents give her cereal instead and try a different vegetable later.*
>
> *Now let's fast-forward to Olivia, age 4, seated at the table with her two parents, and her baby brother, Kevin. It's Kevin's turn to try peas for the first time. He looks at the spoon and then looks to each of his family members, who are all looking on with great interest. He tries the peas, but has a similar look of disgust on his face. The parents laugh and Olivia asks, "Why are you laughing?" Her mother responds, "You don't remember, but when you tried peas for the first time, you made the same exact face!" Olivia smiles as she looks at Kevin.*

Comment

The story of the peas is now part of a family narrative that is evolving with the addition of Kevin. Olivia is now part of this co-construction, and may add further meaning to it with time.

Follow-up at 5 years

In this chapter, we jump to age 5, as we continue to explore triangular communication at this stage. Do the families continue with the same style as they used at the implicit level during infancy and toddlerhood, just reconfigured now that they can engage in narrative tasks? What happens to triangular communication when you add siblings to the mix? How do children manage communication with even more people? To explore these questions further at age 5, we brought back the same families we had been following at the Centre for Studies of the Family (Centre d'Etude de la Famille – CEF), part of the University of Lausanne Institute for Psychotherapy.

New tools for the 5-year follow-up

With all of the changes seen in families by this stage of development, we needed new observational tools that took into account narrative communication and the presence of siblings. We describe three variants of Lausanne Trilogue Play (LTP) (Fivaz-Depeursinge & Corboz-Warner, 1999) developed for this stage below. Additional tools were added for the follow-up at 5 years to examine the child's behavior, theory of mind, and predominant emotional themes. These are described in Appendix 5.1.

The Lausanne Narrative Trilogue Play

Because of the central role of narratives in early childhood, we needed a task with this focus. The *Lausanne Narrative Trilogue Play* (LNP) was used with the mother, father, and first-born child. With toy dolls representing each family member, the parents and child are asked to play out a story: the parents are leaving for the weekend, and the child or children stay with a known and trusted caregiver. In other words, the main topic is the separation of the child from her parents, still an emotionally charged topic for children this age. Implicit in this story is also the parents' intimacy as a couple, another potential challenge for children at this stage of development.

The family is asked to follow the same four LTP configurations. In part I, one parent begins the story with the child, while the other is asked to remain simply present. In part II, the parents reverse roles, so the first parent now watches, and the other helps to continue the story with the child. During part III, the parents must work together to help the child finish the story about the weekend getaway. Finally, in part IV, the parents talk with one another while the child continues playing or drawing.

The Lausanne Family Play

In order to involve siblings we also needed a second adaptation of the LTP, this time *Lausanne Family Play* (LFP). The format is similar to the original LTP or the LNP; however, by adding just one sibling to a family the number of possible configurations goes from 4 to 16. So for simplicity's sake, we handle the siblings as a unit and otherwise stick to the four original LTP parts. Instead of playing with one child, one of the parents plays with both or all of the children at the same time during part I, while the other remains simply present. The parents switch roles for part II. In part III the whole family plays together, and during part IV, the parents talk to each other while the siblings remain at the table, but are left to play on their own. The family is seated at an oval table. The two parents face each other on the ends of the table, with the children seated together along one side of the table and facing the camera.

Assessment of the family interactions is similar, although more complex than with the original LTP. The sibling subunit is now also a focus – their relationship with one another, but also the coparenting in this new context. For example, when the children fight, do the parents impose solutions, help the children find their own solutions, or inadvertently amplify the conflict? Do the parents treat the children differently, either by demonstrating a clear understanding of each child's specific needs or through favoritism?

The picnic game

Finally, we wanted a situation that was closer to real-life conditions and would allow us to observe families when roles were not prescribed as they are in the LTP. In the *picnic game* (PNG) the entire family is invited to engage in a pretend family picnic. The room is equipped with a green carpet representing the grass, as well as a bench, a table with chairs, dishes in a basket, and toys in bags for each of the children. The family is instructed to play out their picnic: planning going to the picnic, playing together at the picnic, and then clearing up and returning home. Without the prescribed configurations, the families typically break out into dyads or threesomes, but they shift organically as needed. Sometimes one parent pairs with the eldest child while the other is with the youngest. At other times the children may play together as the parents interact.

The assessment of the PNG looks at similar questions as the LFP, but how the parents set limits and the degree to which the children test them become particularly salient as they are freer to move about the room. So too is the autonomy that the parents allow the children and how ready the children are to explore. As with all variants of the LTP, central to the assessment is the degree of playfulness and how the family manages and shares the highs and lows of the game (see Frascarolo & Favez, 2005).

We now return to Lucas and his family, and present their LNP and PNG to illustrate some of the patterns we see in normative families. We will also meet Sara later in the chapter and discuss her family's LFP. Recall that we chose families that demonstrated "good enough" multiperson communication. As we will see, Lucas' family does not perfectly comply with everything that is asked of them at this stage. It is the overall picture that we are looking at in how families approach these tasks. The primary goals are intersubjective communication (the ability to share other people's feelings or mind states) and playfulness not strict adherence to "the rules."

Lucas at 5 years: Lausanne Narrative Trilogue Play and picnic game

Lucas is now 4 years and 10 months and he has a younger brother, Hugo, who is 29 months old. The family has already completed the LFP, and Hugo has been taken to another room. We join Lucas and his two parents as they begin to play out the story of the children staying with a trusted caregiver while the parents are away for the weekend. The mother has been asked to play first.

LNP parts I–III

With the instructions completed by the facilitator, the mother starts suggesting which doll is who in the story. Lucas, however, makes the final decisions on the characters, vetoing some of his mother's suggestions. She goes along with his choices, even though we later learn some of them were a little unexpected. For example, Lucas picks up the "Lucas" doll and states that he is going to sleep at his paternal grandparents' home. The parents later explain during the video-feedback session that there is actually very little contact with those grandparents. Lucas decides to include his brother, Hugo, in the story as well. We pick up the story just after the parents leave for the weekend.

> *The separation goes without a hitch, and once the parent dolls have driven away, the mother sets them aside, declaring that from now on, they are "gone." The implication is that from now on the story is about the children's weekend and not the parents'. It is at this point that the family starts to transition to part II and the father takes over.*
>
> *He suggests that "Hugo" go fishing with the grandmother and "Lucas" go cut wood with the grandfather. Lucas suddenly gets out of his seat to go look for the real Hugo. The mother interrupts to explain that Hugo is playing elsewhere with the facilitator. The father holds up the Lucas doll and exclaims, "But Lucas is right here!" Lucas takes the doll from his father. As the father plays the role of the grandfather he draws Lucas back into the game by creating a story: "Grandpa leans over to find mushrooms . . . ouch! He fell on his head!" The Grandfather doll gets back up, moaning, "Ouch, my nose hurts . . . darned mushrooms!" Lucas begins to laugh, looking at his father. His laugh is contagious and his father begins to laugh too. Lucas turns to his mother, who gradually smiles as well, and he looks back and forth at both of them laughing.*
>
> *The three of them laugh for more than a minute, and never actually finish the story. The laughing ends when Lucas sees tears in his mother's eyes and asks, "Why are you crying?" She explains, "Sometimes you get tears when you're happy too." The father adds, "Look at me, my eyes are kind of teary too."*

Comment

The 2+1 configurations of parts I and II of the LNP (one parent actively playing with Lucas while the other is simply present) has little by little shifted to a 3-together interaction.

Some of the patterns that we have seen with this family in previous chapters are still there. Lucas' mother is a little more controlling in her style than is his slightly more passive father. Lucas resists some of his mother's suggestions and protests limit setting, but ultimately they are able to work out solutions and move forward in the story. This shows the flexibility in this family to pick up on each other's cues and find compromise.

While they do not fully follow the structure of part III or the story line prescribed by the task, it is clear that there is warmth and three-way intersubjective communication. This could not have been more evident than when they all laugh together about the grandfather falling. In section II of this book we will discuss families who rigidly adhere to the "rules" of the task, but fail to experience this type of sharing. Others may digress completely and still do not experience the three-way sharing and warmth of Lucas' family.

How this family manages the part in the story where the parents leave for the weekend is also significant. Neither the separation nor the fact that the parents are presumably on some intimate weekend alone poses a problem. Rather, Lucas and his mother sail right through the separation as if it would be no issue at all, and the mother lays to rest any discussion of the parents' time away. Instead, they play out the children's weekend with their grandfather. This ease or tendency not to focus on the moment of separation and the parents' time away is actually a positive indicator. The families we discuss in section II struggle with being clear on the roles of parents and the roles of children, what has been referred to as "distorted intergenerational boundaries" (Minuchin, 1974). Those families tend to dwell on how difficult the separation will be for the child and/or play out what the parents were doing while away, rather than focus on the child's experience.

LNP part IV

This last part of any LNP challenges parents to create a clear intergenerational boundary as they discuss among themselves.

> *The father asks Lucas to finish the story on his own. Lucas protests, "You can finish it yourself! . . . Mom can finish it!" The mother firmly adds, "You have to play by yourself for a while or you can draw." Lucas complies. During their discussion, which is as always led by the mother, she states, "It's really hard for me not to get involved when you two are playing with each other. I need to put my two cents in everywhere!" Smiling gently, the father states, "You've always felt that way." In the meantime, Lucas draws, enthusiastically explaining what he is doing. He addresses some of his comments to his father, but on seeing that his parents are talking to each other, he returns to his drawing, still narrating aloud. At one point he stands up and shows his father his drawing, "Did you see Lucas got bigger?" His father smiles at him, but then continues talking with his wife. Lucas sits back down, picks up the dolls, and returns to the story from the LNP. "Grandpa wants to cut wood with Lucas." The father turns to the mother, laughing. "He remembers the story!" Finally, Lucas offers his drawing to his father. As the mother takes the paper to look at it, Lucas protests, "It's for Daddy!" The mother gives it over to the father and soon after she suggests they end the play and call the facilitator back.*

Comment

The parents have made it very clear that they are talking with one another, delineating a clear boundary around themselves as a couple, separate from Lucas, but still aware of him if he needs them. This is what we would call a clear but flexible intergenerational boundary. Lucas challenges the boundary, addressing his father at one point. His father acknowledges Lucas with a smile, but returns to talking with the mother.

Lucas' response to being placed in the third-party position is typical of a family where the parents have a strong relationship and cooperate as coparents – what McHale has referred to as cohesive coparenting (2007). After a brief moment of protest, Lucas embraces being alone in their presence, finding ways to amuse himself, while at the same time intermittently trying to attract their attention. In contrast, when parents cannot cooperate with one another and have non-cohesive coparenting, the children may be drawn into their parents' interaction, particularly if there is conflict, or they might be shut down, not able to find ways to amuse themselves on their own.

Lucas also easily handles the four configurations of the threesome. He plays a bit of a role in balancing the complementary styles of his two parents, but it is not the overriding theme of this interaction and it is part of the normal variations seen in highly coordinated families. Moreover, this dynamic completely disappears during the 3-together play as the family shares in the humor about the grandfather. The interaction is reminiscent in many ways of the threesome we have observed since infancy.

As a couple, Lucas' parents are complementary and cohesive: the mother tends to lead and the father follows, but remains present and ready to intervene with delicacy or humor in moments of tension. The mother is even aware of and open about her somewhat controlling style. Her capacity for self-reflection and the father's nonjudgmental stance in hearing it are once again positive indicators of a strong family alliance.

Lucas and Hugo in the picnic game

Recall that in this task, the whole family, including Hugo, is asked to play out a pretend picnic.

From the outset, the mother takes the lead and the father goes along. She asks Lucas and Hugo, for example, "Are you hungry or do you want to play first?" She playfully accepts Lucas' decisions and Hugo almost always agrees with his older brother, actually repeating Lucas' answers. Throughout, the mother steers and controls a little bit. She tells the boys they have to tidy up the toys before they can set up the picnic table, and later she says, "We all have to have proper table manners when we're eating our lunch." The parents are also quite firm with the children about not stepping outside the limits of the green rug – a limit which Lucas and his brother repeatedly test, especially at the beginning.

During the play, the family tends to split into two dyads, Lucas and his mother in one dyad, with Hugo and his father in the other. However, both parents appear quite aware of the other dyad's play. When Lucas finishes a very tall block tower, he proudly announces his success and the whole family applauds.

There are several interactions between the two siblings as well. During the instructions, Lucas spontaneously helps his brother put on one of the back-packs. Later when they are playing, Lucas notices Hugo holding a pot. With a parental tone in his voice, he asks, "Hugo, did you make coffee?"

There are several brief squabbles between the boys about who got which toys, but they are quickly resolved by a peaceful negotiation firmly mediated by the mother. Only once does Lucas engage in aggressive behavior towards his brother. At one point, he excitedly gets up from the table to go play. His mother insists, "You have to clean up your dishes first," which he does, but quite rambunctiously. His mother makes him do it again more calmly and he complies. Once done, however, he leaves the picnic, and squeezes Hugo's head hard between his hands along the way.

In general Lucas tries to be the center of attention and to make all the decisions. His family goes along with his choices, with Hugo simply intent on imitating his brother most of the time. As for the parents, they share several brief moments of humor and affection between the two of them, just as they did in the LNP. The game ends with the two parents seated on the bench, hold-ing hands while the children play.

Comment

Overall, cooperation is high, with all parties able to manage this multiperson inter-action. A sense of warmth, fun, and flexibility is seen on a number of occasions. Like most 5 year-olds in cooperative families, Lucas wants to lead, and his parents grant him that role, providing his brother is happy and rules are respected. Lucas initiates games, but also keeps testing limits – only to comply and then of course test them again. This testing, however, does not become the sole focus of the PNG as it might in less cooperative families, where true play cannot occur because the family is caught up in testing and limit setting.

Lucas graciously accepts that his parents divide their attention between him, his brother, and one another. He even takes on a caretaker attitude towards Hugo himself. Lucas' caretaking behavior towards Hugo also suggests that he can now hold his brother's experience in mind as well. At other times the boys squabble, and still other times they each interact with one of the parents, ignoring each other. The ease with which the family flows from one formation to the next is another positive indicator.

Sara's family in the Lausanne Family Play

This is the first time we are meeting Sara's family. We will meet her parents again in the prenatal LTP in the next chapter, so you will see the continuity of the couple's cohesive coparenting alliance from a much earlier stage in the couple's development as coparents. At this point her brother, Theo, was 11 months. We join them for the LFP.

The family is seated at the table with the two parents at either end, and the children side-by-side facing the cameras. Sara is sitting on the end nearest to her father and Theo is nearest their mother. Everyone listens to the instructions. The facilitator then lays out the toys: four lions, four cell phones, and four ducks. Before leaving, she asks them to signal her when they are done.

LFP part I

The father has been asked to play first with the children. The father works hard to include both children.

> *Sara immediately takes the four lions. "All four?" says the father. "Yes," she answers. "Shall we make a story?" he asks. Sara agrees and they embark on a story initiated by the father about animals in the zoo. The father casts himself as the zookeeper and Theo as his assistant. Sara then announces, "I'm bringing the lions to the zoo." He calls Sara to discuss how the lions will be brought to the zoo, and then turns to Theo to explain, "There's a lady who's going to bring us some lions. You can play with the ducks while we wait." Later, after Sara delivers the lions, the father helps transition to part II, "I think I need another assistant to tell me where we should put all these lions, because I'm not really sure . . . I'm going to call the animal trainer, OK?" He calls the mother, signaling the transition to part II. The father introduces the animal trainer to Sara, and they shake hands.*

Comment

Note how the father guides the children, managing to include the 11 month-old, despite the fact that Theo is not really able to engage in symbolic play yet. While he is clearly leading the story, he reads Sara's cues. He includes the lions into the story as well as her additions to the story as they proceed. The tone is playful and humorous from the beginning and the transition to the mother's play is smooth. Sara plays her role with ease, showing that she can adopt the narrative theme and engage in pretend play at the verbal level.

LFP part II

As they transition into part II, Sara immediately shows her mother the lions, and her father sits back in his chair. The mother also works to include both children.

> *Theo continues to play with the phone. The scene continues, as the mother comments, "Oh, the lions just got here. They're a bit frightened so we have*

to be gentle with them." Sara nods in agreement. The mother continues to set the scene at the zoo. She suggests they build a lake for the lions and a bird-bath for Theo's ducks. Sara listens and nods, repeating some of her mother's statements. Later, Sara takes the lead, calling the animal trainer to explain that she no longer wants to keep the lions. Her mother pretends to be the trainer. She shakes Sara's hand. "Hello, ma'am, was it you who called about the lions?"

"Yes!"

The mother says, "Let's see now, how are we going to get them into the truck?"

Sara quickly answers, "Let's put the ducks in first and then the lions will want to go in too." They begin to load the animals, as the mother announces that they should call the zookeeper, signaling the transition to part III.

Comment

Sara takes more initiatives. She proposes a way to get the lions to go into the truck. Her mother is open and accepts her suggestion, even though in reality they might not be enticed to follow the ducks. A less flexible mother might have instead chosen to correct Sara, or educate her on typical lions.

The coordination between the parents in shifting from the father's to the mother's play is very smooth. By creatively including Theo as a full partner in this game, they further promote multiperson communication for both children.

LFP part III

The parents easily make the transition to the next part.

The mother picks up a phone so that Sara can call her. "You have to bring your assistant," she tells her mother. Her mother follows Sara's lead and soon after the zookeeper (the father) comes to fetch the lions. Next Sara suggests that the father play the role of the lions and the mother the zookeeper. They decide to put out hurdles for the lions to learn how to jump so that they can do a show. The final scene in part III is the show. Sara and her two parents each make the lions jump over the hurdles while Theo looks on. By the second round, Theo has also joined in and the whole family laughs together as they make the lions jump. They continue, making the tricks harder for the animals, laughing the whole time.

Comment

Sara further elaborates the game in a way that is quite consistent with the story line. The play then comes to its high point: the circus show. Everyone participates in this beautiful moment of foursome sharing of pleasure and humor, even Theo.

LFP part IV

By way of a transition to part IV, Sara's mother suggests that she play out the part about the lions leaving the zoo on her own. The father adds that he wants, "to talk with Mommy for a bit," and asks her to play with Theo, "the assistant."

The parents sit back in their chairs as the two children each look at what toys the other has to play with. Sara begins to make a pretend call, although it is not clear to whom. Theo watches his parents with interest, but then begins to protest and tries to get their attention. The mother then addresses Theo. "Hey, look at what Sara is doing." She then leans towards Sara and asks her, "Do you think you could play with him a little?" Sara complies briefly, making some duck noises for her brother, but then goes back to her pretend phone call. The family continues in this way for a while, with the parents talking quietly with one another, at times even giggling together. Sara and Theo continue amusing themselves on their own, but then Theo begins to fuss again. This time, without being asked, Sara attends to her brother, offering him a toy and removing one from him for herself. Shortly after, the father proposes they end the play, and the mother agrees.

Comment

The children's responses to their parents' dialogue are typical. They check out what their sibling has to play with, they monitor what their parents are doing, and they absorb themselves in their own activities. But at just 11 months, Theo needs more support to remain on his own. The parents suggest that Sara play with him. The parents remain sensitive to both children's needs. When Theo seems to be getting tired, and Sara has already helped him manage twice, the parents signal that they have finished. Children Sara's age like to take on parental roles for brief stretches and even feel proud of having some responsibility. In chapter 13 we discuss families with high conflict between the parents, where this responsibility has turned into a burden.

Research on links between cohesive coparenting and outcomes for 5 year-olds

Family narratives

The quality of family interactions during infancy does appear to be linked to the family at age 5. In particular, the more functional the alliances are in infancy, the more the narratives at age 5 were characterized by warmth, flexibility, and inclusion of the whole family. So just as others have described how children develop a sense of how others will behave based on their experiences with their primary caregivers (Bowlby, 1969; Stern, 1994), there seems to be a parallel process happening at the family level. Not only do families serve as the template for social interactions, but also it is through these interactions that children begin to develop a sense of themselves within these multiperson interactions (Favez et al., 2006).

Theory of mind

The ability to imagine what is in the minds of others is what is referred to as theory of mind (Meltzoff & Gopnick, 1993). We can use measures such as the false belief task (Harris, Johnson, Hutton, Andrews, & Cooke, 1989) to assess theory of mind in very young children (see Appendix 5.1). Historically this capacity has been understood on a dyadic basis – a sensitive mother with good theory of mind herself is more likely to have a child who scores high on such tasks (Harris et al., 1989). Recent results from Favez et al. (2012) have shown that a cooperative alliance in infancy was also correlated with improved scores on the false belief task at age 5. It would seem that being raised in a cohesive coparenting environment improves children's chances of taking other's perspectives. Through direct interactions as well as witnessing the interaction of their parents (when in the third-party position), these infants are perhaps more likely to learn multiple perspectives and therefore better understand other people's perspectives.

Autonomy

These children also showed more autonomy in the PNG. They were more able to play by themselves and demanded less of their parents' attention. The authors of the study suggest that this finding is analogous to what has been described in the attachment literature. A child who senses that his parent will respond to his security needs will engage in more exploration in a new environment (Prior & Glaser, 2006). Similarly, on a family level, children who have experienced cohesive coparenting appear to be better able to tolerate their parents having their own interaction and playing on their own.

Affective outcomes

In a task known as the family doll play (McHale, Neugebauer, Asch, & Schwartz, 1999), children are asked to tell stories about puppet families who feel sad, happy, angry, and anxious (see Appendix 5.1). Children of cohesive coparents have a significantly lower rate of aggressive, confrontational, and emotional themes in their stories than do the children from non-cohesive coparents. Parents were also given the Child Behavior Checklist (CBCL) (Achenbach, Edelbrock, & Howell, 1987), which looks at problem behaviors in children. The children from the cohesive coparent households also had the lowest scores on the CBCL.

Conclusion

Both families presented in this chapter are typical of families with cohesive coparenting and cooperative family alliances. In response, Lucas and Sara at age 5 are developing well in terms of narratives and multiperson communication. The foundations for these interactions were already evident in infancy at the preverbal stages.

These results presented from the follow up at 5 years of these children and their cohort underscore the importance of family-level interactions and communication in early development.

To close section I of this book, we now move back to the prenatal period and the formation of coparenting.

References

Achenbach, T. M., Edelbrock, C., & Howell, C. T. (1987). Empirically based assessment of the behavioral/emotional problems of 2- and 3-year-old children. *Journal of Abnormal Child Psychology, 15*(4), 629–650.

Bowlby, J. (1969). *Attachment and loss* (Vol. 1). New York: Basic Books.

Bruner, J. (1990). *Acts of meaning.* Cambridge, MA: Harvard University Press.

Favez, N., Frascarolo, F., & Lavanchy, C. (2006). From family play to family narratives. *The Signal, 12*(3–4), 1–7.

Favez, N., Lopes, F., Bernard, M., Frascarolo, F., Lavanchy Scaiola, C., Corboz-Warnery, A., & Fivaz-Depeursinge, E. (2012). The development of family alliance from pregnancy to toddlerhood and child outcomes at 5 years. *Family Process, 51*(4), 542–556.

Fiese, B. H., Sameroff, A. J., Grotevant, H. D., Wamboldt, F. S., Dickstein, S., & Fravel, D. L. (1999). *Monographs of the Society for Research in Child Development: Vol. 64. The stories that families tell: Narrative coherence, narrative interaction, and relationship beliefs.* Malden, MA: Blackwell.

Fivaz-Depeursinge, E., & Corboz-Warnery, A. (1999). *The primary triangle: A developmental systems view of fathers, mothers and infants.* New York: Basic Books.

Frascarolo, F., & Favez, N. (2005). Une nouvelle situation pour évaluer le fonctionnement familial: Le jeu du Pique-Nique [A new situation to assess family functioning: The Picnic Game]. *Devenir, 17*, 141–151.

Harris, P., Johnson, C., Hutton, D., Andrews, G., & Cooke, T. (1989). Young children's theory of mind and emotion. *Cognition and Emotion, 3*(4), 379–400.

McHale, J. (2007). *Charting the bumpy road of coparenthood.* Washington, DC: Zero to Three Press.

McHale, J., Neugebauer, A., Asch, A., & Schwartz, A. (1999). Preschoolers' characterizations of multiple family relationships during family doll play. *Journal of Clinical Child Psychology, 28*, 256–268.

Meltzoff, A., & Gopnick, A. (1993). The role of imitation in understanding persons and developing a theory of mind. In S. Baron-Cohen, H. Tagerflusberg, & D. J. Cohen (Eds.), *Understanding other minds: Perspectives from autism* (pp. 335–366). New York: Oxford University Press.

Minuchin, S. (1974). *Families & family therapy.* Boston: Harvard University Press.

Prior, V., & Glaser, D. (2006). *Understanding attachment and attachment disorders.* London: Jessica Kingsley.

Stern, D. (1994). One way to build a clinically relevant baby. *Infant Mental Health Journal, 15*, 9–25.

Appendix 5.1

Child behavior assessment tools at age 5

- **Child's behavior:** Child behavior was assessed by means of the *Child Behavior Checklist* (CBCL) completed by mothers (Achenbach, Edelbrock, & Howell, 1987), yielding scores of internalizing and externalizing problems as well as a total "problems" score.
- **Theory of mind,** or the capacity to understand mental states of other persons, was assessed with the *false belief task* (Harris, Johnson, Hutton, Andrews, & Cooke, 1989). Puppets play out stories where one of the characters has clearly been misled, or has misunderstood a situation. After each story, the child is questioned about what the puppet might have been thinking (theory of mind). The child is also asked to speculate on what the character might have been feeling – hence the child's understanding of emotions.
- **Predominant emotional themes** were evaluated in the *family doll play* (McHale, Neugebauer, Asch, & Schwartz, 1999). Children are asked to use puppets to tell stories of sad, happy, angry, and anxious families. The number of aggressive, confrontational, and emotional events expressed, or played out by the child, is listed, yielding scores for aggressiveness, conflict, and affection. Finally, language and general development were assessed using the *Wechsler Preschool and Primary Scale of Intelligence* (WPPSI III-R) (Wechsler, 1972).

References

Achenbach, T. M., Edelbrock, C., & Howell, C.T. (1987). Empirically based assessment of the behavioral/emotional problems of 2- and 3-year-old children. *Journal of Abnormal Child Psychology, 15*(4), 629–650.

Harris, P., Johnson, C., Hutton, D., Andrews, G., & Cooke, T. (1989). Young children's theory of mind and emotion. *Cognition and Emotion, 3*(4), 379–400.

McHale, J., Neugebauer, A., Asch, A., & Schwartz, A. (1999). Preschoolers' characterizations of multiple family relationships during family doll play. *Journal of Clinical Child Psychology, 28*, 256–268.

Wechsler, D. (1972). *Echelle d'intelligence de Wechsler pour la période préscolaire et primaire: W.P.P.S.I. (traduction Française).* Paris: Editions du centre de psychologie appliquée.

Chapter 6

Pregnancy

Coparenting in formation

With Antoinette Corboz-Warnery

Long before most become parents, the fantasy of what that will look like has already begun (Stern, 1995). Once we have partners, that fantasy becomes even clearer – with the coparent no longer simply a fantasy but rather an actual partner (Philipp & Carr, 1998). By the time a couple is expecting their first child, they have already started the process of becoming a family. Clinicians and researchers alike are increasingly interested in capturing more information about this critical period before the baby's arrival (Favez, Frascarolo, Lavanchy Scaiola, & Corboz-Warnery, 2013). First, it allows us to untangle the infant's contribution to the family, versus the dynamics that were there before she was even born. With the arrival of the baby, it becomes increasingly difficult to sort out the various factors (Kuersten-Hogan, 2011). Second, from a clinical perspective, the earlier we intervene in a family's development, even prenatally, the earlier we can help them set a more adaptive trajectory, avoiding the crystallization of disruptive patterns, and "spillover" of the couple's issues on to their coparenting relationship (Fainsilber Katz & Gottman, 1996).

To date, there has been little research on the expectant couple and family. In keeping with our work, our interest was not just in questionnaires or interviews of parents about their interactions. We were interested also in the "practicing family" and how to observe an expectant family in action, just as we were doing with parents who already had a baby. Reiss (1981) made this distinction between the "represented family," what the family says about their interactions during an interview, and the "practicing family." What we do know from studies that look at parents' representations about the baby when they are expecting is that these representations are predictive of the parents' responses once the baby is born; they also correlate with maternal sensitivity and early attachment (see Mayseless, 2006, for a review). In addition to exploring only representations, most of these studies have looked only at mothers (Stern, 1995; Zeanah & Barton, 1989). The focus of these studies has rarely been on families or the mother-father-infant relationship. Only quite recently has the question of the family as a whole or even the coparenting relationship been explored prior to the arrival of any children. The question is: can we predict what postnatal coparenting and family alliances will look like based on how couples respond, in terms of both their representations of their family-to-be and their actual interactions, prenatally?

A few centers have been exploring this question. Bürgin, von Klitzing, and colleagues have looked at "triadic capacities" in young couples, meaning the degree to which they imagine their future family as a threesome (Bürgin & von Klitzing, 1995; Von Klitzing, Simoni, & Bürgin, 1999). They used a semi-structured interview prenatally and were able to categorize parents into subsets corresponding to the "family dialogue capacities" in Lausanne Trilogue Play (Fivaz-Depeursinge & Corboz-Warnery, 1999) done at 4 months. Others have noted that parents' antenatal expectations are linked with their interactions once the baby is born. For example, if during the pregnancy the couple demonstrates a pessimistic view of the future coparenting relationship, or if there is a discrepancy between what the couple says about their relationship and how they actually interact in the lab, these are predictive of postnatal maladjustment in the family (McHale et al., 2004; Van Egeren, 2003).

Those studies that have used direct observation of the practicing couple have not surprisingly shown that the couple's interactions during pregnancy are linked to their relationship and coparenting after the birth. Negativity and conflict before the baby arrives are predictive of poorer adaptation and interactions between the partners once the baby arrives (Heinicke & Guthrie, 1996). The degree of negativity and conflict early in the couple's pre-baby relationship as well as during the pregnancy also predict postnatal family interactions. Remarkably this negativity in the couple even before pregnancy is also predictive of the infant's emotion regulation during the LTP at 3 months postpartum (Fearnley Shapiro et al., 1997; Gottman & Schwartz Gottman, 2007). While these studies focused on the practicing couple and its later impact on the child, what if the couple were presented with a specifically baby-oriented task? In other words, in order to look at the practicing family before birth, we had to devise an analogous paradigm for expectant couples and this is how the prenatal LTP came to be (Carneiro, Corboz-Warnery, & Fivaz-Depeursinge, 2006).

The prenatal Lausanne Trilogue Play (prenatal LTP)

The prenatal LTP was designed in our lab by A. Corboz-Warnery (Carneiro, Corboz-Warnery, & Fivaz-Depeursinge, 2006). It takes place around the end of the fifth month of pregnancy, when the parents' fantasies about the baby are at a peak (Stern, 1995). In the prenatal LTP protocol, parents are interviewed about their families of origin at an initial meeting. At a second interview they discuss their representations of how they envision their family after the birth. Then the facilitator asks the parents to imagine the delivery has gone well and this is the first time they are alone with the baby. She leaves the room and returns cradling a rag doll wrapped in a blanket. The doll actually has no face, although this is not readily visible at the outset. It is weighted so that it feels more like a real baby. The facilitator then asks the parents to role-play this first encounter using the four configurations of the LTP, presenting the "baby" to its mother and father and drawing the parents into the role-play by addressing the doll in baby-talk. The instructions are as follows.

It's the first time you're alone together and I'm asking you to play out this fabulous moment for us. We ask you to play according to the following four parts. First, one of you plays with the baby – in other words, meets the baby. Next, you switch roles. Then both of you play with the baby together, and finally, you let the baby sleep, and chat together about what you have just been experiencing. You can pick the baby up if you wish. The play usually lasts 4 or 5 minutes. Please signal me when you're done.

The goal is to get parents to play rather than just talk. We want to observe their intuitive parenting behaviors, the specific behaviors that we all use spontaneously when we are with babies (Papousek & Papousek, 1987). We also want to observe how the parents work together during this unusual task, the affection between them and with the "baby."

In this chapter, we once again return to Lucas' family, back when they were still just expecting him. During the prenatal LTP they are typical of ordinary families, with resources and vulnerabilities. Then we return to Sara's family, the one we met in chapter 5 in the LFP. Both families have a cohesive style, but Sara's parents are at the more playful end of the spectrum whereas Lucas' parents are a bit shyer and struggle a little with the task. We present the two families as counterpoints of two functional trajectories about to begin their journeys as families. Be aware that while some of the interactions may appear quite subtle or there may also be some inconsistencies, it is the sum total of the parts that we are looking for in the interaction.

Lucas' parents in the prenatal LTP

The parents have talked about how they imagine their threesome after the birth. They discuss their hopes and anxieties as well as their plans for "who will do what" to share in taking care of the baby. Next the facilitator introduces the role-play, asking them to imagine their first encounter with their baby. As is typical, the parents are initially surprised, but nevertheless graciously accept the task, with some trepidation. They listen attentively as she gives them the instructions. They smile, but look a bit tense as they hear more. At first the mother asks, "So we just describe what we would do?" But slowly they understand that this really is a role-play with a doll. The facilitator leaves, and returns holding the doll wrapped in a blanket and repeats the instructions. She then proceeds to introduce the "baby" to each parent, using baby talk when addressing the doll and commenting on how alert the "baby" is in order to play up that this is a "real" baby. After addressing some more of the parents' questions, the facilitator leaves the room, reminding them to signal her when they are done.

Prenatal LTP part I

The parents are left to choose who will go first and in this family, not surprisingly, the mother starts. You will see how the mother goes back and forth between role-playing and then commenting about the task to her husband.

The mother leans towards the doll in the basket then looks at the father, laughing. She addresses the doll in baby talk, "So did you sleep well? It looks like you're not crying. You're not hungry?" She adds to the father, "This isn't easy." She picks the doll up and cradles it in her left arm to face her, but the doll is now faced away from the father. She continues to talk to the baby, as the father reaches over to help reposition the doll's blanket, "You're not smiling . . . you're too little and you don't see well." The father smiles on and the mother worries, "Are you laughing at me?"

They talk about the doll's head and wonder if it's misshapen from the "delivery." As the mother struggles to comment on the doll's body parts, the father checks in with her to see if she is feeling okay. "Not too tired?" She reassures him she is not and then asks him if he wants a turn.

"No, I'm going to leave him with you . . . If we mess around too much, he won't sleep." She responds, "When they feel like sleeping, they sleep. Don't you think?" They talk a bit more and then the mother once again suggests he take the doll. "Don't you want to hold him?" He agrees and this marks the transition.

Prenatal LTP parts II–IV

Here is a transcript of the actual dialogue between mother and father as he takes the doll.

Mother: Try! . . . Which way do you want to hold him?
Father: I don't know . . . Do you want to see him?
Mother: You haven't really seen him yet, have you? . . . We all have a side we prefer, I think . . . Which one do you prefer?
Father: I don't know . . . perhaps this one . . . *(he takes the baby in his right arm, so the baby is facing the mother)*
Mother: You're left-handed . . .
Father: Well, I'm holding him with my right hand.
Mother: Okay . . . Hey, he glanced at you, then closed his eyes . . .
Father: He's my little one!
Mother: I don't know if it'll always be like this. *(She laughs.)* We'll see when we're back home. *(After a moment she adds)* It's all right; he's sleeping. . . . See, it wasn't that difficult.
Father: Yeah, it was okay. But I'm not the one who had the toughest job!

The parents talk about caring for their infant as the father continues to hold the doll. As they talk, there is no clear transition to the 3-together or to their dialogue. About 10 minutes into the LTP, the facilitator enters the room, stating that she had forgotten to tell them to signal when they were done. She asks them where they are in the task and whether they would like to do the 3-together or their dialogue part. The parents decline, saying they have exhausted their imaginations. The mother comments on how hard it was to imagine without a face on the doll.

Comment

In spite of their discomfort with role-playing, the parents do cooperate with the task. They support each other throughout, attending to and smiling at each other with affection and interest. Their nonverbal interactions with the doll are notably spontaneous and intuitively "baby-like." The mother easily interacts with the doll much like one would with a real baby – using baby talk and holding it appropriately in her arms. She also strokes the body, and shows concern for the "baby's" well-being. Interestingly, in spite of his reticence, when the father finally agrees to take the doll, he is just as much at ease holding it as his wife. From then on, he keeps it in his arms, affectionately addressing it as "my little one."

It is interesting to note that already in the prenatal LTP, the mother takes the lead and the father follows her, resonating with her experience and ready to cooperate with her. This is the very same style we saw in the previous chapters across the first 5 years of Lucas' life.

The most difficult thing for these parents is letting go of their inhibitions about the role-play. The mother pauses several times, appearing embarrassed and self-conscious. She struggles to find new things to talk about or observe. The father rescues her several times with questions about baby care and once with a concern about her being tired. This wavering between engaging with the "baby" and pausing is quite common in the prenatal LTP. Too much engagement in the role-play and it seems false. Too little engagement, outright refusal, or even mocking of the task are also red flags about the family's future cooperation (Carneiro et al., 2006). For Lucas' parents, their discomfort with the role-play was perhaps part of the reason they did not complete all four parts of the task.

Overall, however, there were enough positive signs about their coparenting alliance as well as their affection for the baby. As we will describe below, these are the most critical factors in predicting a positive outcome and good enough coparenting to later scaffold Lucas in developing solid three-person or triangular communication as well as multiperson communication.

Predicting the alliance later

Based on the analyses of the original sample, the following variables in the prenatal LTP turned out to be predictive of the postnatal family alliance up to 18 months and even up to 5 years (work in progress):

- Collaboration with the researchers: Given that this is a kind of unusual situation, it turns out that the degree to which parents take this task as a playful game is important. The happy medium is one where the parents are not too resistant to the task, but also not taking it too seriously.
- The parents' ability to conform to the format in four parts. (Of note, in Lucas' family this was the only problematic variable; however, it alone did not cause the coparenting to be coded as problematic.)

- The cooperation between the coparents, especially faced with this unusual context.
- The expressions of warmth between the spouses as well as towards the "baby."
- Their intuitive parenting behaviors.

The most significant variables were the degree of cooperation between the coparents, their affection towards each other as well as towards the imagined baby, and their intuitive parenting behaviors. These three variables were the most highly correlated with rich triangular interactions and positive affect in the families once the babies arrived and they came in for their first LTP at 3 months. Interestingly, we also found that in this role-play, fathers and mothers access their intuitive parenting behaviors equally.

Variant: Sara's parents in the prenatal LTP

Sara's parents are an example of a couple that is more comfortable with the role-playing format of this task. Their prenatal LTP is easier to follow, as they verbalize their experience and act it out more explicitly. As with Lucas' family, though, we see the same intuitive parenting behaviors that are biologically imprinted in humans (Papousek & Papousek, 1987).

Prenatal LTP part I

The facilitator has given the instructions. As she exits the room, the father begins by playfully leaning towards the doll. Once again we present actual transcript below.

Father: Me first! Me first! *(The mother laughs)*
Mother: You have to do it on your own . . . but make sure you give him over to me afterwards!
Father: I'll give him over to you after . . . *(holding the baby in his arms in a typical feeding position)* Oh, hello, my beautiful baby . . . He's already so big!
Mother: You're right, he is big! . . . but I'm not supposed to say anything . . .
Father: Hello, my baby . . . What beautiful pajamas they gave you . . . you're so beautiful! Look at these tiny hands . . . Did you see his tiny feet? . . . And he already has a tiny bit of hair *(Mother laughs)* . . . Are you making faces? So you see, I am your dad! Oh, boy! You're already so heavy . . . You weigh at least 7 pounds.

   Oh, you are so cute. Oh, I am so proud of you, my little baby! . . . Beautiful, beautiful, beautiful. And you already smell good!
Father (addressing Mother):   What am I supposed to do? Should I pass him to you?

Mother (laughing):   I thought you were going to pass him way earlier!

Father: You've already got him quite a lot!

Mother: I've already got him? But I don't get to see him!

Prenatal LTP part II

Mother (with baby in her arms):   You're right; he is pretty heavy . . . Oh, I'm starting to cry *(Mother very deliberately and playfully turns away from father)* . . . I'm going to cry . . . *(to the doll, holding its arm and addressing it in baby-talk)* I want to give you a kiss! I am going to give you a kiss! Oh, boy, that sure was difficult! You had nobody with you! *(Now in adult talk)* Oh! If it had actual eyes that would be great! *(To father, but still turned away from him)* Am I supposed to be on my own, like all by myself?

Father: Yes.

Mother: He's grabbing my hand . . . *(referring to the real baby inside her, she touches her belly)* it's so cramped in there for him! *(Addressing the father)* It's weird, isn't it? *(and now looking at the doll)* I've waited so long . . . But it was worth it, I think! And we don't know whether it's a girl or a boy!

Father: We'll name him Alex!

Mother: Or Leslie ! . . . It's true he does smell good ! . . . Afterwards, we have to get him to sleep. I think he has to sleep. Right? We can't take him with us, can we?

Father: He's already closed his eyes.

Mother: Just one eye!

Father: We have to put you to bed, baby!

Mother: Wait!

Father: Oh, did you see all the red marks he still has? The delivery was rough.

Mother: Yes, but he's fine like that. It's fine with me; I'll keep him!

Prenatal LTP part III

Father (addressing the doll in the basket):   There you are, you have a super-basket. Is it your auntie who gave you this big basket? Did you see how beautiful it is? And you have your first slippers . . . and your first pajamas . . . It's great! So now it's 3'oclock, time to sleep.

Mother: It's fine! Can we kiss now? *(they kiss)* We're too far apart! . . . This is hard, isn't it?

Father: Do you think he's tired?

Mother: Yes, at any rate, he's not moving!

Father: He's good.

Mother: So good!

Father: Well, we should bundle him up . . . do you think he's warm enough? How can you tell if he's too cold or too warm?

The parents continue, talking about other caretaking issues. After kissing the baby, they mark the transition to their dialogue by sitting up and turning towards each other, with the father laying his arm across the mother's shoulders.

Prenatal LTP part IV

Mother: This is hard, isn't it?
Father: But it is going to happen to us.
Mother: I know. . . . Yikes! *(touching her belly because the baby has kicked again; the couple laughs)* At any rate, this one is reacting . . . very strongly, in there . . .
Father: He's jealous!
Mother: Yeah, maybe . . . What are we going to do now with this baby *(pointing to the doll in the basket)?* Watch him sleep, for hours? . . . Should we call her? I don't know where she is? Can she hear us?

Comment

This prenatal LTP has the same key ingredients of cohesive coparenting that were relevant in Lucas' family. In particular, there is cooperation, affection, and the same type of intuitive parenting behaviors. The difference is more that Sara's parents visibly appreciate role-playing so they act out the encounter with their baby in an open, lively, and playful way. It allows them to engage with the imagined baby with much animation. It particularly gives us a window into a number of their intuitive parenting behaviors already observable during pregnancy. They openly show their feelings towards each other and towards the baby. They follow the structure of the play in four parts, putting on a playful show for the researchers.

An interesting aspect of their style is the mother's tendency to interact more exclusively with the baby during her time as active player; she turns away from the father in an obvious though playful way. The father's response is crucial for the establishment of the family alliance; he does not withdraw, protest, or appear hurt that she is turned away, holding the baby beyond his reach. Rather, he remains attentive to what is going on between them. This particular dynamic will endure across the first 2 years.

With both families there are a number of patterns that are already observable in the prenatal LTP that remain stable through the subsequent months and years. We cited only a couple of things in these descriptions: Lucas' mother takes the lead while his father tends to cooperate and follow; and here Sara's father also cooperates with the mother's slightly exclusive style of interacting with the doll (and later Sara). These types of responses are part of what McHale has described as cohesive coparenting (2007). We turn to the research findings next, where this issue was assessed more empirically.

Research results

From our detailed results on the interactions in the prenatal LTP we have found a number of links between the interactions of the expectant couple and what we later see on LTPs well into the postnatal period. Of particular relevance is that the degree of cooperation in the couple during the prenatal LTP is correlated with almost all dimensions of postnatal family play at 3 and 18 months. Furthermore, the warmth and intuitive parenting in the prenatal LTP are also correlated with several postnatal dimensions on the LTP. For example, warmth and intuitive parenting are correlated with the parents being able to keep to their roles when the infant was 3 and 18 months, and to come up with age-appropriate games together. These early, make-believe interactions in some key ways foreshadow the interactive qualities necessary for mother-father-infant coordination later on in the family's development. In fact, in 80% of families, there was continuity in the quality of the interactions from pregnancy up to 18 months after birth (Favez, Frascarolo, & Fivaz-Depeursinge, 2006; Favez et al., 2013).

Conclusion

The strengths or difficulties that are observable in the couple, even before they are a family, tend to continue to be there in their postnatal interactions. In the next section we turn to the families who followed more problematic trajectories. For them too, the prenatal LTP was predictive of things to come once the baby arrived. The key concerns noted on their prenatal LTPs were a globally negative emotional climate, low warmth towards each other and towards the imagined baby, low cooperation, and a lack of playfulness. In the most problematic cases, even though the parents seemed to understand that this was a role-play, they were most often unable to pretend and imagine their baby-to-be or in some cases overpretended and took the task far too seriously. Either way, the cooperation, playfulness, and warmth were absent.

Given what we now know about these early markers of problematic interactions, the necessity for taking a whole family perspective in understanding young families, or even pre-families, is paramount. Having insight into how the couple is functioning, and to what degree they can coordinate on baby-oriented tasks is critical information if we are to adequately screen expectant families for early intervention.

References

Bürgin, D., & von Klitzing, K. (1995). Prenatal representations and postnatal interactions of a threesome (mother, father and baby). In J. Bitzer & M. Stauber (Eds.), *Psychosomatic obstetrics and gynaecology* (pp. 185–192). Bologna: Monduzzi.

Carneiro, C., Corboz-Warnery, A., & Fivaz-Depeursinge, E. (2006). The prenatal Lausanne Trilogue Play: A new observational assessment tool of the prenatal co-parenting alliance. *Infant Mental Health Journal, 27*(2), 207–228.

Fainsilber Katz, L., & Gottman, J. M. (1996). Spillover effects of marital conflict: In search of parenting and coparenting mechanisms. *New Directions for Child and Adolescent Development, 74,* 57–76. doi:10.1002/cd.23219967406

Favez, N., Frascarolo, F., Carneiro, C., Montfort, V., Corboz-Warnery, A., & Fivaz-Depeursinge, E. (2006). The development of the family alliance from pregnancy to toddlerhood and children outcomes at 18 months. *Infant and Child Development, 15*(1), 59–73. 10.1002/icd.430

Favez, N., Frascarolo, F., & Fivaz-Depeursinge, E. (2006). Family alliance stability and change from pregnancy to toddlerhood and marital correlates. *Swiss Journal of Psychology, 65*(4), 213–220.

Favez, N., Frascarolo, F., Lavanchy Scaiola, C., & Corboz-Warnery, A. (2013). Prenatal representations of family in parents' and coparental interactions as predictors of triadic interactions during infancy. *Infant Mental Health Journal, 34*(1), 25–36.

Fearnley Shapiro, A., Gottman, J., Lubkin, S., Swanson, C., Burgess, P., & Murray, J. (1997). *The transfer of marital conflict to the developing infant: Examining dynamics within the father-mother-baby triad and the roots of emotion regulation.* Paper presented at the Conference on Affects and Systems, Zurich.

Fivaz-Depeursinge, E., & Corboz-Warnery, A. (1999). *The primary triangle: A developmental systems view of fathers, mothers and infants.* New York: Basic Books.

Gottman, J., & Schwartz Gottman, J. (2007). *And baby makes three.* New York: Three Rivers Press.

Heinicke, C. M., & Guthrie, D. (1996). Prebirth marital interactions and postbirth marital development. *Infant Mental Health Journal, 17,* 140–151.

Kuersten-Hogan, R. (2011). *Predicting coparenting dynamics in the early post-partum period: The value of the Prenatal Trilogue Play.* Paper presented at the Biennial meeting of the Society for Research in Child Development, Montreal.

Mayseless, O. (2006). *Parenting representations: Theory, research and applications.* Cambridge, UK: Cambridge University Press.

McHale, J. (2007). *Charting the bumpy road of coparenthood.* Washington, DC: Zero to Three Press.

McHale, J., Kazali, C., Rotman, T., Talbot, J., Carleton, M., & Lieberson, R. (2004). The transition to coparenthood: Parents' prebirth expectations and early coparental adjustment at 3 months postpartum. *Development and Psychopathology, 16*(3), 711–733.

Papousek, H., & Papousek, M. (1987). Intuitive parenting: A dialectic counterpart to the infant's integrative competence. In J. D. Osofsky (Ed.), *Handbook of infant development* (2nd ed., pp. 669–720). New York: Wiley.

Philipp, D. A., & Carr, M. L. (1998). Normal and medically complicated pregnancies. In N. Stotland & D. Stewart (Eds.), *Psychological aspects of women's health care* (2nd ed., pp. 13–32). Washington DC: American Psychiatric Press.

Reiss, D. (1981). *The family's construction of reality.* Cambridge: Harvard University Press.

Stern, D. (1995). *The motherhood constellation.* New York: Basic Books.

Van Egeren, L. A. (2003). Prebirth predictors of coparenting experiences in early infancy. *Infant Mental Health Journal, 24,* 278–295.

Von Klitzing, K., Simoni, H., & Bürgin, D. (1999). Child development and early triadic relationships. *International Journal of Psychoanalysis, 80,* 71–89.

Zeanah, C. H., & Barton, M. L. (1989). Introduction: Internal representations and parent-infant relationship. *Infant Mental Health Journal, 10,* 135–141.

Section II

Growing up with non-cohesive coparenting
Derailed triangular communication

In section II of this book, the three problematic coparenting styles identified by J. McHale and their complementary infant engagement styles are presented through case illustrations. These families come from our non-referred research sample, and therefore were not receiving any treatment. These illustrations allow us to explore the natural development of each of these types of families. This is an invaluable window into problematic family functioning and its associated derailments of the infant's triangular communication. Key concepts from S. Minuchin's Structural Family Therapy model on coalitions (binding, detouring, and triangulation) are also explored through these case examples.

Chapter 7

Coping with excluding coparenting

With Miri Keren

Charlotte is 3 months old. Her parents have come in with her for their first post-natal visit as part of a longitudinal study on non-referred families at the Centre for Studies of the Family (Centre d'Etude de la Famille – CEF), part of the University of Lausanne Institute for Psychotherapy. In the vignette below, they are about to begin doing Lausanne Trilogue Play (LTP) (Fivaz-Depeursinge & Corboz-Warnery, 1999). They are seated facing one another, at equal distances in a triangle for this first part of the play.

> *During the instructions, her mother tells the facilitator that Charlotte prefers to look at her and not at her father. When the LTP starts Charlotte and her mother are supposed to be playing, while her father is "simply present." Charlotte briefly looks at her father, however, and he gleefully points it out to his wife, "You see!" She snaps back, "You're supposed to be quiet." From that point onward, while the mother plays with Charlotte, the father avoids looking at his wife and daughter, gazing at the ceiling, towards the one-way mirror, or at the floor. He is completely cut off from the interaction, not react-ing to any of the highs or lows. To add to it, his wife comes in so close to Charlotte that even if the baby wanted to check her father's reactions, much of the time he would be obscured by her mother's head.*

Comment

Charlotte and her mother are locked into a very close interaction. Not only do they exclude the father, but also he complies by withdrawing. Charlotte misses opportunities to develop skills for managing three-person interactions, always caught up in an exclusive relationship with her mother that by definition excludes her father. It is the sum total of all of these parts that we have come to recog-nize as excluding coparenting, and the formula for this maladaptive pattern goes something like this:

• Charlotte's parents have a history of conflict between them and do not com-municate well as coparents.

- They are unable to resolve it.
- Instead, one of them (self) excludes, while the other one "captures" the child's full engagement.
- Charlotte has an exclusive relationship with the close parent and rejects the excluded parent, thus reinforcing the family pattern.

Recall that in parts I and II of an LTP there is a 2 + 1 structure, where each parent takes a turn actively interacting with the infant, while the other is in the third-party role. In families where the parents work well together, in what McHale (2007) has referred to as cohesive coparenting, the parents understand that "simply present" means not interfering, but definitely resonating with the interaction. If the infant does turn to look at the non-active parent, the couple handles it flexibly. The non-active parent resonates with the infant's experience, but then allows the infant to return to play with the active parent (see section I of this book for more detail).

With non-cohesive couples, like Charlotte's parents, they seem to lack a sense of what a triad should look like if one parent is supposed to be active and the other simply present. It is as if they understand the instructions as meaning there should be a split in the triad, where one parent is active and the other is "absent" and should be excluded. The infant, who obviously is aware of the other parent, must experience confusion in this split interaction – close with one parent and cut off from the other, who is only inches away. Taken together, the excluding coparenting and the infant's split engagement form what Minuchin (1974) referred to as a binding coalition (see Table 7.1). All three problematic family interactions that we are discussing in this section of the book are listed in Table 7.1, with the focus of this chapter in bold.

Table 7.1 Associations between infant engagement styles, coparenting styles, and resulting family structure

Infant engagement style	Coparenting style	Family structure
Triangular engagement	Cohesive	Alliance
Split engagement	**Excluding**	**Binding coalition**
Role reversed	Child-at-center	Detouring coalition
Go-between/withdrawal	Competitive	Triangulation coalition

Split engagement

In split engagement (Fivaz-Depeursinge, Lopes, Python, & Favez, 2009) the infant exclusively interacts with one parent, the "capturing" one, often in an over-engaged way, and therefore excludes the other parent. The exclusion can be in the form of ignoring or directly opposing that parent's attempts to interact. The infant's affects are mostly positive with the "capturing parent" and mostly negative with the one she excludes. She exclusively addresses dyadic bids to the "capturing parent" throughout the LTP, hardly ever looking over to the third-party parent. This behavior persists even when the "excluded parent" is supposed to be the active parent while the "capturing parent" is the third party. In this 2 + 1 configuration, the infant may still address what is referred to as direct dyadic bids to just the capturing parent, as if seeking help from her. In part IV, when the infant is in the role of third party, she continues trying to engage the same parent, while excluding the other. This form of engagement may be observed in early infancy and continue up to toddlerhood. Thus, in split engagement the infant's frequency of triangular bids is quite low compared to norms for infants her age.

Excluding coparenting

It is easy to understand how the infant's split engagement emerges in the context of how the parents work together or coparent (Elliston, McHale, Talbot, Parmley, & Kuersten-Hogan, 2008). McHale (2007) first described excluding coparenting, identifying the large imbalance in the parents' levels of engagement, but also an absence of warmth, poor cooperation, yet minimal antagonism between the parents. In other words, the infant is also dealing with parents who are disconnected from one another. It is not surprising then that a young infant might be led to exclusively interact with the capturing parent and to go along with excluding the other, particularly when that other parent is already self-excluding.

Binding coalition

Minuchin (1974) described this type of family structure in much older families as a binding coalition. In these instances there is a violation of the "intergenerational boundary." Ideally, parents form a clear but flexible boundary around themselves as the coparents, at times consulting with one another even in the child's presence. This type of intergenerational boundary is what occurs in cohesive coparenting and family alliances. In a binding coalition it is as if there is now a boundary around one of the parents and the child instead, excluding the other parent.

From excluding coparenting in the 2 + 1s to other non-cohesive styles in parts III and IV

The tendency to use excluding strategies in parts I and II is typical of families with non-cohesive coparenting (14/15 in our sample). Most families with non-cohesive coparenting engage in other patterns of interaction in part III of the LTP, when the family is to play together as a threesome, and part IV, when the couple is to talk on their own. Among the 15 families with non-cohesive coparenting, five couples adopted a child-centered style, and two a competitive style (see chapters 7 and 8). Among the remaining seven families, five adopted a variety of problematic styles of coparenting, and even engaged in cohesive patterns some of the time. Finally, only in two extreme cases the pattern of exclusive coparenting continued beyond the 2 + 1 parts. Charlotte's family was one of these two cases. The LTPs for this family highlight the effect of rigid, excluding coparenting on an infant's triangular communication, her ability to communicate with two people at the same time (see section I).

Charlotte at 3 months

LTP parts I and II

We have already presented part I of this family's LTP, which began with the mother scolding the father for his comment about the baby looking at him the one time. After that Charlotte rarely looked at him, and each time he very conspicuously looked away. Now we move on to part II, where the father and Charlotte are to interact, while the mother is "simply present." Watch how Charlotte and her parents manage now that she is to interact with the excluded parent.

> *The father also comes in too close to his daughter; however now, rather than engaging, Charlotte looks away, cutting her father off. Undaunted, he pokes his head around to the other side, getting in close to her face once again. She cuts him off once more. And so the pattern continues. Meanwhile, the mother over-resonates with Charlotte – her facial expressions seem to say, "Poor you! Your father doesn't know what he's doing." As a result, Charlotte does not simply dodge her father, but she also looks to her mother in those moments. On reviewing this segment, it became unclear whether Charlotte is escaping her father, or pursuing her mother. A circular pattern is established, with no clear initiator but with all three participants involved: the father, with his intrusive chase; the mother with her overly engaged behavior as the third party; and Charlotte dodging Dad and pursuing Mom.*

Comment

While the parents try hard, there are problems in this couple's interaction with their baby and no true play occurs in either part I or II of this LTP. Both parents are fairly intrusive with Charlotte, getting in too close and at times poking and prodding her. While Charlotte appears to tolerate this behavior from her mother, she does not from her father. What develops is a "chase and dodge" interaction between Charlotte and her father (Beebe & Lachmann, 2002). The infant uses the only resource she has, to look away or cut off in the face of an intrusive partner. But unlike the classic descriptions of chase and dodge in dyadic play, here we have three people, including a mother who is far too engaged and not "simply present."

LTP part III

> *Part III of the LTP is notably rushed. The couple tends to split their time playing with Charlotte, as if they understand the instruction, "play together as a*

family" to mean "take turns playing with her," while the other sits back and watches. Charlotte continues to look exclusively at her mother, cutting off her father whenever he does come in to play with her.

Comment

We have come to recognize clinically that difficulties in parts III or IV of the LTP, including rushing through, are indicators of difficulties in the marital subunit, the coparenting, or the family dynamic. It is as though they cannot manage being together, and so they move on (see section III). As well, even with the turn taking, once again, no true play ever occurs in this part. It simply looks like a repeat of parts I and II except the parent sitting back at least is not cut off and remains psychologically present.

LTP part IV

The transition to part IV takes a while as the parents struggle to focus on one another and not the baby. As they begin to banter and laugh, the content is about how they never talk. For Charlotte, there is a distinct change. With her parents no longer engaging with her, she makes protest bids. Many more of these bids are just to her mother, but for the first time she begins to address some of these protests as triangular bids, looking back and forth at both parents.

Comment

While still quite short, this part is in fact the longest of the whole LTP. The parents manage to have a discussion, but the hostility between them is quite clear from the content of what they are saying. Without knowing what they were saying, however, you might think it quite flirtatious. Charlotte makes more bids during the parents' dialogue than throughout the rest of this LTP. They are exclusively negative bids, indicating her wish to change the situation, but with the parents' attention turned to each other, Charlotte is finally able to exercise some triangular capacities.

Overall the LTP at 3 months has a number of problems. While the parents manage to complete the task, no true play ever occurs in any part. Throughout there is the mother-baby alignment, with the mother drawing her daughter's attention to herself and Charlotte still directing more bids to her mother than to her father. For his part, the father appears both passive and hostile, coming up with few initiatives other than chasing his dodging daughter, and bantering aggressively with his wife. Finally, Charlotte's triangular communication appears to be compromised with an absence of triangular bids until part IV.

Charlotte at 9 months

All the patterns of the 3-month LTP are further solidified in the LTP at 9 months. There are now some moments of actual play and joy, as the mother has found age-appropriate ways to engage Charlotte, albeit still intrusive and a bit too fast-paced for a child of this age. Charlotte smiles along much of the time, but must accommodate to her mother's pace. The father still self-excludes but seems to have actually given up at this stage, and Charlotte makes even fewer triangular bids, all negative.

LTP parts I–II

Briefly, in part I Charlotte's mother engages in a rapid succession of boisterous and intrusive games, and while Charlotte manages to steal a few glances at her father, he looks away each time. In part II when Charlotte and her father are to play, the same chase and dodge is seen. His style is quite intrusive – moving Charlotte's body and face to try to get her to look at him, but very quickly he gives up and states, "Should we move on to part III?"

LTP parts III–IV

The mother initially plays quite intrusively with Charlotte, insisting Charlotte say, "Ahhhh" while she taps on her mouth. Charlotte smiles, but does not say, "Ahhhh." The father sits passively, looking on, but very quietly holds Charlotte's foot in his hand and gently strokes it, unnoticed by his wife. The mother suddenly tells the father, "You're supposed to play too," and then she sits back in her chair to look on while the father moves in to play with Charlotte. This time, he sits passively and just continues to stroke Charlotte's foot. The mother mocks him for his passivity, and then tells him to do the same mouth tapping game she was doing. He very gently tries tapping Charlotte's mouth, turning to his wife with an awkward grin as if mocking the situation. "It doesn't work when I do it."

During the dialogue of part IV the parents face each other to talk. Their discussion, however, is again quite hostile, still with a flirtatious tone. The topic shifts to Charlotte, with the father noting somewhat angrily, "She's not even looking at us; she couldn't care less." Charlotte plays with her seatbelt and looks away, making no attempts to regain their attention.

Comment

The patterns from 3 months appear to have solidified at 9 months: the mother-daughter alignment, the father's (self) exclusion, and Charlotte's unilateral engagement with her mother, all undermining Charlotte's triangular communication. Charlotte no longer makes any direct bids to her father. Her engagement is all the more split, as she practically ignores his presence.

Charlotte at 18 months

We rejoin the family at 18 months and they are expecting a second child. We always begin taping families during the LTP instructions, as clinically rich information often emerges. We also learn a bit about how the family interacts with an outsider and how receptive they might be to intervention. During the instructions, Charlotte is showing her father the toys, and her father is responding with muted but appropriate animation. This is a pleasant change in their interaction from what we saw before. With the presence of toys and Charlotte's emerging language skills, the father appears much more engaged, facilitating his daughter's play with better ideas of what to do.

While evidence of well-negotiated coparenting is generally nonexistent, there is certainly not the blatant hostility we saw at 9 months and the whole LTP feels much calmer and more cooperative. There are now at least some lovely moments in each of the play parts, but there is also a deepening of some of the patterns we were seeing before. Watch for what seems familiar, and what is starting to shift, particularly in her relationship with her father.

LTP parts I–II

During part I, the mother's play is intrusive: she grabs at the toys and directs all of the play. On three occasions Charlotte looks at her father with a perplexed expression, seemingly making a social reference to better understand her mother's behavior. Twice, he is very conspicuously turned away and so Charlotte gets no feedback from him. On the third occasion there is the briefest moment where they look at each other directly and then both father and daughter look away as though it never happened.

In part II the father-baby play is mostly quite serious and notably joyless, with Charlotte engaging her more passive father. During this play the mother does sit back in her chair appropriately, but she seems angry, her face tense and her arms folded across her chest.

There is one brief interaction that is quite sweet. Charlotte offers to brush her father's hair, something she did with her mother in part I. Her father initially refuses. "No, thanks, I've already brushed my hair. Why don't you brush your own hair?" Charlotte briefly complies but then makes a second attempt, holding out the brush silently as if to ask, "Can I brush your hair, Daddy?" With this second invitation, the father decides to play along and with a sheepish smile he leans forward and allows Charlotte to brush his hair. It is the one moment of sheer pleasure, and the father seems pleased for quite a few moments afterwards. The mother smiles too, but then abruptly interrupts and suggests they move on to the third part.

Comment

While the father's flat reaction to his daughter's triangular bid in part I is not likely to promote her triangular communication, it appears as if something has shifted in the family. There is the hint of a new connection between father and daughter, most evident when the mother is distracted and talking to the researcher before they even begin and during the hair brushing sequence.

The mother's angry stance throughout part II, and her inopportune termination of the only playful interaction, leaves one wondering if she can tolerate any father-daughter connection. Moving to the second half of the LTP, we see some changes here as well.

LTP parts III–IV

In the 3-together play, the mother still mostly leads, and the father is mostly passive, but they are both leaned forward, no longer simply taking turns playing with Charlotte as they did in part III of the earlier LTPs.

After a long stretch of disorganized play, there is one interesting sequence. Handing Charlotte a cup, the mother says, "Give Daddy some coffee." Charlotte passes the cup to her father, who sips his "coffee." The mother then looks at Charlotte. "You have some too." Charlotte tips her head back and drinks from her cup. The mother then asks, "And Mommy? Can Mommy have some coffee too?" Charlotte, not seeing the third cup on the table, seems confused and hands her mother a piece of Lego instead. The mother continues to ask for coffee, holding out her hand and repeating, "And Mommy . . . and Mommy?" She seems to be almost begging Charlotte now. At a loss, Charlotte complies by giving her mother her own cup. The father then shows Charlotte, "Look, there's another cup for you," and hands it to Charlotte. Next there is one lovely, if very brief, moment where they all share a cup of coffee. Later, the interaction sours once again as the parents struggle to control how the coffee party should be cleared away.

Moving to part IV, there is very clear tension between the parents. Charlotte notices they have turned to face each other and she applauds with enthusiasm. She offers them a toy and they laugh. Despite Charlotte's attempts to distract, the parents go on to comply with the goal of part IV, but it is a quiet and still overtly hostile discussion.

Comment

With a second child on the way, things are beginning to shift, while others remain the same. Charlotte is still overly engaged with her mother, but there is a new connection emerging with her father. He is also becoming a bit more assertive in the family, intervening to help Charlotte find the missing coffee cup and struggling with his wife about how to clear the coffee party. While the dominant theme is still exclusion of the father, there is also some evidence of the parents competing for Charlotte's attention. By 18 months the father seems more prepared to push for his own relationship with his daughter.

As for Charlotte, she has been poorly prepared for triangular communication. Although we have seen a few triangular bids, especially at 3 months and again at 18 months, these mainly negative signals are often ignored or invalidated. In part IV her attempt to distract her parents is an example of "triangular over-engagement."

Toddlers use a number of strategies to contend with tension or conflict between their parents. In over-engagement, children try to bring the parents' attention to themselves. It may be through misbehavior, or as in this case, charm. Based on our experience with many families, the timing of Charlotte's charming distraction right at a tense transition to part IV seems to be more than simply coincidence.

Prenatal indicators

If we rewind to the prenatal period, for this family the coparenting alliance is already particularly poor. At this stage the research families come in at the beginning of the third trimester to go through the same four parts but with a rag doll as the "baby" (chapter 6). Charlotte's mother declares she simply cannot role-play an imaginary interaction with a doll, and undermines any attempts the father makes to play. The father alternates between trying to comply with the task and then joining the mother in mocking it. The hostility between them is already evident, barely camouflaged by the mother's flirtatiousness and by the father clowning around – elements we later observe in their LTPs. We know from our sample that how the family does on the prenatal LTP is correlated not only with how they will do on later LTPs but also with how the child functions outside of the lab situation.

Follow-up at 5 years

Now let's fast-forward to when Charlotte is 5 years old, with a little brother, Raphael, age 2 1/2 years. We present all four of them together in the Lausanne Family Play situation (LFP), but also in the less structured picnic simulation (PNG).

Lausanne Family Play

In the LFP, families are asked to interact in the same four parts; however, the children are treated as a unit. We will see some familiar patterns, but also more tension between the parents throughout parts I–III.

> During part I, the father goes first as the active parent and plays with the two children while the mother is simply present. He keeps coming up with ideas, but never actually succeeds in engaging the children. Instead, Charlotte is focused on getting Raphael's ducks and cell phone. Raphael refuses to give them to her, despite the father adding, "Raphael, can you please give that one to Charlotte?" The mother leans in very close to the action, drawing attention to herself – for instance, by laughing too conspicuously.
>
> During part II, the mother is a bit more successful at involving the children in play, but the rivalry over the toys continues and the play soon breaks down. As for the father, now that he is no longer the active parent, he turns away from the family just as he did when Charlotte was a baby. At one point the

mother turns to him to laugh at the children. She has introduced a game where the animals are biting her and the children are frightened. The father laughs along, but never actually looks her way.

As the family moves to play all together, the tension grows. The parents undermine one another as they each try to find a game to play as a family. The children continue to argue about the toys, and then the parents get involved and end up bickering about whose turn it is with the duck – Raphael's or Charlotte's. During this interchange the children basically stop fighting and just watch the parents struggle.

Finally, in part IV the affect in the room shifts. The parents speak calmly to one another and the children play on their own. At some point the two children start banging on the table together, checking on the parents' reactions. The parents tell them to stop and are able to redirect the children and return to their own quiet discussion.

Comment

For Charlotte and her family some things have improved. The parents are able to create a clear and flexible boundary. The flexibility is evident when we see that the children test it by banging on the table, and the parents respond by redirecting them and are able to continue with their discussion. This cooperation we see in part IV is an example of a resource in the family. With problematic family interactions it is far easier to focus on the difficulties. Clinically, however, these very strengths will often serve as an entry point into facilitating change (see chapter 10).

In other ways many of the difficulties have deepened with the transition to a two-child family. The parents often fail to work together and have considerable difficulty handling the sibling rivalry. Instead, the children's struggle over the toys moves up a generation, becoming a battle between the parents, with the children caught in between. It begs the question of whether the inverse is also true. Does the parents' conflict spill down a generation, causing rivalry between the children? Certainly the siblings were much more cooperative when left on their own to play with each other during part IV of the LFP.

Picnic game

How will this family behave in a less structured task such as the Lausanne Picnic Game (PNG)? The family is given toy picnic supplies and asked to play out a picnic with a large green carpet and a park bench for atmosphere. Pay attention to how the exclusive coparenting and binding coalition have developed now that there are four of them.

Sadly, the family never gets beyond setting up their picnic. They get bogged down in struggles about who is going to do what and then the siblings squabble once again over the toys. Each child has received a bag of toys and the parents agree that the children should take everything out of their bags so they can count them. Charlotte, however, refuses, so her mother threatens, "Well, if you're not going to do it, I'll just do it!" But then instead she invites Raphael to go make some "coffee" with her. As Raphael joins his mother, Charlotte starts to follow them. "No, this is only for Raphael," her mother announces, thus excluding Charlotte. Charlotte withdraws.

Soon after, the struggle over toys starts up again, now between the parents, while the children appear almost frozen. It begins with the father counting out their toys. The mother snips, "Raphael doesn't have as many toys, and they're not as good as Charlotte's." The father then removes one toy from Charlotte, and she cries for the rest of the PNG. Each of the parents tries to manage the situation. The mother offers a choice: "Charlotte, you can either give Raphael your dragon or your knight." The father tries to distract and redirect: "Hey, everybody, it's time to eat!" Neither strategy works, and the parents continue bickering over how to manage the children's "sharing problem." In the end they lecture Charlotte about her bad behavior as she gets more upset. The mother abruptly calls the facilitator back, ending the picnic. Even more distressed, Charlotte now exclaims, "I didn't even get a chance to play!" With a big smile the mother tells the facilitator, "Well, that was a total failure!"

Comment

By the time Charlotte is 5, her mother and brother have become quite close. The parents report that Charlotte's jealousy of her brother is "the problem" in the family. Since we did not see the family around the time of Raphael's birth, we can only imagine Charlotte's distress and confusion when she found herself being replaced by her brother in the overly close role with their mother. For this family, it simply reinforces the overarching pattern of "two-(or three)-minus one" – Raphael is now "in" and Charlotte is "out."

In the earlier LTPs with just Charlotte there is a clear pattern of a family-level binding coalition. In the foursome, there is still a binding coalition, with the mother and Raphael now aligned against the father and Charlotte. But the family also engages in other types of coalitions that we will explore in the next chapters. For example, when the parents are arguing over the toys, leaving the children frozen and perhaps frightened, this is actually an example of triangulation (see chapter 9), and there is also evidence of detouring (see chapter 8), when the parents join in attacking Charlotte in the picnic simulation.

So what about Charlotte's triangular and multiperson communication? It is clear that the conflicts limit how she handles any of the family configurations; so too presumably for Raphael. At times Charlotte withdraws. Other times both children are frozen during their parents' conflict. These actions stand as obstacles to the children practicing the actual skills they need for multiperson communication.

Discussion

We chose to present the case of Charlotte's family because, while it is an extreme example, it highlights the major elements of binding coalitions. The parents' problematic coparenting style is already observable in the prenatal LTP even before Charlotte's arrival. Their excluding style continues right up to toddlerhood, along with Charlotte's split engagement.

By 18 months family patterns have typically consolidated, in particular the ways in which infants respond to their parents. At this stage there were 15 non-cohesive families in our sample (Fivaz-Depeursinge, Lopes, Python, & Favez, 2009) and the vast majority of them (14/15) engaged in an excluding coparenting or "two-minus-one" pattern in either part I or II of the LTP. In parallel, approximately two thirds of these infants responded with a split engagement style, making few if any triangular bids. In the remaining cases the infants did make a few attempts at connecting with the third-party parent, but most of these bids were negative and ignored or invalidated by the parents. Thus the frequency of triangular bids in the first half of the LTP was significantly lower than in the group of infants faced with cohesive coparenting (N = 23).

Split engagement and triangular communication

In this chapter, we asked the question, How do infants cope with excluding coparenting? Although early on all infants exhibit some degree of competence for triangular communication, this group had little opportunity for practice. They learned to resort to splitting their engagement, which probably contributed to the cut-off parents further excluding themselves.

As noted, Charlotte's trajectory is extreme but demonstrates the way infants cope with an excluding coparenting style. Already at 9 months, she has learned to strictly follow the "two minus one" rule: systematically ignoring her father when playing with her mother and averting from him in part II or III when he is supposed to play. Interestingly, a change comes with toddlerhood. Charlotte is now able to interact with her father through the medium of objects. The context has also changed somewhat. Sometimes Charlotte and her father engage and her mother, now pregnant, is excluded. Regardless, the rule of two minus one remains, and there is still a serious toll being taken on Charlotte's emergent triangular communication.

For children growing up in this context, right from the start they make far fewer triangular bids than the norm. In parts I and II what triangular or even direct dyadic bids they do make to the non-active parent are almost always ignored, so these children tend not to expect help and do not ask for it from their third-party parent. They rarely, if ever, use social referencing in the LTP. For Charlotte, this situation largely continues even in the 3-together and dialogue parts; however, as we will see in chapters 8 and 9, a majority of non-cohesive families adopt other styles of engagement for these parts.

Excluding coparenting style

Cohesive coparents intuitively understand that simply present means being a participant-observer and they flexibly handle the infant's bids. In comparison the excluding coparenting style leaves little doubt of an underlying problem in the coparenting. In the most problematic cases the third party is almost completely cut off from the dyad as the active parent monopolizes the interaction with the infant. In between there are several variants. Sometimes only one parent behaves inappropriately. For example, the active parent engages in chase and dodge, while the third-party parent maintains the proper participant-observer stance. Alternatively, the active parent engages appropriately with the infant but the third-party parent looks away. In both of these examples, the two-minus-one rule is still in effect, although mediated somewhat by the appropriate parent.

The stability of excluding coparenting from early infancy to toddlerhood is remarkable. For Charlotte's family it is still observable at 5 years and has developed into a two-by-two binding coalition in the picnic game. The father-Charlotte dyad is excluded and opposes the mother-Raphael dyad and vice versa.

Clinical comment

This case illustrates how much things can deteriorate in families with the lowest coordination already observable during pregnancy. All participants were given video-feedback after each data point in the research. Charlotte's family was offered referrals for intervention as part of these video-feedback sessions, but always declined.

When families come to therapy, we anchor the intervention in their resources. At 18 months it might be the moment where the father gives Charlotte a cup to complete the coffee party. At the 5-year follow-up, we might show how well the parents create a clear and flexible boundary in part IV of the LFP. From there, other videoclips with more problematic interactions are used – for example, when the parents begin fighting over the toys in the PNG. The discussion focuses on helping the parents reflect on the children's experience in those moments and discussing alternative strategies.

References

Beebe, B., & Lachmann, F. (2002). *Infant research and adult treatment: Co-constructing interactions.* Hillsdale, NJ: Analytic Press.

Elliston, D., McHale, J., Talbot, J., Parmley, M., & Kuersten-Hogan, R. (2008). Withdrawal from coparenting interactions during early infancy. *Family Process, 47*(4), 481–499.

Fivaz-Depeursinge, E., & Corboz-Warnery, A. (1999). *The primary triangle: A developmental systems view of fathers, mothers and infants.* New York: Basic Books.

Fivaz-Depeursinge, E., Lopes, F., Python, M., & Favez, N. (2009). The toddler's role in family coalitions. *Family Process, 48*, 500–516.

McHale, J. (2007). When infants grow up in multiperson relationship systems. *Infant-Mental Health Journal, 28*, 370–392.

Minuchin, S. (1974). *Families & family therapy.* Boston: Harvard University Press.

Chapter 8

Coping with child-at-center coparenting

Alex is 18 months old, seated facing his two parents. The family is in part III of Lausanne Trilogue Play (Fivaz-Depeursinge & Corboz-Warnery, 1999), and the mother, father, and toddler should be playing together as a threesome. Alex is very intently brushing his mother's hair, while his father is sitting back in his seat, as if not really part of the play. Suddenly the father turns to the mother and says, "No." Without saying a word to her husband, the mother quietly stops her activity with Alex. Alex in turn appears confused, as he looks first at his mother and then at his father. His father says in a whining tone, "Daddy's the only one who can't get his hair brushed today?" He leans in towards Alex as if to invite him to brush his hair but then says, "You can't brush my hair, because I don't have any." Alex looks quizzically at his father's bald head, and then at his father's sad expression. His father adds, "Daddy's sad." Alex finally turns to his mother, who looks quite serious as well. She nods and agrees, "Daddy's sad." Suddenly Alex throws down the brush angrily. His parents both exclaim, "Alex! That's not nice!"

Even on first pass, there is something uncomfortable in this interaction. At the outset, Alex and his mother are the only ones interacting, rather than the whole family. Later it switches to the father and Alex. Alex tries to engage with each of his parents. But their reactions are a bit too serious, lacking the normal exaggeration parents do in play that lets children know that they are not actually "sad," just playing "sad." As a result we see Alex's confusion – "Is Daddy really sad?" and his subsequent reaction, which is to throw the brush down. Finally, there is the father's behavior towards the mother, demanding she stop playing with a simple "No," and her silent consent. There is no clear communication between the two parents about it at all. It is the sum total of all of these parts that we have come to recognize as child-at-center coparenting, and the formula for this maladaptive pattern goes something like this:

- Couple A has a history of conflict between them.
- They are unable to resolve it.

- Instead, they put the child in a leadership or role-reversed position:

  o As scapegoat
  o As entertainer
  o As victim

- The parents can then react to the child.
- The parents avoid reacting to one another.

How infants cope with child-at-center coparenting is the second type of problematic family interaction listed in Table 8.1. All three problematic family interactions that we are discussing in this section of the book are listed in Table 8.1, with the focus of this chapter in bold.

Table 8.1 Associations between infant engagement styles, coparenting styles, and resulting family structure

Infant engagement style	Coparenting style	Family structure
Triangular engagement	Cohesive	Alliance
Split engagement	Excluding	Binding coalition
Role reversed	**Child-at-center**	**Detouring coalition**
Go-between/withdrawal	Competitive	Triangulation coalition

We know that families set themselves on this maladaptive trajectory long before children such as Alex reach 18 months of age, but it is at this point in development that the pattern is fully recognizable. With toddlerhood play can now be much more complex and rich due to the emergence of language and the possibility for pretend play. Yet it is also a time of tension between the social rules that adults are trying to instill in the child and the child's desire to assert his autonomy (Kochanska, 2001). Children now begin to experience the pleasures and pains of emotions such as pride, enthusiasm, empathy, embarrassment, guilt, and shame, referred to as "moral emotions" (Emde, Biringen, Clyman, & Oppenheim, 1991). The toddler now has more elaborate triangular strategies to share his emotions with both parents, but also to manipulate the relationship and test the limits they set.

Child-at-center coparenting and role reversals

Needless to say, these new developments not only challenge the solidarity between the parents but also can exacerbate any tensions and aggravate any boundary diffusion between the couple and the toddler. So it makes sense that it is most often at this "moral symbolic" stage that problems become more obvious. For some families, conflict or tension between parents is displaced, or, as Minuchin termed it, "detoured" onto the toddler (1974). As a result, the child functions to regulate the relationship between his parents, placing him in a role-reversed position. Depending on a number of factors, this role-reversal may take on different forms. The child may become oppositional, taking on the role of the badly behaved child or scapegoat. This is what we saw with Alex throwing down the brush earlier, allowing his parents to focus on his naughty behavior instead of on the awkwardness between them. Or the child might adopt the role of the "good" child. He may take on a caretaker stance, more like a parent, spouse, or peer, or perhaps adopt the role of "entertainer." Under other circumstances, such as illness, he may be considered the victim. Finally, the infant may alternate between various roles.

While at times even children in well-coordinated families can briefly find themselves adopting one of these strategies, it is the exception and not the rule. In families who use detouring regularly as a way to deflect marital conflict, the role of regulating the parents' relationship places the child in what has been referred to as an "over-engaged" position, playing too significant a role in their interactions. It is important to stress that in all of these instances, once the child takes this "over-engaged" position (Fivaz-Depeursinge, Lopes, Python, & Favez, 2009), the parents then react in a unified manner – for example, scolding Alex for throwing the brush. It is because of the unified front that such dynamics have also been described as "detouring coalitions" (Minuchin, 1974).

In our study of this type of family interaction at 18 months there were some very clear patterns, not only in part III but also throughout the LTPs of these families. Let's now return to the case of Alex, and go through it in more detail.

Alex at 18 months

We should start by pointing out how hard Alex's parents worked throughout the session to engage their toddler in play. Unfortunately, their repertoire lacked coordination and flexibility and they seemed misattuned to Alex's cues much of the time. As well, while the focus of this chapter is the challenges for infants coping with child-at-center coparenting, these families also engage in a pattern of exclusion, particularly in parts I and II of the LTP (chapter 7). We begin with these two parts.

LTP parts I and II

The task begins with Alex and his mother playing while the father is supposed to be "simply present." Later they will switch roles for part II. As the active parent each of them tends to be quite didactic and controlling, and the interaction is not particularly playful, with little evidence of affect sharing. In part I, the father's behavior as third party is striking. He does not watch his wife and son as they play; rather he looks down at the floor most of the time and occasionally checks the time on the clock. Because he is not watching the interaction, he fails to resonate with any of the high points in the mother-son play. When the mother is the third party in part II, for the most part she also averts her gaze and does not resonate with the father-son interaction. On the few occasions that Alex looks at the third-party parent, they are looking away and unresponsive to his gaze.

Comment

The concern at this point in the LTP is that at the very least, Alex is set on an alternate trajectory in terms of his triangular communication. Even if only one parent is active and the other is simply present, we expect infants to share some of their experience with the third-party parent. This can be simply shifting their gaze over to that parent and then back again to the active one in what is called a triangular bid. It can also be a more complex series of nonverbal behaviors, such as is seen in social referencing. Typically the inactive parent smiles along when the active parent and child are doing something cute or fun, or he or she might look concerned when the child shows some distress. For Alex's parents, instead of being "simply present" in these first two parts, they each self-exclude, and so he can not share his experience with the non-active parent. The few bids he addresses to his third-party parent are ignored or unseen. We will see that the track record for unrequited triangular bids was already set in previous LTPs, and so by 18 months Alex in fact addresses far fewer triangular bids than is expected for a child of his age. This is one of the patterns seen in children confronted with exclusion (chapter 7).

LTP part III

We began this chapter with a small excerpt from the 3-together play since it was here that the pattern of conflict was most representative of child-at-center coparenting. As in the situation with the brush, through most of these next two parts the parents presented a united front. The father imposed rules and the mother strictly complied without further discussion. We pick up the interaction shortly after the situation with the brush.

> *The parents have built a fence for the toy farm animals. When it is ready, Alex playfully knocks the barrier down and throws it on the floor. His father complains, "Oh, now I don't have anywhere to live . . ." but as with the brush situation, it does not register as playful. Alex looks anxiously at his father. Then, in a typical triangular social referencing bid, he looks at his mother, who confirms once more that "Daddy's sad." Alex reacts by throwing down another animal. At this point, the mother suggests to the father that they move on to Part IV. "I think we should move on, darling, because we have to . . ." The father ignores her and addresses Alex. "Yeah, like maybe we can eat something with Alex?" The mother goes along with this plan. "Alex, can you make us something to eat?" But Alex does not cooperate, continuing to play with the farm fencing instead. The parents both try cajoling Alex into making them something to eat, even teasing him for not doing it. "I guess we're not going to get to eat anything . . ." Finally the mother says, "Fine then, we'll leave you to play on your own," and she and her husband turn to face each other to start part IV.*

Comment

The parents work together but in the service of correcting or shaming Alex for his actions. One of the few attempts at direct communication between them happens when the mother first suggests they move on to part IV, and the father ignores her completely. Alex copes with his parents' united, negative front by ignoring and frankly opposing their games, even throwing them on the floor and scoring as the "bad child." In part IV he will change his tactic somewhat.

LTP part IV

The father reminds the mother not to look at Alex in part IV and they move on to talk about their plans for the afternoon. Meanwhile, Alex rebuilds the farm fence and proudly presents it to his parents – to no avail. The parents completely ignore him. Next, he stands up in his high chair, ready to climb out. His mother admonishes him, wagging her finger. "Mommy and Daddy are talking. You have to stay in your seat." When she addresses Alex a second time, the father warns her, "We're not supposed to look at him."

"But he's going to fall down," the mother responds, to which the father rebuts, "No, I'll catch him!" Eventually they do stop the session in order to prevent Alex from falling.

Comment

Alex starts out this part with a new strategy. He reconstructs the farm fencing, to score as the "good child," but his actions go unnoticed. Any opportunity to repair the relationship has been missed. This is when Alex decidedly turns up the volume on his opposition and tries to get out of his seat. The parents presumably feel that their strategy of scolding is for their "bad" child's own good. But what are the origins of this joint, rigid control?

We can now recognize this type of pattern as one where parents might be detouring some of the tension between themselves onto the child, pushing him into a position where he alternates between opposition and repair. Ironically, this dynamic also allows the parents to feel close with one another, in opposition to their child. In the case of Alex's parents, a subsequent interview did reveal that they were struggling with some unresolved marital conflict.

The emergence of moral emotions such as pride, empathy, guilt, and shame provides parents with new leverage to control their child's behavior. In Alex's family there is an imbalance in these emotions, with the negative weighing more heavily than the positive. It is clearly related to the absence of playfulness and limited positive affect sharing we see. If we can generalize from this LTP what Alex's experience of being with his two parents outside the LTP might look like, then it would be one of feeling alone, anxious, and guilty.

Trajectory towards role reversal

Clearly Alex and his parents did not arrive at this pattern the moment he became a toddler. Even as early as the prenatal assessment, the father tended to be quite rigid and controlling, while the mother typically followed his lead, without discussion or confrontation. This meant that already by the 3-month LTP the parents controlled which games they played with Alex. They also engaged in the same self-exclusion in parts I and II. In part IV they focus so exclusively on each other that they miss all of Alex's nonverbal cues. Each time they do an LTP Alex becomes increasingly difficult and unwilling to submit to the wishes of his parents. By the time they reach the 3-together part at 3 months, and even more so at 9 months, Alex's parents see him as fussy, oppositional, and unable to regulate his negative affects. To the outside observer, however, it feels like the parents' rigid control and lack of attunement might be reason enough for the difficulties observed in the child.

Follow up at 5 years

Lausanne Family Play

The family has expanded. Alex has a little brother, Jack, who is 15 months old. In the standard protocol, families first play together in the Lausanne Family Play (LFP). Then the eldest plays alone with his parents in the Lausanne Narrative Play (LNP). While not described here, the sibling rejoins them for the family picnic simulation (PNG) at the end.

The instructions for the LFP, described in chapter 5, are identical to the LTP; however, in parts I and II, the active parent plays with both children, while the other parent is simply present. In part III the entire family plays together, and then in part IV the children are left to play on their own, while the adults discuss. The whole family is seated at a table, with the parents at the ends, and the two children together along the length of the table (in order to both face the camera).

LFP parts I and II

The play starts out looking very familiar. The mother is playing with Alex and Jack, and the father once again is not watching the scene unfold. However, their play is animated, in particular by Alex's introduction of a story. "Let's pretend I'm the gardener." Alex picks up one of the four toy phones and proceeds to call his mother. "Hi, Daddy asked me to come over to your house to work and I'm gonna take care of Jack while you and Daddy are at work." The mother interjects, "Oh, Jack loves being with you so much!"

Next, the mother suggests the transition to the father's play. During the play between the boys and their father, the mother sits enjoying the interaction, without interfering. The father works to include both brothers in the play. Again, it is Alex who leads. He is extremely attentive to his little brother – for instance, gently helping him hold the phone correctly.

Comment

It is important to stress that we are already seeing some notable differences now that Jack is part of the interaction. While the father still excludes himself during the mother's play with the children, there are small changes that make this family's interactions appear far more functional now.

During part II the mother no longer excludes herself as third party. She looks on and even resonates with the play. Likewise, rather than imposing his own agenda, the father is now able to go along with the pretend play initiated by Alex. He even finds ways to keep Jack included in the play.

As for Alex's play, we see both his resourcefulness as well as possible areas of concern. By age 5 children often want to lead, and to take care of their younger siblings, but for Alex these behaviors also raise the question of role reversal as he tries to play the adult. But let's leave this question open for now and move on to the second half of this LFP.

LFP parts III and IV

Alex initiates the next transition. "Now all four of us have to play together."
He distributes the animals and the cell phones to the parents and children.
The three other family members willingly go along with him and his par-
ents even praise him for it. Later the whole family playfully tries to get Jack
to choose a cell phone. He refuses one phone after another. Suddenly Alex
announces in a very loud voice, "I have to go shopping now!"

The mother very skillfully negotiates the next transition with the children
and they easily move on to part IV. During the parents' dialogue the boys
play nicely together, with Alex taking the lead. Alex "calls" his brother on the
phone, and then patiently tries to get Jack to respond, "Say that you're com-
ing over to my house, okay?" In the meantime, the parents talk about the day's
events, but are not so cut off from the children that they are unaware of them.

Comment

Clearly there are some strengths seen in this family now that they are four. They join together playfully around a shared activity, helping Jack choose a phone. The mother is more assertive at negotiating a clear but flexible boundary between the adults and the children in part IV. The father participates more fluidly. He does not seem controlling and is able to play more cooperatively.

Areas of concern that remain are around the role of Alex in this family. If we saw only this LFP we might be less concerned about the possibility of role reversal. Boszormenyi-Nagy and Spark (1973) identified "normal parentification" where children learn about caretaking roles through play. Likewise, according to Jurkovic (1997), intergenerational boundaries can and are crossed in healthy families – but only temporarily and with clear recognition of the violation. It can occur as an exception due to extenuating circumstances, or during play, where children should take the lead. For Alex, the previous LTPs lead us to wonder if this might be a more maladaptive form of leading.

We see possible parentification in several places as Alex directs the transition to part III; finds an activity for the whole family; and takes care of his brother so that the parents can have an uninterrupted dialogue in part IV. Now, rather than being difficult or fussy, the parents can compliment Alex on how wonderful he is.

It is interesting to see how the presence of a sibling changes the family's interactions. Jack, for the moment, seems to be protected by his brother from the detouring coalition and child-at-center dynamics. Alex is no longer the scapegoat, but is complimented for his caretaking, and there are many examples of him managing multiperson communication. Both parents seem more flexible and actually playful for the first time. In this four-way interaction, Alex has many opportunities to use multiperson communication. There are still areas of concern, but if this were our first encounter with this family, their LFP would be unremarkable as their interactions were not actually out of the norm.

Lausanne Narrative Play

Next the parents and Alex do an LNP (see chapter 7) while Jack is supervised in another room. The two parents and child are seated in a triangle, at a round table. They are provided with dolls representing each family member – a mother, a father and two boys, plus two dolls representing "trusted caregivers."

The instructions are to help Alex tell the following story: The parents are going away, just the two of them, for the weekend. The children are going to be looked after by trusted caregivers. In part I of the LNP, one of the parents helps the child to begin playing out the story. In part II, the second parent continues the story with the child. In part III, mother, father, and child end the story together. During part IV, when the parents are to have their own discussion, the child is to play or draw on his own at the table.

LNP parts I and II

Alex and his mother start out the story and the father as third party once again excludes himself by looking down. The mother helps Alex select the characters and decide where he and his brother will stay for the weekend. They decide the trusted caregivers should be the grandparents, and the figures drive to the grandparents' home. The parents and children in the story kiss and say good-bye, and then the mother has the parents drive away for their weekend in the mountains.

At this point, the father announces, "It's my turn now," and the mother quietly withdraws. The father asks Alex to explain. "So who's who here? I wasn't listening." Alex explains, but things quickly get confused as Alex asks his father to play the grandmother cooking dinner. Alex's father seems unable to see how he could play a different role. "I'm supposed to play the husband away for the weekend with his wife." Alex looks frustrated, and still wants his father to play other roles as need be. He keeps asking his father, "Come on, let's play now!" His father complains, "This game's too complicated," and repeatedly states, "I'm supposed to play out the part where Mommy and I are away for a romantic weekend." He takes the parent dolls, and plays out the two walking, swimming, and going to a restaurant. Alex sits and watches for a bit, but then asks to go to the bathroom. His father stops him. "No, Alex, pay attention to the game!" Finally the father announces, "Okay, the mommy and daddy are back from their weekend away! They're here to pick the kids up and take them home." They transition to the third part.

Comment

Some things have changed, and some have not. Typically in families with problematic coparenting, at the point in the story where the doll parents leave for their weekend away, parents have a tendency to make a bit of a fuss, making statements like, "Oh, no, now it's time for us to go away. Will you be okay without us?" Interestingly, Alex and his mother skim right over the separation just as normative families do.

With language now a primary vehicle for interactions, the mother is able to playfully set limits and engage in more imaginative games. In fact, aside from the father's self-exclusion, the interaction between Alex and his mother in part I of the LNP is fairly typical. Of course the father does self-exclude in the third-party position, so cut off that he apparently has not even caught the storyline.

When it is time for him to play with Alex, the father is unable to follow his son's lead and takes over completely. There is a change in how Alex now manages his father's control. As a toddler he alternated between compliance and opposition, but at 5 he has adopted mostly a compliant/caretaking stance. He tries to explain to his father how to play the game (caretaking), or simply allows his father to act out the story (compliance). When overwhelmed by his circumstances, he no longer resorts to overt opposition like he did as a toddler, angrily throwing down the brush. Instead he first begs his father to play, and then eventually asks to leave instead of watching his father play out the uncomfortable story on his own. Asking to leave is a subtler, more indirect form of opposition.

As for the mother in the third-party position, she no longer looks away but rather resonates in an exaggerated way so it is unclear how she would respond to Alex if he did turn to her. In fact Alex does not look to his mother to help him sort out this conundrum with his father. Not expecting and not asking for her help are typical of children faced with excluding coparenting and we have seen this in Alex since infancy. So while there are some positive changes, the excluding coparenting style is still present in parts I and II of the LNP.

LNP parts III and IV

The mother now gently tries to clarify the situation for her husband, but he instead interrupts with, "We have to play!" She complies, and plays out the reunion with the parents and children. She takes on various roles while the father sits and watches. Several times she praises Alex for how "good" he is. Suddenly, the father interjects, "I want to kiss my children." While Alex and his mother watch, he has the father doll kiss the children dolls and then tuck them in bed. Once again Alex asks to go to the bathroom. His mother joins his father to tell Alex, "No, you should stay, sweetie, the researchers will be disappointed if you're not in the video." Alex complies and the parents move to their dialogue.

The father begins by talking about how confused he was during the task. The mother simply listens. After a while, Alex asks his parents, "Mommy . . . Daddy . . . is it true, you're going away on a romantic weekend?" Alex gets no response, other than hushed murmurings between his parents, who appear visibly embarrassed. He repeats his question several times, getting louder and louder. The parents finally move on to another theme and Alex gets permission to go out.

Comment

While there is some improvement in this interaction, in general the same patterns are still much more evident than when the family was together with Jack. The mother and Alex play together, flexibly taking on various roles. Yet the father still excludes himself as the third party. When he plays with Alex, the father insists on literally sticking to his "real" role in the story and frequently interrupts to control or redirect the play. His literalness is actually quite striking and during the subsequent debriefing the father does spontaneously comment that he wishes he were more "relaxed." This self-awareness is another positive marker of some flexibility or change in this family.

The child-at-center style of coparenting, however, is still present. When Alex asks to go to the bathroom in both parts III and IV, his parents join together to insist he stay. They even resort to guilt about disappointing the researchers, leaving the team uncomfortable with being cast as overly controlling.

The timing of Alex's requests to leave is actually quite consistent. In the first two instances it happens when the father imposes his own agenda on the game instead of hearing Alex's wishes. For example, in Part II, he has to watch his father play out the parents' weekend away, which is not only not what Alex wants but also quite atypical in this task. Normally, families play out the children's story at the caregivers' home, leaving the parent dolls off to the side. In part IV, Alex repeatedly asks about the parents' romantic weekend and they do not answer. His wishes are once again not met and so he asks to leave again.

There is also consistency around when the mother joins the father "against" Alex in a classic child-at-center pattern. It happens around enforcing the "rules" of the LTP, as the parents understand them. In other words, both parents join together against Alex to keep him in the room and on task so as not to "disappoint" the researchers. They also still avoid looking at Alex during part IV. It is as if they believe they must defer their own better judgment to the authority of the researchers, even if their child needs them. This type of rigid adherence to the "rules" of the researchers is a frequent pattern in child-at-center coparenting, and likely reflects how these parents deal with authority in general. It is a critical piece of information clinically, which we discuss in chapter 10.

As for Alex, the unanswered question about the romantic weekend getaway is telling. Clearly the romantic weekend has piqued his imagination. Is it an unspoken wish for this child to be relieved of the burden of his parents' covert conflict? When the family first arrived that day, the parents spoke at length about a serious conflict, which they had been trying to resolve of late, so clearly their marital conflict is ongoing.

Alternatively the idea of romance between his parents might be a frightening change for Alex. He stands to lose his central position regulating his parents' marriage, and the control that comes with it. Perhaps both possibilities are true – the wish for a more peaceful and loving relationship between his parents, and the fear of what such a change would bring.

While the detouring coalition is still evident when Alex plays alone with his parents, the presence of a sibling changes the family's interactions. When all four are together, Jack seems to be protected by his brother from the detouring coalition and child-at-center dynamics. Alex, as noted, finds himself in a leadership role. Both parents seem more flexible and actually playful for the first time. All told, the family interactions appear more functional when all four play together. We point this out as a marker for how, within the same family system, different subsystems articulate with the whole, but can function quite differently.

Discussion

Alex's family is representative of the five cases in our sample with severe child-at-center coparenting, resulting in a detouring coalition. The parents' problematic coparenting style was already forming prior to the birth of their children, as observed in the prenatal LTPs. It endures to varying degrees, well into early childhood.

By toddlerhood, Alex has adopted various forms of role reversal, but mostly he has learned to resort to confrontation to cope with his parents. At 5 years, Alex is on the caretaking side of role reversal, particularly with his father in the three-person LNP. Interestingly, when the family plays together as a foursome, his caretaking of his little brother is much closer to age-appropriate parentification (Kerig, 2003). Other children in the same subgroup learned to use animation or caretaking strategies by toddlerhood as well.

Role reversal and triangular communication

So how do we assess the development of triangular communication of these role-reversed children? As infants in parts I and II, their bids to the third-party parents are ignored, and so they are left on their own to understand and manage whatever inappropriate or uncomfortable behaviors the active parent proposes. In parallel these infants tend not to ask for help from their third-party parents. They make far fewer bids than the normative sample, just like all infants faced with excluding coparenting. In contrast, in the 3-together play and when they are in the third-party position themselves, these children tend to overuse triangular communication. Into toddlerhood Alex uses mostly negative bids of protest or confrontation, while other children tried positive bids of animation or charm.

These bids do not serve the usual function of sharing affects with the parents. Rather, they serve to regulate the couple's conflict, so that not only is the child's social and affective communication derailed, but so too is the development of his triangular communication.

Child-at-center coparenting style

Parents in this group seem to be cut off from one another, each having an exclusive interaction with their child in parts I and II of the LTP. It seems to contradict the united front they present in the second half of the LTP. However, on closer examination there is another contradiction: under the banner of a united front, there are more or less subtle signs of tension between the parents. For example, Alex's mother complies with the rules set by her husband not to look at their son in part IV, but it is unclear whether she actually agrees with those rules, given that he needs to keep reminding her of them. Interactions between the two parents are almost exclusively about managing Alex's behavior. It is important to note the paradoxes:

- the divided couple of the first half and the united couple of the second half
- the superficially united front yet underlying signs of un-negotiated agreement

These signs are confusing and difficult to assess exactly because of their paradoxical nature. Observers typically oscillate between these poles, calling the coparents divided or united if they do not take all elements into account at the same time.

Detouring coalitions

How do the infant's role reversal and the child-at-center coparenting style precisely play into the dynamics of a detouring coalition? By the time they reach toddlerhood, the children are controlling the family interactions during the 3-together play and the parents' dialogue through provocation or caretaking strategies. The net function of the infants' triangular bids is to monitor and control the family interactions, rather than to share intersubjective experiences as a threesome.

The parents as a coparenting subsystem allow the toddlers to control their relationship seemingly in order to avoid confronting their own conflict. These parents reported in the interviews that a united front was good for Alex – without acknowledging or perhaps even being aware that it was forced. This belief contradicts the exclusion we see in parts I and II. The parents' responses and comments during the video-feedbacks indicate that they do not see those first two parts as triadic. It was as if, for them, the LTP's four configurations were a succession of separate parts rather than four different ways of being together as a threesome.

In the sample there were five families with detouring coalitions at 18 months. Two showed improvement by 5 years, Alex's family and another one not described here. They were also the families with a second child. Did having a second child offer them the opportunity to change? Or were they already changing, and it allowed them to have the second child? Either way, while there were certainly cohesive couples that did not go on to have a second child, it is important to note among the families with the lowest coordination in infancy none had a second child by the 5-year follow-up. We have to wonder whether something about their poor coordination played a role in this decision, but imagine the burden for an only child with parents in chronic conflict, who rely on him in order to remain united.

Clinical comment

All the cases in the longitudinal study were brought in for a video-feedback session after each LTP. This was a way in which the research team could give back to the families who volunteered to participate in the study. For some families, this was also an opportunity to recommend interventions if they were thought necessary. A family intervention was certainly suggested to Alex's parents during the video-feedback at 18 months; however, they declined. Fortunately they were beginning to see that there were problems in their marital relationship, and did get couple's treatment after Jack was born. While there were still issues at the 5-year follow-up, there was also clear evidence of progress in this family. Sadly, not all of the families in this study who struggled agreed to intervention.

References

Boszormenyi-Nagy, I., & Spark, G. M. (1973). *Invisible loyalties: Reciprocity in intergenerational family therapy.* Hagerstown, MD: Harper & Row.

Emde, R., Biringen, Z., Clyman, R., & Oppenheim, D. (1991). The moral self of infancy: Affective core and procedural knowledge. *Developmental Review, 11,* 251–270.

Fivaz-Depeursinge, E., & Corboz-Warnery, A. (1999). *The primary triangle: A developmental systems view of fathers, mothers and infants.* New York: Basic Books.

Fivaz-Depeursinge, E., Lopes, F., Python, M., & Favez, N. (2009). The toddler's role in family coalitions. *Family Process, 48,* 500–516.

Jurkovic, G. (1997). *Lost childhoods: The plight of the parentified child.* Philadelphia: Brunner/Mazel.

Kerig, P. K. (2003). Boundary dissolution. In J. Ponzetti, R. Hamon, Y. Kellar-Guenther, P. K. Kerig, L. Scales, & J. White (Eds.), *International encyclopedia of marital and family relationships* (pp. 164–170). New York: Macmillan.

Kochanska, G. (2001). Emotional development in children with different attachment histories: The first three years. *Child Development, 72,* 474–490.

Minuchin, S. (1974). *Families & family therapy.* Boston: Harvard University Press.

Chapter 9

Coping with competitive coparenting

With France Frascarolo-Moutinot

In this chapter, we begin by meeting Myriam and her parents. The family was seen as part of a longitudinal study on non-referred families at the Centre for Studies of the Family (Centre d'Etude de la Famille – CEF), part of the University of Lausanne Institute for Psychotherapy. Their interactions were recorded during Lausanne Trilogue Play (LTP) (Fivaz-Depeursinge & Corboz-Warnery, 1999) as well as its variants. Myriam's family illustrates how infants cope with what McHale has termed "competitive coparenting" (2007). Myriam will alternate between what we call a "go-between" and a "withdrawal" style of infant engagement. The cycle can be summarized below:

- Myriam's parents have a history of unresolved conflict and do not communicate well as coparents.
- Instead, each parent tries to capture Myriam's attention.
- Myriam is overstimulated; she looks back and forth at her parents, signaling her distress.
- Each parent tries harder to soothe her in their own way.
- Myriam gets more distressed and withdraws.

By "go-between" we are referring to when Myriam looks back and forth at her two parents in the face of their competing behaviors. She signals to the parents that she wants to change the situation and we refer to this back-and-forth distress signal as a triangular protest bid.

During the first two parts of the LTP, she also makes what we call "direct bids" (see chapter 9). She signals directly to the "other" parent, the one inactive at the time, as if seeking help. Were she to signal only to the parent playing with her, it would be a "dyadic protest" bid, but some of the time during the first two parts of the LTP, Myriam protests to the inactive parent only, and so here "direct" refers to those protest bids directed only to the inactive parent. It seems as if she is already learning to draw each third-party parent into the conflict, in the same way that her parents draw her into their conflict.

This family dynamic results in what has been called a *triangulation coalition* by Minuchin (1974) and is the third type of problematic family interaction that we

Table 9.1 Associations between infant engagement styles, coparenting styles, and resulting family structure

Infant engagement style	Coparenting style	Family structure
Triangular engagement	Cohesive	Alliance
Split engagement	Excluding	Binding coalition
Role reversed	Child-at-center	Detouring coalition
Go-between/withdrawal	**Competitive**	**Triangulation coalition**

describe in section II of this book. All three problematic family interactions are listed in Table 9.1, with the focus of this chapter in bold.

The term triangulation may be confusing, because it has different meanings according to different schools of thought. Here we clarify the definitions we are using in this book.

- *Triangulation coalition:* The term triangulation is used in family therapy when "two parents, in overt or covert conflict, are each attempting to enlist the child's sympathy or support against the other, causing intense conflict of loyalty" (Hoffman, 1981, p. 150). When referring to this concept we will exclusively use "triangulation coalition."
- *The infant's triangular capacity:* We systematically associate the terms "capacity" or "competence" to the adjective triangular to describe the infant's ability in connecting with two partners at the same time, in particular by means of triangular bids. The infant then engages in "triangular communication."
- *Normative triangular communication:* The ability to handle the four possible configurations of a triad.

Myriam at 9 months

This time, we start describing the triangulation coalition at 9 months because in Myriam's case it reaches its peak at this stage. As described in chapter 3, this age corresponds to the emergence of a new form of intentionality, often referred to as the "intentional stance." The infant is able to set himself a goal and use different means to reach it (Bretherton, 1992). However, in the context of competitive coparenting, the infant's autonomy is visibly restricted.

LTP parts I–II

As with many families with seriously non-cohesive coparenting, in the first two parts the coparenting style is "excluding." The interaction is particularly stressful for all parties. Already in part I, the father and Myriam engage in a "chase and dodge" pattern, with the father intruding and Myriam averting him each time (Beebe & Lachmann, 2002). In part II the mother also intrudes, but Myriam paradoxically fusses when her mother backs away.

Myriam starts off by turning to explore the headrest of her seat. And her father immediately exclaims, "No, no, no!" Holding onto the headrest, Myriam turns her head to look at him, puzzled. He grabs hold of her hands and pulls her around to face him square on. She of course protests. He leans his face even closer, and in response Myriam arches her back and protests some more but still looks at him.

Now Myriam turns to her mother and makes the same protest signal. Instead of responding to her baby's bid for help, her mother ignores her and even turns away very conspicuously.

Myriam becomes increasingly frustrated. She partially covers her face with her hands, still protesting to both parents. After two more rounds, during which Myriam escalates her bids, she finally breaks down crying.

In part II, the mother overpowers Myriam by looming close, with exaggerated gestures and non-stop chatter, mimicking the baby, "No no no no no no . . ." Myriam, frozen in what looks like a mix of fascination and fear, fusses as soon as her mother backs off a bit. She makes one bid to her father but it is ignored.

Comment

Already in the first part of the LTP, even though it is an example of excluding coparenting, we see evidence of the triangulation coalition. In both parts I and II, Myriam protests to the active parent, but she also makes direct bids to the non-active parent.

This interaction between Myriam and her two parents nevertheless is excluding coparenting, in particular because neither parent responds to her protests when in the third-party position. In cohesive coparenting, parents resonate with bids nonverbally, neither ignoring nor intruding on the active parent's interaction with the infant. Halfway into this LTP, we already have concerns for how these parents will scaffold Myriam's triangular communication.

LTP parts III–IV

By the time they reach the 3-together, Myriam is even fussier. She oscillates between aversion, freezing, and seeking help by making bids of distress or pick-me-up gestures to both parents.

Myriam is faced with intense stimulation from both of her parents, each following their own repertoire. Towards the very end of part III there is one brief stretch of togetherness, where the parents sit at a more appropriate social distance, each playing with her feet. Myriam shows interest looking back and forth at both of them with a faint smile. The father immediately comes in closer, which in turn triggers Myriam to dodge him once again.

The parents are next supposed to talk in part IV; however, their dialogue is almost immediately dispensed with as Myriam tries to get out of her seat and then starts to cry. It is clear to all that she needs to end the task.

Comment

Myriam faces two parents who engage in non-stop uncoordinated stimulation, forcing her into protest and self-protection. Through her triangular protest bids Myriam tries to let her parents know she is not happy with her situation. The back and forth is then interposed with moments of withdrawal in order to recuperate.

There is one short-lived moment of 3-together sharing, with the foot game. This resource is one we would use clinically. For the most part, however, there is no space for Myriam to do anything other than to react.

Finally, the couple's dialogue is essentially skipped. In the LTP this is a frequent clinical marker of marital discord and as with many couples, the infant soon learns ways to rescue them, as does Myriam by crying. In fact the couple later reports that this is the part they most disliked.

Myriam copes with the excluding coparenting of parts I and II by means of direct bids, and the competitive coparenting of part III by adopting a go-between/withdrawal position. These strategies prove ineffective in altering her parents' style. If anything, her coping strategies strengthen the parents' competition. Finally, many of her multiple bids are ignored, giving her no sense of her own agency.

Myriam at 18 months

LTP parts I–II

At 18 months, Myriam seems to have lost her stamina. Her mood is sad; she shows little interest or pleasure, no enthusiasm or pride. Any attempts at challenging her parents or testing limits, as would be typical for a toddler at this stage, are mostly aborted.

> During the play with her father, the chase and dodge pattern observed at 9 months surfaces only in moments of increased tension, probably thanks to the fact that there are now toys that can serve as a buffer. The play is still unsuccessful. The father maintains a very fast pace, picking up one toy after another. Myriam lags behind most of the time. Without looking at her father, she turns twice to her mother in a direct bid. Her mother ignores these bids, and appears tense. She keeps checking the time and trying to get the father's attention to let him know it is her turn, which he ignores. Myriam no longer tries at all to share her affects with her parents by means of triangular bids here or in part II.
>
> In part II, the mother-Myriam play is similar to what we saw at 9 months – intense non-stop stimulation from the mother met with relative inaction from Myriam. At one point, Myriam lets an object fall on the floor and, pointing to it, she exclaims, "Fall?" in a tone that sounds both questioning as well as angry. The mother repeats, "Fall," but changes its affective connotation by making it exaggeratedly sad.

Comment

Myriam's triangular communication is completely shut down in these first two parts of the LTP. She no longer makes the direct bids we saw at 9 months, and certainly no triangular bids.

We also want to highlight the moment in part II when the mother repeats the word "fall" to her daughter. This is what Stern (1985) described as "distorting attunement," where the parent alters the meaning of the child's expression in their response, rather than conveying that they understand the true sense.

LTP parts III–IV

During the 3-together play, the father joins the mother a few times in this distorting attunement when repeating the word "fall." These will be the only episodes with joint parental responses, yet joined together "against" their child's feelings.

After a while, Myriam hits the table more in tune with her own original angry affect than the one the parents have ascribed – or perhaps also reflective of some frustration with their misattunement. Eventually, however, she too adopts the parents' sad sounding tone.

Near the end of part III, mother and daughter are engaged, and the father leans back in his chair, resting his hands in his lap, looking defeated. Myriam and her mother continue to play and ignore him. He makes one last attempt to reengage by offering a cup to Myriam. The mother comments, "There's not enough space for everyone here . . ."

In part IV, during their dialogue, the tension between the parents is obvious. They reorient towards Myriam within less than a minute, talking about her as they look at her. Myriam mostly keeps herself busy with the toys. For the most part, she does not try to get their attention or even look at them. Once, when a toy falls to the floor, she looks up at her mother, exclaiming with a sad voice, "Fall!" The mother does not respond, but the father moves to pick up the toy. The mother then unilaterally decides that the time is up and waves to the facilitator to end the LTP.

Comment

Myriam has shifted to a mostly withdrawn position. She makes almost no attempts anymore to oppose or even solicit her parents' attention. Rather, she tends to submit, as illustrated by her joining her parents in their distorting attunement, accommodating to them rather than the inverse. This restriction of her triangular affect sharing to a negative, distorted emotion is in sharp contrast with other toddlers her age. For the typical toddler, affect sharing includes pride and playfulness as well as the feelings that come with the toddler's testing of limits, such as apprehension and frustration. Of note, the father also seems to have given up on competing with his wife.

In the dialogue of part IV the parents are unable to maintain a discussion alone for more than a minute, and instead put Myriam at the center and speak about her. The parents are unable to create a boundary around their relationship as separate from Myriam (Minuchin, 1974). Their only communication is centered around Myriam, as we have seen in child-at-center coparenting in chapter 8.

Myriam is mostly withdrawn. There is the one occasion where she looks at her mother in what might be an "approach," a toddler strategy to get the parent's attention back in part IV of the LTP. She makes reference to the word "fall," perhaps trying to get her mother's attention and gain her favor by adopting the same (distorted) sad affect.

Myriam at 3 months

When we rewind to 3 months, a number of the patterns that we see at 9 months are already becoming evident.

> *The parents are both hyper-stimulating throughout. Myriam makes direct bids to her mother when playing with her father. The mother over-resonates with the interaction when in the third-party position. Myriam makes no direct bids to her father when interacting with her mother. In part III, the parents are uncoordinated and engage in competing actions during the 3-together, with Myriam dodging both of them. The tension between the parents is evident in part IV, and they focus on their baby during their dialogue.*

Comment

The hint of the triangulation coalition we see in parts I and II at 9 months is not yet evident at 3 months as Myriam makes direct bids only to her mother. We see these bids as precursors of the strategies typical of triangulation coalitions in older families, although in this part of the LTP they look a bit more like a mother-daughter binding coalition against the father. The competition between the parents, however, becomes quite clear in part III.

Prenatal LTP

If we go back even further, we can see that the couple's tension was visible already during the prenatal LTP, which the parents dutifully executed without the usual mutual support or warmth we see in expectant couples doing this play task. They are asked to role-play the same four parts of an LTP, with a rag doll posing as their soon-to-be-born baby. At one point in part IV the mother exclaims that the baby fortunately does not have its father's nose. They finally end after a debate over petty details about the medical aspects of the delivery.

Comment

It is important to note that throughout the study, although the parents were intent on cooperating and came regularly, they were also quite critical of the tasks they were asked to do. The father also commented that he was not good at "role-playing" when referring to his play with Myriam in the LTP.

During most LTPs the mother turned several times towards the facilitators behind the one-way mirror, rolling her eyes in an attempt to recruit the research team in deriding the father's actions towards Myriam.

The parents repeatedly complained that their child was difficult – stating there were feeding problems and severe sleep disturbances and, at 18 months, that Myriam had "extreme" tantrums involving head-banging. Their response to the Symptom Check List (Favez et al., 2006), a validated questionnaire on child functional problems, was one of the most severe scores of the sample. Although they repeatedly claimed to be open to getting help, they did not follow up on several therapeutic recommendations.

While the concerns about Myriam's difficulties are possibly in part due to her own temperament, two observations point to the maladaptive coparenting style as contributing to her disregulation. First, both at 3 and 9 months, when the family reaches part IV of the LTP and she is left more or less to her own devices, she consistently is more active and better regulated than when having to contend with her parents' endless splitting and competition.

Second, at 9 months all of the infants spent a brief time interacting with an unfamiliar, experienced adult. In Myriam's case, she actually initiated more with the stranger, and appeared less withdrawn, than she had with her own parents.

Follow-up at 5 years

At the 5-year follow-up, the parents have separated, but not surprisingly, they have negotiated a joint custody agreement. Myriam lives halftime with her father and halftime with her mother. The parents state that they are getting along fine when it comes to Myriam's care.

Myriam has been evaluated by the school and there is a concern about her "extreme shyness." The parents do not agree with the assessment nor do they agree to the proposed treatment.

The mother describes Myriam as a "cry-baby," a difficult child that she has to spank in order to get her to obey. The father also describes Myriam as difficult. The mother feels the father is not strict enough with Myriam and that she is left having to be "the bad guy." In spite of her insistence that they get along fine as parents, the mother keeps making indirect criticisms about the father's parenting style. As always, he does not defend himself.

The parents see no problem in coming for the follow-up together. They agree to do a video-taped free play session in one of their homes, as well as to come to the center to do an adapted Lausanne Narrative Play (LNP), given their separation, as well as the picnic game. Finally, all children in the study had a series of assessments at age 5 (see Appendix 5.1 for more details on the measures used). Myriam was noted to have attentional difficulties as well as scoring below average for her ability to imagine the perspective of others, or "theory of mind."

Free family play

The researchers asked the family to play together as they would normally for about 10 minutes. Note that despite the separation, this was a family that still occasionally spent time together.

> The play begins with Myriam announcing, "You guys can play whatever you want, but I'm not playing." Her parents will take turns trying to get her to play. Her mother tends to use threats, such as "Santa Claus is watching!" and insisting that Myriam must do what the researchers ask of her.
> Her father tries making up games to entice her to play with him or mirroring back statements. When Myriam says, "I can't take this!" her father responds, "You can't take this . . . why don't you want to play today, Myriam?" At one point Myriam explains that she does not want to play because she is "yucky." The family never actually plays during the 10 minutes.

Comment

In video-feedback sessions with families we always try to begin with resources, sometimes not easy to find. Here, the parents are remarkably persistent in trying to engage Myriam in play.

On the other hand, despite their claims to the contrary, they are still in competition for their child. They are at no time coordinated with one another. The mother primarily uses threats, while the father uses mirroring or attempts to distract.

Myriam struggles in the face of the parents' badly coordinated and often awkward attempts to engage her in play. She appears distressed and disorganized. Just as she did in infancy, Myriam oscillates between openly opposing her parents and withdrawing. She finally resorts to putting herself down: "I'm yucky."

Modified narrative LTP

For separated parents, the format of the LNP theme is modified to mirror their situation: one parent picks up the child at the other parent's home and brings her to a trusted caregiver's home. The other parent picks up the child at the end of the weekend. They are asked to tell the story with the doll figures provided, and to follow the same four parts.

Narrative play

What follows is a brief synopsis of the narrative play. While not described here, as Myriam and her father play, the mother laughs loudly, once again drawing attention to herself when she is supposed to be just simply present. The father's competition and hostility towards his ex-partner are more evident in a creative choice he makes in the story.

> *The family is not able to keep to the structure of the story. They digress into a completely different and somewhat disturbing story line as Myriam introduces a monster. The father soon turns it into a mother-eating-monster during his part of the narrative. The mother suggests a potion that kills mother-eating-monsters when she plays with Myriam. At the end the mother in the story refuses to pick the child in the story up at the caregiver and instead throws her into the fire.*

Comment

The parents try to stick to the format of four parts, yet the storyline digresses radically and disturbingly from the one prescribed. The hostility between the two parents seems quite transparent in the story itself. We will end the case of Myriam with the family's picnic game.

Adapted picnic game

For separated or divorced families the PNG is modified to take place in a restaurant instead of a picnic in a park. The parents agree that the task is not out of keeping for their family, who sometimes do go out together to restaurants. Not surprisingly, the parents begin with diverging agendas.

> *The two parents immediately propose different food and different beverages at the restaurant, and Myriam announces in a low growl, "I'm not hungry." The father quickly proposes a toast, and they all say "Cheers" together, although it is quite flat.*
>
> *The parents then work together to get Myriam to "eat" her lunch. She obeys, even though her mother continually nags at her about her table manners during this pretend meal. Later, when her parents are interacting briefly, Myriam will purposefully eat very loudly and rudely. Once more her mother reprimands her, and then both parents encourage her to play in the restaurant's play area.*
>
> *The mother next starts to mock the father for not having a girlfriend and Myriam suddenly stands up on a chair, facing the camera and doing a silly dance as she screams, "Monster! Monster! We need the Monster!" The parents scold her. "No shouting in the restaurant!" Myriam counters with, "We're not in a restaurant," but then gets down from the bench anyway.*

Near the end, the father asks Myriam to give him a taste of her ice cream and Myriam serves him. Then the mother asks for a taste too and Myriam complies again. The parents both thank her, but there is no moment of playful or positive affect sharing during this interaction. Finally, they decide to leave the restaurant, amid Myriam's loud protests: "This is not a restaurant!"

Comment

Again, if we start with the resources, in this less structured paradigm we see at least a couple of moments of cooperation between the parents as well as with Myriam, although it is quite flat. What stands out much more is the competition and hostility between the parents as they each suggest different foods for the picnic, and employ different, not coordinated strategies to get Myriam to go along with the task.

Myriam once again uses withdrawal but she also defies her parents. When she does her silly dance for the camera, they both scold her, and so here she is again for a moment in a child-at-center position as the "bad child" (see chapter 8).

Myriam's family interaction at 5 years represents an extreme case of triangulation. Among the 15 cases of family coalitions in our sample, patterns of triangulation were typically less extreme and mostly emerged only in part III, but in a more covert form. Typically these families alternated much more between different coalition dynamics in the latter half of the LTP. Ahead we discuss this more common phenomenon of shifting coparenting styles.

Discussion

Shifting coparenting styles

Our results at 18 months (Fivaz-Depeursinge, Lopes, Python, & Favez, 2009) showed that among the 15 non-cohesive cases in our sample, only one infant – namely, Myriam – experienced competitive coparenting as the dominant, enduring pattern; six other infants experienced it at times. These other families shifted much more between various coalition patterns, including triangulation. The children learned to cope with these shifts by adopting different strategies. We see the shifting process between various patterns first as a resource, in that shifting is less rigid than keeping to a single pattern. Thus, shifts may be understood as repair attempts, even if failed. The second advantage over the more rigidly competitive pattern seen in Myriam's family seems to be that the child has some more leeway. Yet the child's practice of triangular communication remains very restricted even in these families.

Go-between/withdrawal style and triangular communication

In this chapter, we asked: How do infants cope with competitive coparenting? The most striking characteristic is that in the face of the parents' antagonism, the infant signals her distress to both. Her bids are not appropriately validated. Unsuccessful, she eventually withdraws.

By 18 months, Myriam has given up protesting. She disengages from direct interaction with her parents and focuses on objects or withdraws, with one important exception, during the "fall" incident.

Without exception, the triangular bids these infants address are all negative (mostly protest) and are not validated by the other parent. The negative bids and the infant's withdrawal simply exacerbate the parents' competitive style. Consequently the infant has almost no opportunity to share interest or pleasure, at least at the triadic level, despite the fact that the goal of the task is "play."

These infants engage in a high frequency of triangular bids when engaged as a go-between, but then drop to a low frequency during withdrawal. As a result, the average frequency ends up within norms but this average does not reflect what is happening in the triad. As well, the valence is not within norms, being predominantly negative.

The case presented here had a negative outcome in early childhood. Myriam's development was clearly disturbed, from the perspective of emotion regulation, sociability, and to some extent cognitively. The other six cases who shifted between triangulation and other types of coalitions had less negative outcomes. More moderate role reversals still place children at risk for later socio-affective adaptation, all the more so that they may go unnoticed.

Finally, returning to our definition of normative triangular communication – namely, the handling of the four configurations in a three-person interaction – we see that the competitive coparenting style is clearly detrimental to the practice of children's triangular communication.

Competitive coparenting style

It is important to keep in mind that competition between the parents arises in the context of trying to help an infant who is not ready to engage, and is mostly in distress. The problem is that each parent acts in an inappropriate way in trying to outdo the other one, apparently feeling that the other one is not acting appropriately. Thus, the competitive coparenting style leaves little doubt as to a mistrust of the other parent for whatever reason, and an underlying conflict between them. Competition is by definition prone to escalation; however, at some point the stakes get too high and the parties exhaust themselves for a breather.

In Myriam's case the enduring competitive coparenting from early infancy to toddlerhood was remarkable. It remained unchanged by 5 years in all three play situations.

Triangulation coalition

How do the infant's go-between/withdrawal and the competitive coparenting styles precisely play into the dynamics of a triangulation coalition? We have seen throughout this chapter how the child's and the parents' styles seem to exacerbate the problems rather than fix them. The absence of a sibling for Myriam, as was the case for our most severely problematic families, may have had a detrimental influence, perhaps rendering the family dynamics more rigid. Consider Alex's family (chapter 8), where the arrival of a sibling seemed to allow some flexibility and for other styles of relating to emerge. Finally, note that the child's temperament is likely to be a component: an infant inclined to actively protest may more easily activate competition between parents, while a less active child may foster an exclusion process. By 18 months in our sample, there did seem to be this correlation (Favez et al., 2006).

Triangulation in the lab versus the clinic

It is curious that triangulation as the predominant coalition pattern is so little represented in our sample, given that in the clinical literature, it is the most cited coalition and often stands for coalitions in general (Hoffman, 1981). Clearly, the competitive coparenting style is the most blatant among non-cohesive coparenting styles. It is perhaps more obvious to the observer than the excluding style, which in many ways is a cultural stereotype that can pass for "normal": the over-engaged mother paired with the withdrawn father.

As emphasized in chapter 8, child-at-center coparenting often goes unnoticed, given the apparent coordination between the parents. Beyond the small size of our sample, the low frequency of triangulation coalition in our study may be a question of definition, perhaps stricter in our study. It may also be that a couple with a competitive style may be less inclined to participate in a community study, not wanting to have to look at their struggle, or perhaps they are even referred or self-refer to clinical services instead.

These findings point to the importance of a developmentally informed family approach already in infancy and toddlerhood, for preventive as well as for therapeutic work. In the section III of this book, we will see how the semi-standardized LTP procedure and the criteria we have used to define coalitions are helpful in clinical research and family therapy. As clinicians become trained in its clinical uses, we hope the LTP will be included as standard practice (Keren, Fivaz-Depeursinge, & Tyano, 2001). It is important to stress, however, that this procedure was designed in the systems perspective, which considers assessment to be in and of itself an intervention. Going through the LTP procedure is often experienced by families as a growth-enhancing process, especially when it is associated with video-feedback, as we will discuss more in the next section.

References

Beebe, B., & Lachmann, F. (2002). *Infant research and adult treatment: Co-constructing interactions.* Hillsdale, NJ: Analytic Press.

Bretherton, I. (1992). Social referencing, intentional communication, and the interfacing of minds in infancy. In S. Feinman (Ed.), *Social referencing and the social construction of reality in infancy* (pp. 55–77). New York: Plenum Press.

Favez, N., Frascarolo, F., Carneiro, C., Montfort, V., Corboz-Warnery, A., & Fivaz-Depeursinge, E. (2006). The development of the family alliance from pregnancy to toddler-hood and children outcomes at 18 months. *Infant and Child Development, 15*(1), 59–73.

Fivaz-Depeursinge, E., & Corboz-Warnery, A. (1999). *The primary triangle: A developmental systems view of fathers, mothers and infants.* New York: Basic Books.

Fivaz-Depeursinge, E., Lopes, F., Python, M., & Favez, N. (2009). The toddler's role in family coalitions. *Family Process, 48*, 500–516.

Hoffman, L. (1981). *Foundations of family therapy: A conceptual framework for systems change.* New York: Basic Books.

Keren, M., Fivaz-Depeursinge, E., & Tyano, S. (2001). Using the Lausanne family model in training: An Israeli experience. *The Signal, 9,* 5–10.

McHale, J. (2007). When infants grow up in multiperson relationship systems. *Infant-Mental Health Journal, 28,* 370–392.

Minuchin, S. (1974). *Families & family therapy.* Boston: Harvard University Press.

Stern, D. (1985). *The interpersonal world of the infant.* New York: Basic Books.

Section III

Clinical applications of the LTP paradigm

In this final section of the book, some of the main clinical applications that have developed out of the LTP paradigm are described.

Chapter 10

The LTP paradigm as a model for clinical consultations

With Joëlle Darwiche

Up to this point we have focused our attentions on understanding how infants and their parents progress in well-coordinated alliances versus problematic ones. Now we veer from description and observation to clinical application. Since its birth in the 1980s, the Lausanne Trilogue Play (LTP) has always been intimately linked to the clinical world. Right from the outset, families were being referred for consultations to the Centre for Studies of the Family (Centre d'Etude de la Famille – CEF), part of the University of Lausanne Institute for Psychotherapy. The goal in these consultations was to help clinicians working in hospitals in the context of maternal postpartum breakdown, as well as in the community (Fivaz-Depeursinge & Corboz-Warnery, 1999). In this chapter we will describe consultation models that capitalize on the LTP as a systematic way of understanding young families:

- The Developmental Systems Consultation: This model is a two-session assessment and intervention (Fivaz-Depeursinge, Corboz-Warnery, & Keren, 2004).
- Trial Intervention: This model is a way to intervene during an LTP; it may be part of a Developmental Systems Consultation.
- The Longitudinal Developmental Consultation: This model uses the two-session format, but the family is seen at various ages and stages, according to the protocol presented in sections I and II of this book.

All three are described in this chapter using clinical vignettes, but first we explore what is lost when we limit how we assess families.

The infant as part of the family system

We begin with an exercise we did to better understand what we stand to gain or lose by assessing only dyads (mothers and babies or fathers and babies) or assessing only the whole family when we see clinically referred families (Philipp, Hervé, & Keren, 2008). In this exercise, one family was videotaped in different contexts and these were shared with three different clinicians. The first clinician received all of the videos, but the other two did not. The second clinician was provided video only of the baby playing alone with her mother and then playing alone with her father. The third clinician was provided only the LTP for this family. The second and third clinicians did have a number of convergent observations, but they both missed certain strengths and weaknesses in this family that only the first clinician could assess.

Both parents played very differently with their daughter when they were alone with her than when they each played with her while the other was "simply present" in the room. The father was more intrusive when alone with the daughter. The opposite was true for the mother. During the LTP there were problems with how the parents worked together or coparented. Most notably, they tended to compete for the baby's attention in the part where they were supposed to be playing together as a family. The clinician who observed only the dyads was not aware of these coparenting difficulties.

Families can run into a variety difficulties in the LTP that are not seen during dyadic play alone. To be clear, we are not suggesting we dispense with dyadic assessments, as there is so much we can learn from these observations. We are simply suggesting we observe the whole family together as well.

The LTP is a way to observe the family in action or "the practicing family" (Reiss, 1989), and not simply ask them about how they interact. It allows us to observe all the possible configurations of interaction within the context of the family. Furthermore, it asks the family to navigate a number of transitions, as they must do in everyday life. Managing transitions is particularly challenging to many clinical families for a variety of reasons, and so the LTP can at times bring out the presenting problem in a way that some of the more traditional, dyadic, and interview-based assessment tools are not able to do (Philipp, 2012; Philipp & Hayos, 2013).

Now let's turn to the clinical cases to illustrate the use of the LTP in both assessment and intervention. The first case presented illustrates both a Developmental Systems Consultation and Trial Interventions.

The Developmental Systems Consultation

The two-session Developmental Systems Consultation was based on a model developed by Wynne, McDaniel, and Weber (1986). In their "systems consultation" a therapist working with a family asks for consultation around a particular stumbling block in the treatment. The hope was to adapt this model to the infant and preschool population. In the first meeting the LTP provides a framework for exploring family communication, the family alliance, and the infant's contribution. In a second session, video clips from the LTP are then used to provide feedback to the parents and their referring clinician. The whole family is the focus, including any siblings. How do the family members work together in carrying out a task? What is the style of coparenting? How does the child[1] respond to the parents – what is the child's style of engagement?

Referral process

There are a number of things that are unique to this sort of consultation. First, the interventions developed at the CEF provide a model for a bridge between research and intervention. Families referred to the center were offered the expertise of consultants who were both researchers as well as trained family therapists. In exchange, they were asked to participate in the research protocol, alongside the volunteer families discussed in parts I and II. Some came for only a two-session consultation, but many agreed to be followed for a full Longitudinal Developmental Consultation.

Second, both the family and the referring therapist were invited to participate in the consultation. Finally, because there was a therapist already managing the case, the consulting team chose not to hear the reason for referral until after the play session had been completed. In this way, the team was not biased by this information during the initial assessment.

Structure

All LTPs start with a warm-up phase, which allows parents, and especially infants or children, to acclimatize to the new setting. Unlike in the strange situation (Ainsworth, Blehar, Waters, & Wall, 1978), where we challenge families with a stressful situation in order to assess security of attachment, the aim of the LTP is for the family to attain the common goal of play, cooperation, and affect sharing between family members. Consequently we want the families to feel at ease in the space. We also see this warm-up as part of developing a strong therapeutic alliance with the family, which is critical if we are to move forward with observations, interventions, and recommendations. Typically the warm-up will involve a feed and a diaper change or a snack and a chat, depending on the age of the child.

After the warm-up the next step is to provide the family with the instructions for the LTP. Parents are left to decide who will be first to play with the child while the other is in the third-party role. In this way, we begin the assessment with a coparenting challenge. How will the parents decide who will play first? Or will they allow their child to somehow make that decision for them?

The remainder of the instructions is the same as in any other LTP: in parts I and II, each parent has the opportunity to play with the child actively, while the other parent is "simply present." In part III, the whole family plays together. In part IV the parents are asked to interact as a couple on their own.

After giving the instructions, the clinician leaves the room, asking the family to signal when they are done. The duration of the task will vary depending on the age of the child. In infancy it is typically between 8 and 12 minutes; however, with older, more verbal children it may take 12–15 minutes.

With the task completed, the clinician rejoins the family and thanks them for their efforts. It is critical to check in with the family, particularly in a clinical context, about whether what was observed is "typical" of family interactions, given the somewhat unusual context. It is at this point, after the LTP, that the referral question is heard.

Next steps

In the interceding weeks, the consultant and usually one other member of the team at the CEF will review the video. Borrowing from principles of Interaction Guidance (Rusconi-Serpa, Sancho-Rossignol, & McDonough, 2009), they choose representative clips from each of the four parts of the LTP that highlight the family's resources, as well as areas of difficulty. The focus is especially on the initial referral question.

The parents return with their referring therapist (some may choose to bring their child to this session). Maintaining a good therapeutic alliance with both the family and the referring therapist remains a priority. For example, when the video clips are reviewed, it is important to check in with them again about whether they are representative of the family's interactions. Having the parents' buy-in is critical to the therapeutic alliance and the success of any possible intervention or recommendation (Fivaz-Depeursinge et al., 2004).

Video-feedback

With each clip, the consultant explores with the parents what their experience was at the time and how they see it and feel about it now, reviewing it on video. It is at this point that the consultant brings up the referral question, tailoring his responses to what is observable in the video clips chosen. It is essential, both for the therapeutic alliance and for the success of any intervention, that the focus always remain not just on areas of deficit but also on resources. In this way, any intervention can be anchored in the family's strengths and therefore have the greatest chance of success.

After the feedback session the family returns to work with their own therapist, integrating what they choose from their consultation at the CEF. Of course the option to return at a later date for a subsequent consultation is always there, and can occur after several months or even years.

The case of Felix

Felix[2] and his family were referred to the Centre by the parents' couple's therapist. For this particular family the Lausanne Narrative Play was chosen as the assessment tool, as there were no siblings and Felix was already 6 years old. The referral question was not discussed before the observation.

Felix and his parents in the Lausanne Narrative Play (LNP)

After the warm-up, the consultant gives the family the instructions for the LNP (chapter 5). Recall that the parents are asked to help their child tell a story, using dolls to represent the different members of the family. The theme is that the parents are leaving for the weekend and the child is staying behind with trusted caretakers. One of the parents starts the story with the child while the other is simply present. In part II, the other parent continues, and then in part III they conclude the story together as a family. Finally, the parents talk about this experience while the child draws or plays by himself. The main steps of the LNP are illustrated in Figure 10.1.

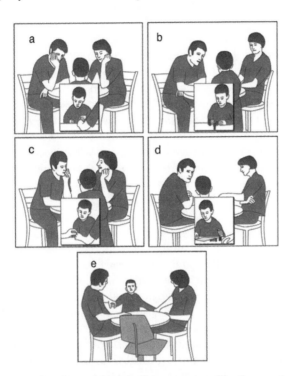

Figure 10.1 Body configurations during the four contexts of family narrative play: everyone is included, but displays of third-party roles are problematic
  a) During mother-child play, father leans in as if active partner
  b) During father-child play, mother's moves in (not shown) and out to signal to proceed to next context are ignored
  c) During three-together play, the three partners are active and appropriately display it
  d) During father-mother dialogue, father orients towards son, and son is not on his own
  e) Child tries to remove parents from setting (father-mother dialogue cont.)

Drawings by Roland Fivaz (first published in Fivaz-Depeursinge & Fivaz, 2006, pp. 120–121)

For this family the negotiation about who should initiate play with Felix goes quite smoothly. The mother starts out the story with Felix, artfully helping him choose the characters and set the scene. However, the father keeps leaning on the table, as if he were an active partner (Figure 10.1a). Bit-by-bit the mother lets him take over, without any clear transition to part II. The father and son continue the story, acting out a rich and exciting story, but seem to have forgotten about moving on to part III, despite clear signals from the mother. More specifically, she alternates between leaning back in the observer position, but looking increasingly unhappy about being excluded (Figure 10.1b), or she tries to lean in and engage, but goes completely unnoticed by the father and son. She finally gains entrance, taking on a role in their story (Figure 10.1c). For the transition to part IV, it is again the mother who must remind them of the instructions. She is met with limited cooperation from her husband and son. The father remains engrossed by his son, turned towards Felix, rather than towards his wife. Felix continues to demand his father's attention, not fully aware that his parents are supposed to be interacting with each other (Figure 10.1d). At some point, the mother actually asks the father to turn to face her, and Felix stands up and grabs his two parents by the hands, trying to pull them out of their seats and away from the table (Figure 10.1e). What follows is a negotiation. With Felix back in his chair, his father turns to him, asking, "Felix please, you need to be patient while Mom and I talk!" At the same time the mother pleads with the father, "Stop talking to him, you're supposed to be talking to me!"

Comment

There are clear strengths in this family. The story is extremely creative and colorful and much of the time the family looks ready and willing to participate. The difficulties are that the father ignores many of the mother's signals as he engages with his son. The mother then ends up marginalized or excluded in what we have called excluding coparenting (see chapter 7). This non-cohesive style of coparenting typically results in a binding coalition (Minuchin, 1974) with the child "bound" too closely to one parent (in this case the father) and going along with excluding the other. This dynamic is most obvious in part III, when the mother is unable to join in on the play, and part IV, when the parents cannot talk because the father continues to engage with his son. As a result, Felix has a "split engagement" style with his two parents (see chapter 7). He excludes his mother in preference for his father. There is little opportunity for this family to feel a sense of threesome sharing and togetherness. These difficulties are often observed in families with child behavior problems like Felix's parents describe later in the session. The next thing that happened in this case was a Trial Intervention, so let's take a moment to discuss what that is before continuing.

Trial Interventions

Trial Interventions are brief, nonverbal strategies that can be part of a Developmental Systems Consultation and done at the time of the LTP. They are used by the consultant to elicit change and can be quite simple maneuvers. The consultant might use her voice tone, keeping it soft and gentle in contrast to the family, in order to lower the volume and affect in the room. Alternatively she might ask the parents to shift their positions in order to create clearer nonverbal, positional cues of who is actively interacting, and who is to be simply present. These strategies can be containing to struggling parents, or help define boundaries, all of which may facilitate the family's interactions. It is typically done in the context of a clinical referral, when there have been very concerning behaviors in the LTP, and yet the consultant feels that the therapeutic alliance with the family is sufficient to try to push for change.

At the simplest level, a Trial Intervention can occur when for some reason a family does not do a part of the LTP. At times it can be quite confusing for the observer, and so the consultant will typically return to the room and might ask them, for example, "We were just wondering about part IV? Did we miss it? Sometimes families forget one part, so is that what happened?" Even if the parents believe they did do part IV, but they spent the whole time continuing to face their child and engage with him as Felix's parents did, the clinician would then suggest a Trial Intervention. "I'm wondering if you could try something for me. I'm going to ask you to just do part IV again [or *now* if they have established that it was forgotten]."

Felix and his parents – A Trial Intervention

Watching from behind the mirror, it seems a Trial Intervention focusing on part IV is warranted. It was here that the binding coalition was most visible. If the consultant were to tell the family all the problems observed, she would run the risk of rupturing any potential therapeutic alliance. Instead, she decides to try to initiate a change by more implicit means. The Trial Intervention involves repositioning the parents to make their interaction with one another clearer to everyone. Sensing the family will be receptive, the consultant intervenes when they are still trying to do part IV, and remains in the room to help them through it. The trial intervention is illustrated in Figure 10.2.

Figure 10.2 Trial intervention by consultant
   a) Consultant orients father towards mother; child watches, intrigued
   b) Consultant orients mother towards father; child watches, intrigued

Drawings by Roland Fivaz (first published in Fivaz-Depeursinge & Fivaz, 2006, pp. 120–121)

After the mother's third unsuccessful attempt to reengage the father in dialogue, the consultant reenters the room and asks for permission to try something. Intrigued, the parents accept, and Felix watches closely. First, she approaches the father, firmly takes him by the shoulders and actually turns him away from Felix to face the mother (see Figure 10.2a). Second, she approaches the mother, holds her by the shoulders and helps her to further orient towards the father (see Figure 10.2b). Throughout, the parents and the consultant laugh together, while Felix watches the scene in silent fascination. Now she asks them to continue their dialogue. "What about?" asks the mother. "Just go on with what you were talking about before . . . like what you're going to do tonight; something that concerns just the two of you . . ." After a moment of hesitation, they resume their conversation. Soon the father starts turning even further away from Felix – perhaps to counter an impulse to turn towards him. The consultant remains close to him and stops him, "No, not too far . . ." The father exclaims, "Oh, so it's not a wall here!" indicating the space between him and his son. The mother adds, "The wall is here," indicating the space between herself and the father. Felix adds, "There are walls everywhere in here!" The parents continue talking. The consultant remains close by, stopping the father twice more from turning towards his son, even though Felix is no longer demanding his father's attention and is drawing quietly. The mother, coming close to the father, adds in a playful tone, "It's hard for you to just talk to me."

Comment

The Trial Intervention seems to help clarify difficulties the couple was having setting a clearer boundary around their relationship, as separate from Felix. The family's metaphor of walls is perfect, stressing the idea that the boundary needs to be flexible – they are aware of their son, but only if he needs them.

Near the end of the session the couple's therapist explains that the parents have been very concerned about their son. Felix has been sleeping in their bed and has been a behavior problem both at home and at school. He has no friends and they wonder whether he is hyperactive. The father clarifies that he is not so worried, since he was just like this as a boy and grew out of it.

Video-feedback

The parents come back with the therapist 2 weeks later for the video-feedback session. They report progress – Felix is sleeping on his own and his behavior is improving at school. They feel they have already learned something about their family from just doing the LNP.

During the video-feedback, clips are used to illustrate the strengths of the family. The consultant and therapist also do an exercise to reinforce the Trial

Intervention. Using the TV to represent Felix, they have the couple reproduce the same body positions – for instance, in part IV, facing each other but keeping the "child" in their periphery. In each configuration they explore how each parent feels. The parents once again see the importance of providing clear and consistent signals, including body positioning, to help define limits for their child.

Follow-up

At follow-up 3 months later, the parents are happy with the progress and report proudly that their son is making friends at school and is infatuated with a little girl in his class. The couple's relationship has benefited from the change as well. The case is closed, but the door is left open for the family to return should they run into trouble at a later developmental stage.

Comment

How can we understand the process of change in this family? Through the Trial Intervention, the family and consultant come to an understanding about the "walls" or boundaries being in the wrong place. The physicality of the intervention, moving each parent's shoulders, allows them to see this in a far more powerful way than had it simply been discussed or described to them. The video-feedback session then reinforced the change that was already happening.

Felix's parents were very insightful and not only adopted the change quite readily but also understood the process. Trial Interventions have also proven quite useful in working with parents who were not ready to reflect on their interactions. They respond to the intervention without necessarily having insight into it – for example, at times of acute crises during psychiatric illness (for other examples, see Favez, Frascarolo, Keren, & Fivaz-Depeursinge, 2009; Fivaz-Depeursinge, Corboz-Warnery, & Keren, 2004).

Using the LTP paradigm in a Longitudinal Developmental Consultation

Developmental Systems Consultations may also be repeated as a family progresses through different ages and stages and encounters new obstacles in their interactions. This format is particularly useful with high-risk families where one or both parents have a psychiatric illness or substance abuse and are already in other forms of treatment. We have offered these families, as well as less acute families, the chance to participate alongside the research protocol, bringing them in for assessments and video-feedback sessions to give additional support to them and their outside therapists. We have called this type of intervention Longitudinal Developmental Consultations.

The case of Gabriella

Gabriella's parents were referred by their therapists for preventive support concerning their child. They were both in treatment for serious psychiatric problems when the mother became pregnant. Their relationship is both strong and highly conflictual. After an initial interview, they agree to participate alongside the research protocol. As we follow the case through time, we will see patterns that are there from the outset, and how the consultant works with this family to shift some of their interactions.

The prenatal LTP

The prenatal LTP is preceded by an interview about how the couple imagines their family after the birth of their baby. They are then asked to role-play a first encounter with their infant using a doll (chapter 6). Normally, the prenatal LTP is done at 5 months, but the mother is already 8 months pregnant by the time it takes place.

The consultant explains the premise of the task and then leaves to go get "the baby." She returns, carrying the doll in her arms and is completely in character, cooing over the couple's gorgeous "infant," and introducing the "baby" to each of the parents. The instructions for the task follow the same four parts as other LTPs: first one parent plays with the doll while the other is simply present. In part II they switch roles and in part III they play together with the doll. They are asked to decide who will play first and can choose whether to pick the "baby" up, or leave it in the basket. In part IV they are to let the "baby" sleep and talk among themselves. The whole exercise is about 4–5 minutes. We quickly summarize the LTP as well as the debriefing after.

> *The first three parts of this prenatal LTP can be described as stilted and awkward with a decided distance or coldness between the two parents. The father seems frozen, staring straight ahead at times. The mother mocks the task a bit, making fun of the doll's face. In contrast, they both are very gentle and sweet when they interact with the "baby." They cradle it appropriately in their arms and talk to it gently. At the end they decide the "baby" should have a nap and they put it back in the basket.*
>
> *Both parents sit back in their chairs and the mother leans towards the father, smiling at him and touching his shoulder. Uncertain what to talk about, the couple flounders to find something to say. At one point the mother makes a quip to the father about the doll. "Too bad she has your nose!" The father looks at the one-way mirror and abruptly tells the team he wants to end the task. The mother laughs, rolling her eyes at him, and then tells him, "She's beautiful, just like you." Still looking at the one-way mirror, he reiterates to the team, "Okay, we're done," and then adds to the mother, "That was not okay."*

Debriefing with the couple

With the consultant back in the room, the parents each share how difficult this task was for them. The consultant begins by normalizing their experience. "We know this is hard for people. We do it that way on purpose, you know, so that you're just left with your imagination, but at the same time we know it's hard for a lot of parents. Truthfully, it was really quite moving to see each of you interacting with the 'baby,' though." She listens and further validates each of their concerns about the experience and then reminds them that they will have a chance to process it further at the video-feedback.

Comment

The strengths for this couple are the intuitive parenting behaviors they each showed when they cradled the doll and spoke to it gently. The mother also tried to reach out to the father, touching him on the shoulder at the very beginning of part IV. Unfortunately the hostility between them made any true sharing of this experience difficult.

Video-feedback

It's a few weeks later and the couple has returned to the CEF for their video-feedback session with the consultant. Like other parents we have worked with, they initially express some discomfort with seeing themselves on video, but then participate fully. The facilitator begins with the resources, showing clips of each parent holding the doll tenderly and using some of their intuitive parenting behaviors. The parents are in fact quite surprised by how well they played and report that since then they can more clearly imagine the baby.

The consultant moves on to the more difficult parts, when they had the spat about the nose. The couple acknowledges that this sort of interaction is quite typical for them. The mother explains, "When we have to do something stressful together, we usually don't talk. Eventually I break the silence, but I guess I'm often irritated with him at that point, so I may make a mean joke, like what happened around the nose." With the support of the consultant the mother continues. "I'll try to repair the damage, but only manage to make it worse. And then at some point he'll just leave because he's too angry." Near the end of the meeting the consultant returns to this pattern of handling conflict. "It sounds like that kind of interaction tends to happen when the two of you are feeling stressed. That's something for all of us to keep in mind given the baby's upcoming arrival, as that's going to be a pretty stressful time for you two."

Comment

By starting with the resources, the intuitive parenting behaviors, the consultant not only reinforces these behaviors but also strengthens the therapeutic alliance. She is then able to embark on some of the areas of concern and use the conflict between the parents during the prenatal LTP to explore other struggles in their relationship that they may need to address.

LTP at 3 months

The birth was uneventful and the baby is healthy. The parents are in love with their daughter, despite the turmoil of a newborn as well as some problems in the father's work situation. The theme of distance will come up again in the first half of this LTP, followed by hostility again in the second half. The consultant will also look for the resources to use at the beginning of the video-feedback.

> *The family is seated facing one another in a triangle formation. During the instructions, Gabriella sits calmly in the baby seat, but she begins to fuss as soon as they begin part I. The mother is quite sensitive and empathic to Gabriella, as is the father when he plays with her in part II, but she cooperates with either for only very short stretches.*
>
> *As third party in part I, the father turns away from the mother and Gabriella as they play. He gives no sign of resonating with the interaction, or that he is in any way part of a triad. As for the mother as third party, she also turns her body away, but at the same time looks intently at father and daughter, with her hand over her mouth, as if trying to hold back from interfering.*
>
> *During the 3-together part, the parents are unable to coordinate with each other to find games to play. At one point Gabriella is looking at her mother, and her father takes her hands and says, "Gabriella . . . Gabriella!" Gabriella keeps looking at her mother, and the mother comments, "Only Mommy matters." The father doesn't reply but silently moves to part IV.*
>
> *During their dialogue, the father is turned to face the mother, looking at her in a very exaggerated way, but the mother has her whole body still facing Gabriella, and is not looking at him. The tension is high and they do not talk to each other. Gabriella's fussiness increases, she begins to cry, and the parents stop the session.*

Comment

The parents had to contend with a difficult situation; Gabriella was unable to engage with them. While her fussiness may have been partially due to her mood that day and not being familiar with the setting, we cannot exclude the possibility that it was in response to the tension and lack of coordination between the parents. There is evidence of excluding coparenting (see chapter 7) in parts I and II of this LTP. Each parent self-excludes as the third party, leaving Gabriella to interact with the active parent as if the other parent is not even there. With Gabriella looking more at her mother in part III we see the split engagement style infants have in the face of excluding coparenting. There is also evidence of competition between the parents when the mother comments that Gabriella prefers her.

Video-feedback

During the video-feedback session, the consultant shows clips illustrating the parents' sensitivity to Gabriella in parts I and II, as well as how they did manage to capture her attention, if only briefly.

The parents share that they actually feared being judged by the consultant. She acknowledges that their experience is understandable and quite common for parents in this situation. She then goes on to explore the meaning of this experience of feeling judged, given their own histories.

Next the parents bring up other areas of difficulty they observed in their LTP. The father describes his struggle as the third party, and not knowing how far he should be from his wife and daughter when they play. The mother resonates with his experience, admitting her own struggle to find the right distance. At the end they even laugh together about the same pattern of conflict – that the mother teases the father, "Only Mommy matters," and he withdraws even further from her.

Comment

Once again with this family, by starting with resources the consultant strengthens the therapeutic alliance. Feeling some sense of competence as parents, the couple is then able to share with her their fears of being judged by her. When parents share such fears it is critical for the clinician to respond empathically, but it is also an opportunity to further explore these feelings in a broader context, as the consultant did. Finally, given their history of working with the consultant, they are now beginning to recognize the pattern of conflict across sessions.

Dyadic play at 5 months

At the end of the last video-feedback session the parents felt it was too long to wait till Gabriella was 9 months old before returning to the CEF. They were offered a midway session to help contain this anxiety.

Where appropriate, the protocol may include dyadic assessments, to see how each parent functions with the baby outside of the triad. Parents can behave quite differently in the absence of their partner, particularly in the context of marital conflict (McHale, 2007). For dyadic interactions, the parents are instructed to play with their baby in two parts: first, with their baby in the seat and without objects and after a while, freely as they wish. The other parent remains outside of the room and does not see the interaction.

For Gabriella's family, the dyadic assessments confirm the strengths of each parent. Without the other partner in the room, both parents show their resources much more freely. They play with sensitivity and warmth and Gabriella in turn is quite responsive with each of them.

Comment

Had we done only dyadic assessments, we would not have seen any of the concerning interactions or behaviors in this family, or the impact of the couple's conflict on their baby. By doing the purely dyadic interactions, however, we got more data on each parent's resources and what each of them lost, to some extent, when in the presence of the other. Interestingly, their parenting styles alone with Gabriella would actually be complementary if maintained when they were together. The father seems better at supporting Gabriella's emotional regulation, and the mother brings more animation to the interaction. So the target of the work remained: help solidify their coparenting alliance and capitalize on the parents' individual strengths, as well as help the parents protect Gabriella from the spillover of their marital conflict.

LTP at 9 months

In this LTP, given the focus of our intervention as defined above, we are looking for any indications that the coparenting style has shifted towards greater cohesiveness rather than a continuation or a worsening of the exclusion or competition. Likewise, we are looking for any signs that Gabriella's engagement style is moving towards triangular communication.

In parts I and II the parents show no real change, particularly as third parties. Gabriella, however, is now making some triangular bids, looking back and forth to include the third-party parent. Unfortunately they are always ignored by the self-excluding parent. But it suggests that her trajectory is starting to shift. Now let's fast-forward to part III, where we start to see some real change in the coparenting.

LTP part III

Gabriella is leaning out of her seat and both parents try to get her attention. Then, the mother kisses her and says, "Let's do the Itsy Bitsy Spider again." She and Gabriella had played this game in part I, but now she invites the father to join them as well. "Look, Daddy will do it too." The father playfully wiggles his fingers in front of Gabriella and the mother begins to sing while the parents both move their hands. Gabriella looks back and forth at each of them. The father sings along and in the part of the song where the spiders are "washed away," both parents hide their hands behind their backs. Gabriella looks perplexed. "Where are the spiders?" her mother asks. The father repeats the question and then they resume the song, continuing on for a second round of Itsy Bitsy Spider. Gabriella looks back and forth at her parents a number of times. During the third round, Gabriella squawks excitedly. The father leans forward. "Do you like that?" Gabriella cries out again and then turns away.

Comment

At last, the parents have succeeded in coordinating play together. The mother initiates the game, but the father immediately goes along playfully. Gabriella repeatedly shares her pleasure with them, making numerous positive triangular bids. We still do not see any signs of direct nonverbal communication between the parents, but their cooperation is clear. Let's see how things have progressed in part IV as well.

LTP part IV

The parents manage the transition to their dialogue by showing Gabriella the seatbelt in the infant seat. The father then sits up and turns squarely towards the mother as he has done before. He maintains a flat expression and alternates between looking at his wife and looking up at the ceiling. The mother continues to orient her body towards Gabriella, but she turns her head to look at the father.

Gabriella looks at her mother and calls out to her. The parents comment on what she is doing and Gabriella alternates between playing with the belt and looking at her mother. The mother looks again at the father, but he is looking at the ceiling. She laughs and finally turns her body towards him. "I think it's better when we don't pay attention to her. Let's ignore her for a little while . . . She can entertain herself just fine." She looks at Gabriella. "You can entertain yourself just fine!" The parents go on facing each other and talking about Gabriella. They connect with one another about how she has started saying "Mama" in addition to saying "Papa." There is a sense of warmth between them.

Comment

Remarkably, the improvement in coordination between the parents is also observed during their dialogue, particularly when the mother shifts her body to face her partner. The mother does laugh at him just before, when he was looking away from her, but she does not mock him outright. Rather, she uses this as a turning point to shift her own positioning. From then on they are able to connect. At points, it looks like they are turning to the baby again, but then they catch themselves, acknowledging that she can handle being ignored. Gabriella's emotion regulation is age-appropriate. She still looks mostly at her mother, and hardly at her father and still makes no triangular bids in the fourth part. The family is making progress, but there are still some areas of concern.

Video-feedback

In the video-feedback session the consultant once again shows the parents areas of strength in all four parts of the LTP. In terms of the coparenting coordination she shows them the Itsy-Bitsy Spider game in part III, and when the mother finally turned towards the father in part IV. She also shows the couple how age-appropriate Gabriella is: cooperating with the games and regulating her affect in part IV. The parents appreciate seeing Gabriella's reactions and discuss the things they did that made a difference.

Comment

The parents' struggle to improve their family is beginning to pay off. They work hard at cooperating for the baby's benefit. Since their dialogue is exclusively focused on Gabriella we do not have a sense of their marital conflict. As for Gabriella, she is finally beginning to activate some triangular competences, particularly in part III, when the parents were very well coordinated. Finally, seeing Gabriella's cooperation and clear enjoyment of the family play is obviously very gratifying for both parents.

Follow-up

The family was seen again at 18 months, and it was quite a difficult but productive session, dealing again with similar themes. A detailed description of that video-feedback session can be found in chapter 11. The last session took place when Gabriella was 24 months old and was a feedback session only. At the time, there were several major life events; they were expecting a second child, and the father's parents were both ill. The couple reported they were still cooperating as coparents moderately well; Gabriella was developing well, and had remarkable emotion regulation. The consultant left the door open for continued work, and the couple did go on to meet with her for a few more couple's sessions. They also agreed to return for a follow-up at 4 years to complete the research protocol.

Comment

This case is an illustration of the possibilities and limits of working with families at high psychiatric risk using an intermittent longitudinal approach. The focus is always first on strengths, to improve parenting confidence and fortify the therapeutic alliance. The parents were then more open to observing some of their coparenting difficulties. With successive consultations, they were able to build on what they had learned and free Gabriella from some of the burden of their conflict. Limitations were inevitable. While not presented here, there were definite ups and downs in both parents' mental illnesses that impacted on their functioning, but this is inherent in the work with this population.

Conclusion

Developmental Systems Consultations, Trial Interventions, and Longitudinal Developmental Consultations are some of the main clinical tools developed from the LTP paradigm and used at other centers as well now. They combine the advantages of systematic assessment based on research, with brief therapeutic interventions. The goal of this chapter was to give an overview of these methods. In the next chapter, we will slow things down and describe the use of video-feedback in greater detail, using edited transcripts from two different cases seen at the CEF.

Notes

1 For simplicity we refer to "child" even though at times there were siblings as well.
2 Throughout the book names and identifying information have been altered to maintain confidentiality.

References

Ainsworth, M. D. S., Blehar, M. C., Waters, E., & Wall, S. (1978). *Patterns of attachment: A psychological study of the strange situation.* Hillsdale, NJ: Lawrence Erlbaum Associates.

Favez, N., Frascarolo, F., Keren, M., & Fivaz-Depeursinge, E. (2009). Principles of family therapy in infancy. In C. Zeanah (Ed.), *Handbook of infant mental health* (3rd ed., pp. 468–484). New York: Guilford.

Fivaz-Depeursinge, E., & Corboz-Warnery, A. (1999). *The primary triangle: A developmental systems view of mothers, fathers, and infants.* New York: Basic Books.

Fivaz-Depeursinge, E., Corboz-Warnery, A., & Keren, M. (2004). The primary triangle: Treating infants in their families. In A. J. Sameroff, S. C. McDonough, & K. B. Rosenblum (Eds.), *Treating parent-infant relationship problems: Strategies for intervention* (pp. 123–151). New York: Guilford Press.

Fivaz-Depeursinge, E., & Fivaz, R. (2006). Implizite Kommunikation une experimentelle Intervention im Rahmen einer systemischen Beratung. In B. Hildebrand (Ed.), *Erhalten und Verändern: Rosmarie Welter-Enderlins Beitrag zur Entwicklung des systemischen Therapie und Beratung* (112–123). Heidelberg: Carl-Auer Verlag.

McHale, J. (2007). When infants grow up in multiperson relationship systems. *Infant Mental Health Journal, 28,* 370–392.

Minuchin, S. (1974). *Families & family therapy.* Boston: Harvard University Press.

Philipp, D. (2012). Reflective Family Play: A brief family therapy model for the infant and preschool population. *Infant Mental Health Journal, 33*(6), 599–608.

Philipp, D., & Hayos, C. (2013). Le Reflective Family Play: Un traitement de la famille entière centré sur l'attachement et le système familial. In N. Favez, F. Frascarolo & H. Tissot (Eds.), *Naître et grandir au sein de la triade* (pp. 227–250). Brussels: De Boeck.

Philipp, D., Hervé, M. J., & Keren, M. (2008). Does the portal of entry determine our view? Interfaces between dyadic and three-way assessment of a clinical family transitioning to parenthood. *Infant Mental Health Journal, 29*(3), 259–277.

Reiss, D. (1989). The represented and practicing family: Contrasting visions of family continuity. In A. J. Sameroff & R. N. Emde (Eds.), *Relationship disturbances in early childhood* (pp. 191–220). New York: Basic Books.

Rusconi-Serpa, S., Sancho-Rossignol, A., & McDonough, S. (2009). Video-feedback in parent-infant treatments. *Child and Adolescent Psychiatric Clinics of North America, 18*(3), 735–751.

Wynne, L., McDaniel, S., & Weber, T. (1986). *Systems consultation: A new perspective for family therapy.* New York: Guilford Press.

Chapter 11

An in-depth look at the LTP and video-feedback

With Antoinette Corboz-Warnery

In the previous chapter, we shared case material to provide an overview of some of the interventions developed at the University of Lausanne Centre for Studies of the Family (Centre d'Etude de la Famille – CEF). In this chapter we use in-depth transcripts from video-feedback sessions in order to better illustrate the techniques used.

The cases are once again drawn from the data on clinically referred families seen at the CEF. Recall that in addition to the volunteer families who participated in the longitudinal study of family interactions (see sections I and II of this book), there were always clinical families who participated alongside, following the same research protocol. They were seen for several years by one of the research consultants trained in family therapy and received video-feedback a few weeks after each Lausanne Trilogue Play (LTP) session (Fivaz-Depeursinge & Corboz-Warnery, 1999).

Other families came with their referring therapists for just a two-session Developmental Systems Consultation with a clinical research consultant from the CEF. The family's interactions were recorded during an LTP in the first session, and the family and referring therapist received video-feedback in the second session (see chapter 10 for details).

The first case we describe is Gabriella's family, who we presented in chapter 10. They were followed for a few years in the research protocol as one of the clinical families. In this chapter we provide more detail from the LTP done when the baby was 18 months. In the second case we have edited transcript from the video-feedback of a Developmental Systems Consultation.

The case of Gabriella at 18 months

Context

Recall that Gabriella's parents were referred late in pregnancy. They agreed to participate in the research protocol, in exchange for some support around their parenting. Both parents had mental health issues and were already receiving help outside the CEF. In addition to the video-feedback sessions with the consultant at the CEF, the couple had also met with her a few times in between to deal with marital issues.

Rather than describing the LTP at 18 months first, we will share the relevant excerpts as we go through the video-feedback session. One last note before we go into the session; on the day of the LTP the parents quarreled on their way to the center and arrived late, and both in very bad moods. You can see spillover of the argument in the parents' behavior throughout the LTP. The therapist will try to address it at the beginning of the video-feedback.

Video-feedback

The parents come without Gabriella for the video-feedback. The tension, so glaring on the day of the LTP, has clearly waned and the couple seems ready to work with the team. As in all video-feedback sessions, the consultant begins by emphasizing the family's resources. The parents tried their best to do the task, despite whatever difficulties they were experiencing that day. Also, Gabriella showed age-appropriate behaviors and remarkable emotion regulation.

The consultant next begins to probe further about the tension between the parents. "When you arrived there was some tension between the two of you?" The mother remembers, "Right, we had that fight." The father does not, "To be honest, I don't recall."

Comment

It is important to stress that this consultant has worked with the couple intermittently for the last 2 years – using the LTP and video-feedback, as well as the marital sessions. For this reason, there is already a comfort level between her and the couple that allows her to jump in so early in the session and address the tension seen on the day of the LTP. That being said, even with further discussion, the father was unable to recall the tension. While frustrating for the mother, and perhaps for the consultant, it was important data. Either he really could not recall the tension or he was not yet feeling comfortable enough to discuss it. Rather than getting stuck here, the consultant moves on to show the first clip of the play where the mother was visibly overwhelmed by Gabriella. Over the next three clips, the consultant will bring up the tension again, and they will arrive at a point that they can talk about it.

Part I – Clip I

In this part the mother and Gabriella are playing while the father is simply present. There are some brief moments of cooperation but still longer episodes where Gabriella throws toys on the floor, openly defying her mother. The mother alternates between trying to contain Gabriella versus getting into a power struggle with her about throwing the toys. In the meantime, the father self-excludes and looks visibly angry, although he picks up toys when the mother asks. On one occasion Gabriella looks challengingly back and forth at both parents immediately after throwing a toy. This back-and-forth communication to both parents is known as a "triangular bid." The bid is ignored by the father while the mother once again reprimands Gabriella.

Consultant:	Gabriella's throwing everything on the floor here, which is pretty typical for this age.
Mother:	I find it really annoying.
Consultant:	It seemed that way. We certainly see a lot of throwing toys at this age, but we also wondered if it was just about her being a typical toddler, or whether she was maybe diffusing some of the tension she was picking up on? You were trying to contain it, but . . .
Mother:	She does that stuff all the time though . . .
Consultant:	Hm. So you're not so sure about that idea?
Father:	What, of her diffusing tension?
Consultant:	Yeah.
Father:	I just think she's too young to know anything about it.
Mother:	I just thought she does that to get a reaction out of me . . . and it works.
Consultant:	Okay. Well, let's just hold that thought and watch a little more.

Part I – Clip 2

In the next segment of video, we see Gabriella looking at her mother provocatively, holding yet another toy to throw down, and then looking at her father questioningly. The consultant continues:

Consultant:	She's looking at Daddy . . . is she looking for your help there? Or just to see if you're still there?
Father:	Uhm . . . I'm not sure.
Consultant:	Let's watch a little more.

Part I – Clip 3

Later in the clip, on seeing himself in the video looking both tense and absent at the same time, the father remarks.

Father:	I didn't realize it was so obvious!
Consultant:	That the tension was that noticeable . . .?
Father:	Yeah. That's what I'm realizing . . . so Gabriella must also be able to feel it.
Mother:	Feel the tension between us? . . . That's not good.
Father:	No . . . It's not.
Mother:	We've really been trying to keep that stuff to ourselves.
Consultant:	You've wanted to protect her from the conflict between you.
Mother:	Yeah, totally.

Comment

The power of video is that moment-to-moment interactions often move too quickly for us to perceive the multiple levels of communication. This is perhaps even more the case for clinical families, so caught up in their interactions. But it is also true for the clinicians working with them. Video allows them to return to the moment of tension to either recall it (since the father initially says he cannot even remember) or feel comfortable exploring the role it plays in their family.

By providing appropriate clips and then allowing the parents to sit with the material, the consultant creates space for the couple to now acknowledge the conflict. In their wish to protect Gabriella from it, they were in fact drawing her into their conflict. So often couples believe they should somehow avoid any conflict in front of their children, and that if it does happen, their silence will protect their children. Since conflict is inevitable, what Gabriella really needed was for her parents to learn ways to manage it in front of her, which would give her a template for managing conflict and resolution.

This same theme is further explored after they view part II, but let's skip ahead to part III and the one moment where the family did work together as a threesome.

Part III

> In contrast to earlier in the LTP, now the parents try to coordinate. At one point they all join hands to sing "Ring-around-the-Rosie." The whole way through, the family looks quite serious, with no true joy or affect sharing between the partners. We rejoin them just as they are watching it.

Mother: Look at our hands!
Consultant: It's lovely to see how nicely you worked together. It's not easy to play together. It's so sweet, all three of you there. It seems that the tension is a little bit forgotten here, which is nice to see.

The parents appear more connected as they now reflect on this clip.

Comment

Given how heavy the affect was in this normally fun game, in some ways it is not an ideal clip to show. At 9 months they had a much more joyful game of Itsy-Bitsy-Spider. The consultant chose to use the Ring-around-the-Rosie clip because it shows the place where the parents were most coordinated or cohesive during this LTP. It would hopefully help the couple continue to move towards greater coordination. This strategy mirrors Interaction Guidance (McDonough, 1993), where the clinician capitalizes on positive interactions, with the goal of shaping the family's behavior further in that direction.

They next move on to the parents' dialogue in part IV.

Part IV

The hostility between the parents is most evident during their dialogue. They speak for the first minute, but then fall silent. They both stare at one another for a few more seconds, and then turn their focus to Gabriella. Meanwhile Gabriella is amazingly well regulated, playing on her own, but not watching them.

The consultant chooses to comment on when the parents looked at one another without speaking.

Consultant:	It's hard to be just sitting there, not saying anything.
Mother:	I wanted to strangle him . . . I remember, because he asked me, "Do we have to talk?" and I told him, "Yes," and he stayed totally mute.
Father:	I thought the instructions were that we weren't supposed to pay attention to the baby – that she had to manage on her own.
Consultant:	She certainly managed quite well on her own, not really asking for your attention much. I wondered if you hadn't understood or whether you just didn't know what to do. You looked confused.
Father:	Yeah, I guess in those kinds of situations, I just don't know what I'm supposed to be doing.
Consultant:	And what was that like for you to be feeling . . . I guess kind of helpless, is that fair to say?
Father:	Yeah, I guess so.
Consultant:	Okay. So what's that like?

Comment

The consultant starts with an empathic statement about it being difficult to sit in silence. The mother is able to resonate with it and will go on to identify her feelings of exclusion and abandonment when her partner absents himself in this way. With the further probe about him looking "confused" the father is also able to feel supported enough to talk. Finally, the consultant also manages to reinforce the idea that Gabriella can manage on her own and they can take the time for themselves as a couple when she is around. At the end, the therapist returns to the initial goal of their work together: to protect Gabriella from the parents' conflict.

Consultant:	So despite the tension between you two there are ways in which you do succeed in protecting Gabriella. There were some lovely moments where all three of you came together and shared in something, like with the Ring-around-the-Rosie game. That's a real strength that we want you to keep.

Follow-up

The parents returned for a follow-up visit when Gabriella was 2 years old. Many of the gains had been sustained, in particular the improved coopera- tion between the coparents. The door was left open for them to return at any time in the future.

Comment

How do we understand the process of change in this session? By using carefully selected video clips the consultant helped the parents observe themselves in action and gain new insights into the impact of their conflict on their baby. The clips were not necessarily perfect, but they were "good enough" to move them towards, for example, better coordination as coparents. Finally, seeing Gabriella manage in part IV reinforced the notion that infants can and should learn how to manage on their own.

Let's move on to a case referred for consultation.

The case of Miles at 5 years: Video-feedback in a Developmental Systems Consultation

Context and structure

Miles is 5 and he has a brother, Duncan, who is 3. The parents are worried about Miles' behavior, and the degree of violence between the boys. They are at a loss as to how to react. A Developmental Systems Consultation has been requested by the parents' two couple's therapists.

The parents come to the consultation with their referring clinicians, in this case the couple's therapists. Because this is a family of four, they will do the Lausanne Family Play situation (LFP; see chapter 5) during this first meeting. In the ensuing weeks, two separate consultants evaluate the videotapes of the play session – the consultant who attended the LFP and an additional consultant who did not attend and therefore does not know the referral question. The consultant then chooses clips that illustrate the strengths and weaknesses identified in the LFP.

Video-feedback

Two weeks after the play session the parents return for video-feedback, along with their couple's therapists. The consultant explains what has happened with the video since they last met and how they are going to proceed today. We join them as she begins to clarify some terms.

Consultant: I want to just make a distinction between "parenting," which is how you function on your own as a parent, and "coparenting," how you two are as a couple parenting your kids together, and finally "marital,"[1] which is how the two of you are just as a couple, separate from your parenting and your coparenting. So what I'm going to show you first is from part I, when Lise, you were playing and I want to show you something quite lovely, of you as a "parent."

Part I

The family is seated around an oval-shaped table. The parents are at the two ends, with the children along one side between them and facing the cameras. The mother is playing on her own with the two boys, while the father is supposed to be simply present:

> *After briefly playing with the telephones, Miles grabs one of the puppets and Duncan follows his lead. The boys immediately play out a scene of the puppets wrestling. The mother seems to tolerate the aggressive play quite well, even engaging with the boys in a containing but not controlling way. At one point she suggests they tell a story about the lion family on the table instead, but the boys continue with the puppet fight. The mother comments, "Okay, no story, just wrestling."*
>
> *Meanwhile, the father wavers between leaning on the table with his elbows as though ready to engage in the play, and then sitting back in his chair. Miles repeatedly tries to get his father to play. He asks him a number of questions and even offers him a puppet. Duncan also tries to get the father's attention on one occasion. Throughout, the mother repeatedly explains, "Daddy is going to play with you guys in a moment." The consultant pauses the tape.*

Consultant: My goodness, so let's start with the boys and how excited they are, particularly when they were playing with the puppets. It's classic at this age. They play pretty violent games. Actually, we get concerned when they don't. So what we're really interested in is how the parents handle the aggression. And you, Lise, you were so lovely with them. You tried to contain them a little, but at the same time you were also flexible. You didn't try to stop them by saying, "No, don't do that, don't make so much noise, calm down, etc." Instead you were like, "Okay, you guys prefer to play with the puppets, and make them wrestle." Right away you understood that was more fun for them. It's really impressive given this kind of stressful situation, where we're asking you to play in front of a one-way mirror, and be filmed and watched by us. You were totally able to parent your two boys appropriately.

Comment

The consultant has done two important things here. First, she has started with a strength in Lise's parenting, and pointing it out helps the therapeutic alliance right at the outset of the session. But she also is setting the stage for talking about how the parents feel about being in this situation – being asked to do things by the team and then being observed. As we continue through the next part she will make a similar comment to Greg.

Consultant: So now I have a question for you, Greg. How were you feeling while Lise was playing with the boys and we had asked you to be simply present? How was it for you?

Greg: I think I wanted to get in on the action too.

Consultant: You would have . . . can you say more about that?

Greg: In which sense, in terms of the relationships . . .

Consultant: Yeah. Do you feel comfortable in the role of just watching, or as you just said, maybe not because you did want to get involved?

Greg: Normally I would get involved in that kind of a situation.

Consultant: You'd get involved . . .

Greg: So it was a bit unnatural to just watch.

Consultant: Okay, yes . . . I could see that. There you are watching them and at times you were more like this *(the consultant leans forward as the father did in the clip)*. And then there were times where you were more leaned back *(the consultant now leans back in her chair)*. And did you see what happened each time? Miles tried to engage you each time you sat forward, and you'll see he does it a lot. I wondered what that was like for you when Miles kept trying to engage you and, you know, we'd asked you to be simply present.

Greg: Difficult to resist.

Consultant: Mhm, I see . . . I wondered why you didn't say to him something like, "Right now I'm not supposed to play; I'll play with you a little later." I wondered whether it was your understanding that you weren't supposed to say anything in this part?

Greg: Yeah, that's what I thought.

Consultant: Okay, sure. So you saw our team as very, very strict!

Father: Mhm.

Consultant (addressing the couple's therapists):   I think that's really interesting. We didn't tell them what we meant by being "simply present." We do that on purpose, leave it kind of vague just to see how people will understand it *(turning to Greg again)* and you understood it as that we were very strict, which is interesting . . . *(next addressing all in the room)* Correct me if I'm wrong, but I somehow imagine that Greg has this idea that people in authority are very strict or severe . . . authority figures, like us, because you came here to see the "specialists," so we're also kind of authority figures. And if that's Greg's perspective, it's important for us to understand it.

Comment

Here the consultant again introduces the question of how the parents felt knowing they were being observed. This time she asks Greg what it was like for him given that "we had asked you to be simply present." The consultant is conveying her empathy for Greg's position, but she is also talking a bit about the therapeutic relationship – whether the parents are okay with this whole idea of being observed. We did not see this in the previous case with Gabriella's parents, in large part because they had already been working together for 2 years.

The consultant soon after floats her hypothesis that Greg over-interpreted "simply present" because of his response to authority in general. This interpretation is based on experience with others in the context of the LTP. During debriefing sessions with families from the longitudinal study, certain parents reported feeling they had to strictly adhere to the "rules" set by the researchers. This pattern occurred most often in families with problematic coparenting, such as those presented in section II of this book. It seemed reasonable to think that this might be the case for Greg, and he agreed. This insight and the discussion that follows address the therapeutic relationship, reframing the consultant's role as maybe not so "strict" and easing the way for further work to be done in the session. The consultant focuses next on the parents' coparenting in the same clip, but we also want to draw your attention to the way the consultant and other therapists in the room begin to reflect with each other.

Consultant:	Now I want to come back to Lise, and when the kids kept turning to ask their dad to get involved. So Lise, there . . .
Lise:	What did I say?
Consultant:	You said, "Daddy is supposed to just. . . ."
Lise:	. . . "just watch for a little bit."
Consultant:	That was a really interesting moment. We imagined that – Lise – you saw Greg was kind of in a bind and you helped him out by telling Miles, "Daddy can't answer you right now." So in a sense that helped Miles understand Greg's behavior, because otherwise for Miles, Greg's reactions would have seemed a bit weird. Miles probably didn't totally understand the instructions like you did. For us, that was a real sign of cooperation between you two. *(The parents both smile).*
Therapist:	Yes, you could see that Miles tried several times to get his father's attention, so you're right, he probably didn't really understand why his dad was acting like that. But at the same time he coped with it, you know.
Consultant:	Yes, he coped with it, but I do get the sense that he's a little anxious or worried.
Therapist:	Yeah.

Consultant: A little worried that his father be included . . . and I get the impression that he really wanted to play with his father, but that he was worried that maybe his father wasn't happy.

Therapist: Because he was on the sidelines . . .

Consultant: Yes. . . . I understand Miles can be quite noisy and difficult at times, but I also learned from this that he's extremely sensitive and that he gets anxious, or to be more specific, anxious about his father, about his parents, I don't know . . .

Comment

The consultant and therapists have worked together to try to shift how the parents see Miles. While the consultant is empathic to him being "noisy and difficult" at times, she proposes that perhaps he is also very concerned about his parents, his father in particular. While not explicitly stated, the implication is that some of Miles' difficulties may be related to how sensitive he is to the parents.

The way the consultant and referring therapists work together is somewhat akin to a Reflecting Team (Andersen, 1987). At various points in the session, the clinicians share their own thoughts and observations about the family right in front of the couple. In a traditional Reflecting Team, the transitions are more formally marked. The family is asked if they would like to hear what the team has to say. It is a powerful tool that has been used in other forms of family therapy with much older children, and so even without the "marking," there is a parallel. This technique allows families to observe themselves through the eyes of the observers. They hopefully see their interactions in a different light – different enough to trigger change, but not so different as to overwhelm them.

Part II

The consultant proceeds to show the group a clip where the father became the active parent and the mother was simply present.

As the father begins, the boys become even more agitated, "wrestling" through their puppets. The father comments, "Oh, they love to wrestle, those guys!" and then asks Miles to trade. "I'll give you my puppet if you give me the police officer." Right then, Lise leans forward as if to intervene, only to sit back again in her chair, covering her mouth with her hand. Moments later, she starts up again, suggesting that they could use the grandmother puppet, but then, wincing, she excuses herself and sits back once again. Miles and Lise will actually have two brief interchanges before the end of the clip.

Consultant: Okay, so now with you in the role of being "simply present," Lise, that was pretty hard for you to hold back and not intervene. And actually you ended up jumping in a few times *(Lise giggles)*. The reality is that each time you intervened, maybe you just wanted to help your husband out, because you thought he was having a hard time, but then that could give him the message that he can't manage on his own.

Lise: Totally.

Consultant: So it's a bit of a double edged sword . . .

Comment

With this second clip, the consultant is able to point out a parallel between the two parents: they both struggled with remaining simply present in the third-party role. This is an important strategy for working with couples around coparenting. While the consultant ultimately is pointing out a problem in each of them, at the same time they feel connected, neither shamed more than the other, both able to admit their difficulty. This vulnerability opens the door to further explore other areas where they may struggle and allows them to entertain alternatives.

The consultant leads the discussion back to Greg's role as a parent in the same clip. Of note, when Greg first saw the puppets at the LFP, he commented that he was uncomfortable with them.

Consultant: So what was again really lovely was that even though you said you weren't comfortable with the puppets, you were very responsive to what the kids wanted to do and you tried to join them, while . . . containing them . . . So as a parent you were terrific here, you know, you used your own gut instincts as a dad in that situation, and that was great *(once again there is smiling and laughter in the room as the father receives this acknowledgment).*

Lise: Perfect . . .

Comment

Having earlier acknowledged Lise's parenting strength, now the consultant does the same for Greg. Finding a complementary way to reinforce the second parent goes even further towards strengthening the therapeutic alliance – between the consultant and the couple, but also the alliance between Lise and Greg. Part of the goal is to improve the quality of the parents' coparenting style to help them find ways of becoming more cooperative or, in McHale's terms, to guide them towards more cohesive coparenting (McHale, 2007). They turn to one another and smile, pleased with themselves, and share more about how hard it is not to intervene with each other's parenting.

Part III

The consultant transitions on to part III, where the focus is even more on the coparenting. After a couple of false starts by Lise, the parents work together to come up with a brief hugging game for the puppets, and they play together as a family.

Comment

The consultant focuses on the "good enough" moment in the hugging game in her feedback, rather than the struggle to get there, or the fact that it quickly ends.

Part IV

At the outset of part IV the consultant summarizes for the parents what they are about to watch. This technique is helpful, particularly in more chaotic vignettes when there is a lot going on in the room.

Consultant: The transition to your dialogue was nice. But then the kids started making lots of noise and – Lise – you decided to intervene. Greg, you didn't agree with her. You told her that you weren't supposed to talk to them *(his understanding of the instructions)*. It's interesting because just after that you ended up having a disagreement about something totally unrelated. Let's watch:

Miles climbs on to the table, and the mother makes him get down. The father reminds her that she is not supposed to intervene with the boys, but the mother disagrees with him. The father continues talking anyway, and tells her about something at work. She listens to him, and once again intervenes with the boys, asking them to lower their voices. The father is still talking about work when the mother suddenly cuts him off. "I have to see an apartment for my dad this afternoon."
"No, I have to take the car into the garage then."
"You have to take it just then!?" she says, leaning back in her chair. They talk further and manage to come to a compromise.

Consultant: So Lise, you decided to ask the kids to be quiet . . . and whether that's right or wrong is actually not the issue. The concern is that now you have to deal with your disagreement.
Lise: Mhm.
Consultant: So now you're quarrelling. I imagine this kind of thing happens pretty often. One of you does something, like here, Lise intervened, and Greg didn't agree. Later Greg started talking about his work without watching the children, and Lise didn't agree with that. So one of you doesn't agree, but tries to go along, just to keep the peace.
Greg: I think, your earlier point about how I understood the instructions and how important it was for me to follow my interpretation of them exactly, that's why I told Lise she shouldn't be talking to the kids.
Consultant: That makes sense.
Greg: Yeah, I might have handled it differently now.

Consultant: Right . . . So Lise, you went along with Greg, but you can see on your face that . . . It's very difficult to go along when you don't agree . . . even painful *(laughter).*

Greg: My strategy was to keep talking . . .

Consultant: Yes, and Lise went along with it. But after a while, it becomes too difficult to keep going along . . . Lise, you suddenly brought up something about seeing an apartment. Greg said he needed the car and within no time you were back to disagreeing. It seems like a pattern: one of you tries to . . . impose . . . something, the other one tries to go along with it, to make a compromise for peace, but then next round, the disagreement comes back.

There is further discussion around this pattern of trying to sweep disagreements under the rug and go along with each other, only to find themselves butting heads once again.

Comment

The consultant ends by presenting the parents with a formulation of their coparenting pattern and the impact on the children. At times when they find themselves in conflict with one another, Miles, being a sensitive child, sometimes "gets out of control" and draws their attention to him. They can then focus on his "bad" behavior, rather than deal with their own conflict. If we translate this into the terms we have been using throughout, there is a role reversal, where some of the time the parents' undiscussed conflict is detoured onto Miles as he acts out (see chapter 8).

Follow-up

After the consultation, the couple's therapists continue working with the parents, trying to focus on the spillover of the marital conflict into the coparenting. They also work on times when Miles acts out in response to the exclusion of one or the other parent. The door remains open for the family to return to the CEF for future consultations.

Comment

There are several elements from this session that helped the consultant move things forward. She worked throughout to manage the therapeutic alliance. First, as always in video-feedback, she began with the resources. She also acknowledged how the parents felt in this observational model – for example, judged by the consultant or needing to be compliant with the rules. Finally, she found complementary areas of concern in both parents for balance.

By having the other therapists in the room, it was also possible to use Reflecting Team techniques. Through their observations of the family, the clinicians were able to reframe Miles' behavioral challenges in the context of the family relationships.

Conclusion

We should close this segment on video-feedback by highlighting the power of video in these interventions. Video allows clients to experience an interaction in real time, and then to review it on video and re-experience it with some distance. Interactions are slowed down, and it is possible to explore the different levels of communication and affect – verbal, nonverbal, tone, expression, and gaze. The Developmental Systems Consultation has drawn on well-established dyadic work in video-feedback, particularly Interaction Guidance (McDonough, 1993; Rusconi-Serpa, Sancho-Rossignol, & McDonough, 2009), where it has proven to be an invaluable tool for change.

Developmental Systems Consultations and Longitudinal Developmental Consultations, along with Trial Interventions and video-feedback, have remained the mainstay of clinical work at the CEF. These methods have now been applied at other centers, but further adaptations and modifications have also been developed. It is to these other forms of intervention developed from the LTP that we now turn.

Note

1 For common-law relationships, alternate wording may be used.

References

Andersen, T. (1987). The reflecting team: Dialogue and meta-dialogue in clinical work. *Family Process, 26,* 415–428.

Fivaz-Depeursinge, E., & Corboz-Warnery, A. (1999). *The primary triangle: A developmental systems view of fathers, mothers and infants.* New York: Basic Books

McDonough, S. C. (1993). Interaction guidance: Understanding and treating early infant-caregiver relationship disorders. In C. Zeanah (Ed.), *Handbook of infant mental health* (pp. 414–426). New York: Guilford Press.

McHale, J. (2007). *Charting the bumpy road of coparenthood.* Washington, DC: Zero to Three Press.

Rusconi-Serpa, S., Sancho-Rossignol, A., & McDonough, S. (2009). Video-feedback in parent-infant treatments. *Child and Adolescent Psychiatric Clinics of North America, 18*(3), 735–751.

Chapter 12

Reflective Family Play

A brief family therapy combining the LTP with Watch, Wait, and Wonder

With Christie Hayos and Hervé Tissot

Jared[1] is 4 and has come with his family for a consultation. His parents report that he has always been a very hyper child but also quite anxious around separations. In the first few weeks of junior kindergarten, Jared struggled with separating from his parents. More recently he started having severe tantrums when he does not get his way, some lasting up to 45 minutes. Jared's 6 year-old sister, Kayla, is afraid of him as he sometimes attacks her physically. When the family is at home together Kayla spends most of her time hiding in her room to get away from her brother. The parents report feeling overwhelmed and exhausted by Jared's behavior. During a recent speech and language assessment, the therapist initially voiced a concern about Jared's eye contact and urged them to see a child psychiatrist.

This scenario is quite typical of families we assess on the infant and preschool team at the Hincks-Dellcrest Centre (HDC). A number of diagnostic avenues are open to explore: Is this child hyperactive, on the spectrum for an autistic disorder, anxious, or is there a problem in the family relationships? In this chapter we use this case as an illustration of a newer treatment known as Reflective Family Play (RFP) (Philipp, 2012; Philipp & Hayos, 2013), which derives in part from the Lausanne Trilogue Play paradigm (LTP) as a consultation and treatment model. As we have discussed in previous chapters, the LTP can also be used for assessment and treatment planning, and as an outcome measure in the infant and preschool population. As we go through the case we will also discuss the role of the LTP in assessing a clinically referred family.

Reflective Family Play

Reflective Family Play is a brief family therapy model for the infant and preschool population, as well as for younger school-aged children who still communicate best through play. It was created with the intention of bringing two parents into the treatment room, to move beyond the more traditional dyadic treatments (mother-infant or father-infant) available at the time for infants and preschoolers. There are many similarities between RFP and the consultation models using the LTP that we discussed in the two previous chapters (see chapters 10 and 11). There are also a number of differences that are borrowed from recognized dyadic treatments, and in particular the attachment-based parent-child treatment known as Watch, Wait, and Wonder (WWW) (Muir, 1992; Muir, Lojkasek, & Cohen, 1999). Before we go into any further description of the case, we describe some of the basic principles of RFP, pointing out the similarities and differences to these two other models, where pertinent.

Play

Each RFP session is divided into two parts, play and then reflective discussion with a therapist. A wide selection of toys is provided in the consultation room, and parents are asked to get on the floor and to follow their child's[2] lead when playing. The idea of following the child's lead derives from WWW, but because a whole family is in the room, it was necessary to come up with a way to deal with all of the possible configurations of people playing. This is where the LTP comes into the picture. In families with just one infant or child the parents are asked to go through the same four parts of an LTP, but with some slight modifications, which we have highlighted in italics:

Here are the four parts of play in RFP:

I   First one parent plays with the child, *following his lead, not introducing any of his own ideas, and entering the play only when invited to do so by the child.* The other parent is asked to be "simply present."
II   When it feels right, the parents are to switch roles in part II.
III In part III they are instructed to play as a family and to *work together to follow the child's lead.*
IV   In part IV the parents are asked to *reflect with one another about what they observed in the first three parts of play with their child.* The child is left to manage on his own.

All transitions, including who will play first and when the play is over, are left up to the family to negotiate. The family is asked to signal the therapist when they have finished playing. The therapist leaves the room for the play, although in practices without a one-way mirror, the therapist may remain in the room, off to the side, and as inconspicuous as possible. Even if the therapist remains in the room, the family is to still signal when they are done.

Discussion

In the second half of each RFP session there is a discussion of the family's observations. The therapist focuses on following the family's lead. The rationale for this stance comes from WWW – to not bias the family's observations with what the therapist saw, but rather to hear what most stood out for them, that they are ready to discuss.

Mentalization and mindfulness

Reflective questioning is used to help the parents get a better sense of their child's experience. For example, one parent might comment, "I noticed that he played with the doctor's kit today." The therapist can then respond with questions to reflect further on this: "What do you think that was about?" or "What do you think is going on for him?" These questions are aimed at improving both parents' abilities to mentalize or understand their child's experience and become more sensitive to the child's needs (Fonagy, Steele, Steele, & Moran, 1991; Slade, 2008). Recent findings looking at both parents' reflective function or "insightfulness" about their toddler (Marcu, 2013) but also towards one another (Lopes & Favez, 2012) support the idea of working in this way in order to promote overall family functioning.

At the same time the focus is also on the parents' experience, both at the time they were playing as well as during this discussion. This second focus is more of a mindfulness task (Duncan, Coatsworth, & Greenberg, 2009), asking the parents to be more aware of their own internal experiences when they are with their child and with one another. As parents begin to recognize the interplay of their own experiences as affected by but independent of their child's, they will hopefully become more sensitive to what the child needs from them. In RFP there is a parallel process for the coparents, as they become increasingly mindful of themselves as coparents, particularly in part IV of the play.

With an older, verbal child, the ability to mentalize, also referred to as reflective function, is just beginning to develop (Meins et al., 2003) and so asking the parents to mentalize is also an opportunity to model it for the child. For some children we can even begin exploring with them directly during the discussion.

Comment

Unlike the interventions discussed in previous chapters, the pace and style of sessions in RFP are quite different and unfold as the parents begin to make their own observations. This style of discussion is another influence from WWW. At times it can be frustrating for the therapist, who may observe things in the play that the family may not be ready to see.

Video-feedback

In RFP video is used to help support the parents' observations. After a brief discussion about a part of the play, the therapist might ask, "Shall we watch that?" On viewing themselves in the interaction the family is able to experience the interaction at arm's length and to perhaps observe things they did not see or feel before.

While watching the video clip chosen by the family, the therapist still follows their lead in choosing when to stop the video and discuss further.

Comment

In WWW there is no video whatsoever; the parent's observations are based only on what the parent can recall. The use of video in RFP is an influence from the LTP assessment and intervention model: Developmental Systems Consultation (see chapters 10 and 11). This two-session consultation model is much more directive than RFP. Clinically referred families come in to do an LTP with their referring therapist. The group returns at a later date to receive video-feedback from the consultant, showing them the family's strengths and weaknesses as they are understood through the LTP.

Assessment for RFP

Families come into the HDC for an initial intake interview, where they discuss their concerns about their child. This first meeting allows the team to informally observe the family interacting as they get used to the setting and to the clinician. The following week they return to do an LTP as well as dyadic play sessions, with each parent playing alone with each child. Finally, there are opportunities to observe separations and reunions between the identified child and each parent (Clark, Tluczek, & Gallagher, 2004).

In a third meeting we gather further history and background information from the parents about their marital situation and each of their attachment histories. Standardized measures are sent home for the parents and any other caregivers or teachers to complete. At the end of the assessment process, a considerable amount of data has been gathered about the family, including their own narrative about the problem, the standardized measures, phone interviews with any teachers, nannies, or grandparents involved with the child, and of course the play observations of the family.

Pre-treatment LFP

With the family's consent, we were able to send the LFPs of Jared's family to the Centre for Studies of the Family (Centre d'Etude de la Famille – CEF), part of the University of Lausanne Institute for Psychotherapy. Two independent codings were done of the pre- and post-treatment LFPs, and while the coders were aware of which was the pre- and which was the post-treatment session, they were blind to the reason for referral, background information, and nature of the treatment.

What follows are excerpts from the family's pre-treatment LFP. The family was given the standardized instructions for Lausanne Family Play (LFP), intended for families with two or more children. The children are treated as a "unit" and then the same four parts are followed. A rectangular table and toys are provided. The parents are seated at the ends of the table, with the two children facing the camera along one side. The family is asked to remain in their seats throughout the filming and to signal the team when they are done.

As you read through the case consider the principles we expanded on in chapter 1. For example: Is everyone included and keeping to his role? Is the simply present parent resonating with the play, excluded from it, or withdrawing? Is the family all focused on the same activity? Is there a sense of joint affect sharing of these moments of play between all family members?

The pre-treatment LFP for Jared's family is quite chaotic throughout. The children are almost never at the table at the same time, as the parents try to coax and cajole them back into their seats. There is very little communication between the parents. The mother, Jessica, unilaterally decides she will start, and from that point onwards the father, Pete, rigidly times each part, so all transitions are quite abrupt. (Note: At the time this family was first seen, we were not explicitly telling families not to use their phones as timers. We now routinely include this in our LTP instructions.)

Part I

Jessica often is engaged in separate interactions with each child, playfully having a "hot chocolate" party with Jared while scolding Kayla for not participating more. The mother-daughter tension is made all the more uncomfortable given that Jared is equally noncompliant, jumping on the furniture at the back of the room. Kayla alternates between saying she does not want to play, but then making pretend phone calls with her mother, and then withdrawing to the back of the room again. Pete follows the action with his gaze, but his affect is notably flat. Jared tries to engage his father, offering him some pretend hot chocolate. Jessica lets him know, "Daddy is just watching right now. He'll play with you guys in a little bit." Finally, some of the narrative of the play is concerning, as Jared and his mother play out a theme where a family of giraffes all fall off the edge of the table to their deaths.

Part II

Pete's play is radically different from Jessica's exaggerated style. He remains flat and expressionless; any attempts at play with his children are awkward and stilted. He tries ineffectually to coax Kayla back to her seat. Jared eventually starts following Kayla around the room. As Jared works hard to engage his father and sister, he is met with his father's flat responses and Kayla's withdrawal. Jessica sits back appropriately in her seat, resonating with the action.

Eventually the two children end up under the table together. Kayla starts lifting the giraffes up off of the floor and onto the table. As quickly as she does this, Jared pushes them back down. Both children laugh as the parents look on silently. Eventually Pete says, "If you're going to break the rules,

why don't you do something at least helpful while you're breaking them?
Why don't you rescue the giraffes instead of killing them?" Being so flat in
his expression, it is hard to know what he is feeling.

Part III

This part is perhaps the most chaotic with more than one person often talking
at the same time. At one point Pete sits holding his head in his hands, looking
either tired, exasperated, or in pain. Mostly the parents divide the children,
each playing with one of them. Jessica and Kayla talk on the toy phones, and
their interaction is warmer now that Pete and Jared are interacting at the
other end of the table about the giraffes. Jessica, however, occasionally tries
to interject into the father-son play.

Eventually Jared comes up with a story about a bad wolf (Kayla) that is
making "crank calls" and the family works together to send the police and
arrest the wolf. Jared makes the "arrest," pouncing on Kayla and stealing
her phone. Kayla laughs at the time, but then later complains, "Why do I have
to be the wolf?"

Part IV

The parents never truly succeed in talking as a couple. They are easily dis-
tracted by the children and drawn in by Jared's complaints that Kayla will
not play with him. Jared successfully gets his parents' full attention by rein-
troducing the story about the giraffes, but with a happier ending, where the
mother and babies swim and then go to sleep together. Kayla is withdrawn in
the corner throughout this segment.

Coding

As noted earlier, two consultants from the CEF coded this LFP. Neither coder was
familiar with the background information for this family. One consultant used an
empirically validated coding scheme developed at the CEF to assess the family
alliance. The other coder used a more heuristic, clinical read of the family alliance,
the coparenting style, and the engagement styles of the children. This clinical read
would be more typical of what one might use in clinical practice and borrows on the
principles noted earlier such as inclusion versus exclusion, roles, and whether the
family is able to focus together and have moments of shared fun.

The results of these two coding systems were quite consistent with one another.
The family alliance was coded as "disordered," given all of the difficulties noted.
In particular, both Pete and Kayla engaged in self-exclusion at various points
throughout the task. At times Jessica played a role in excluding them by focusing
only on Jared, even when she was supposed to be playing with both children in
part I or sharing play with her husband in part III.

In addition to the exclusion, the coparenting style was also child-at-center; there was minimal direct communication, warmth, or cooperation between the two parents, all of their focus being centered on the children. The children got their parents' attention mainly by means of opposition – for example, throwing the giraffes back on the floor when they were told to pick them up.

Clinical background

There are a number of issues salient to the background of this family. This is not the first time they presented to our center. Kayla had selective mutism when she was 4, and the parents sought treatment for her at that time. When her spot came up on the waiting list, Kayla had spontaneously begun to talk at school, and so the family declined meeting with the team. Pete struggles with chronic health issues resulting in fatigue as well as some mood difficulties. Jessica reports feeling overwhelmed at times by all of the caregiving she has done in the last few years. She has also struggled with her mood in the past.

At the end of the assessment the therapist presents our impressions to the parents and together they explore possible treatment options. It is felt that Jared's relationship with his father has suffered from his father's illness. Pete's low energy means that most of his interactions with Jared are quite subdued and not at all physical. Jared's only rough-and-tumble play is with his mother, who is feeling exhausted. The parents' focus on Kayla and her selective mutism has also meant less attention for Jared. Kayla remains a demanding child who struggles with separation anxiety and often wakes her parents at night to sleep in their bed.

Finally, there is the parents' concern that Jared might have Attention Deficit Hyperactivity Disorder (ADHD). The standardized measures given to his teacher show no indication of ADHD, and during a telephone interview she reports some separation anxiety, but that Jared is otherwise doing well in junior kindergarten. The day care also reports no concerns about Jared's behavior.

Formulation and treatment plan

The formulation is of a little boy lacking the kind of physical attention he needs from both of his parents, but particularly his father. He is acting out only at home, and struggling with separations from his parents at school. The plan is to address the relationship difficulties in the family and to monitor Jared further for ADHD in the meantime.

Watch, Wait, and Wonder dyadic sessions

The first step is to prioritize the father-son relationship and then use a treatment modality that can address the family-level dynamics. Jared and his father come in for some focused sessions of dyadic treatment before starting RFP. They meet with a clinician for four WWW sessions. Jared's behavior is remarkably calm during these four sessions alone with his father. During the second half of the sessions, Pete reflects on the calm in Jared's play as well as the closeness the two of them are developing at home.

Reflective Family Play

With the father-son relationship beginning to shift, Jared and his family attend eight RFP sessions, rescheduling only on two occasions.

Sessions 1–3 – Play

In the first three sessions Jared starts out crying in his mother's arms, unable to begin play. It is clear that the shift from the WWW play alone with his father is a difficult transition. His mother jumps through hoops to try to engage the children, just as she did in the LFP. Once settled, Jared remains calm and playful for the rest of each session. In these early sessions the family is still unable to play together during part III; each parent plays with one child, at times trading off, but never engaging as a foursome. Early discussions focus on this struggle, with Pete and Jessica attributing much of their difficulties to Jared's challenging behavior. On one occasion as they are trying to transition to their discussion, Pete tells the children, "You two need to play together now." Jessica turns an empathic face to Kayla and says, "Good luck with that!"

In part IV, the parents are unable to set a limit and actually discuss anything, often turning and interacting with the children, or just watching them as Jared follows Kayla about the room and Kayla dodges him.

Sessions 1–3 – Discussion

With each successive session Jared and Kayla begin to play more independently during the discussions with the therapist, although the parents do not seem to notice it. They speak with the therapist about how difficult it is to play as a family. The family tends to focus exclusively on part III.

Session 4 – Play

A breakthrough occurs in session 4. During part III, Jessica and Kayla are playing with the construction kit while Pete and Jared build side-by-side towers. At some point Kayla comes over to interact with her father and Pete accidentally knocks down Jared's tower. Jared protests briefly, "Hey! You knocked down my tower!" but then he quickly starts a new one. Shortly after Jared looks up at his father's tower, which is now much bigger than his own. He gently flicks his hand and quite intentionally knocks over Pete's tower. Pete repeatedly asks Jared, "Why did you knock over my tower?" Jared has no explanation and simply continues building his tower, showing it to his parents. Pete rebuilds his tower, ignoring Jared after that. Jessica continues to play with Kayla, acknowledging Jared only when he throws himself into her arms for a hug.

In part IV, Pete comments to Jessica about the tower, "When it's the other way around, and his things get knocked over, he's not okay with that." As the parents speak, the children actually play together for the first time. Kayla tickles Jared at one point, and later crawls around the room with him on her back.

Session 4 – Discussion

When the therapist is back in the room, the first thing that the parents choose to bring up is the children's relationship. What follows is the transcript from this point in the session.

Jessica: It was a lot more fun for Kayla when we were all playing together. She's told us she really hates part IV, but today I think she kind of took a deep breath and said, "I'm gonna be a big sister."

Kayla: And that's when I started tickling him! *(Everyone laughs).*

Therapist (addressing no one in particular):   What do you think it was like for Jared when Kayla started tickling him?

Jessica: Oh, I think he really likes it when his older sister pays attention to him.

Kayla: Yeah, I even play with him after school in the playground.

Therapist: So Jared really likes it when Kayla pays attention to him?

Comment

The therapist's question, "What do you think it was like for Jared when Kayla started tickling him?" is directed to the whole family, including Kayla. She is modeling for all of them the idea of reflecting on Jared's experience. The therapist did this in previous sessions, but this was the session where it first started to click.

Change is starting to begin outside of the sessions as Kayla is starting to play with her younger brother. Taking on the "big sister" role has given her a sense of pride. While Kayla says very little after this it seems she is feeling quite proud of herself as she has also heard her parents recognize her efforts to be "a big sister."

Session 4 – Discussion continued

In the next segment the therapist will ask more reflective questions that push the parents to consider alternatives to Jared's motivations other than the ones they have been holding until now.

After a pause to enjoy some more of the children's play in the moment, the therapist continues. "Any other observations of today's play?" There is a long silence and then Jessica turns to ask Pete.

Jessica:	Do you want me to answer?
Pete:	No. . . . It's just that with Jared, and the tower. I asked him why he knocked over my tower. You know, it's okay if he knocks over somebody else's stuff, but if you knock something of his down then he gets really mad.
Therapist:	How do you understand that – that he wanted to knock your tower over, Pete?
Pete:	I don't know. He just does stuff like that.
Jessica:	I think he thinks it's fun to knock stuff over.
Therapist:	So one hypothesis is that it's fun for Jared to knock stuff over. Any other thoughts on what it might be about for him?
Pete:	Competition maybe? He doesn't like it if you make something bigger than him.
Therapist:	So he might be feeling upset by you making a bigger tower than him. Interesting. Should we watch that bit and see what was going on?

The family watches the video from where Pete first knocks down Jared's tower and Jessica turns to Pete and exclaims, "He was mad at you!"

Comment

This session is the first time that the parents understand Jared's behavior as not simply attention-seeking or provocative. During the discussion around the tower, the parents initially see Jared's actions as more of a provocation, typical of child-at-center coparenting (see chapter 8). In other words, the child's provocation allows the parents to focus on the child as the problem, rather than directly confronting some distance or disconnect between them as a couple. With Jessica and Pete there is not so much an explicit conflict in the couple but rather a lack of connection between them. Jared's provocations allow the parents to connect through him, placing him in an over-engaged, role-reversed position.

The therapist has the family consider other motives than provocation by saying, "So one hypothesis is that it's fun for Jared to knock stuff over. Any other thoughts on what it might be about for him?" Pete is then able to suggest that it might be difficult for Jared to see his father making something bigger and better than him. With the help of the video they understand Jared's motivations further and as connected to Pete having knocked Jared's tower over first.

Sessions 5 and 6 – Play

During these sessions there are definitely some setbacks, both at home and in the treatment room; however, for the most part the gains made are consolidated. During part III the family finally starts to play together as a group. The uniting activity is a game of catch. With successive sessions, these games become more boisterous and joyful.

In part IV the parents are still not able to create a clear boundary for themselves, and spend most of their time responding to and interacting with their children instead.

Sessions 5 and 6 – Discussion

With so much focus on part III, this issue does not come up in the discussions with the therapist until the end of session 6, when the parents mention that while the children are doing better, they are not able to find time for themselves at home. The children continue to invade the parents' space, both in the evenings as well as during the night.

Comment

In the last sessions, the therapist tries to put some emphasis on the importance of part IV when delivering the instructions to the parents. To clarify, the instructions for the play in RFP are repeated weekly, at the beginning of each session. It is the one place where the therapist can stress some area of focus for the family. In this instance the therapist stresses part IV.

Leading up to the last three sessions the team despair somewhat that while the family is clearly making progress, the parents are still struggling with creating a coparental boundary. It is with this in mind that the instructions are geared to encourage them to work on setting the limit.

Session 7 and 8 – Play and discussion

On the heels of the discussion from session 6, in session 7 the therapist phrases the instructions for part IV even more clearly.

Therapist: Thinking about what we were talking about last time, about how the two of you are still struggling with finding your own space as a couple, part IV is for the two of you to practice finding that time in here with the kids.

Jessica: Well, we could always threaten the kids that we'll start smooching. They hate it when we do that!

Therapist: Whatever works for you. Just signal me when you've done all four parts.

In session 7 the parents do threaten the children that they will "smooch," and for a stretch Kayla and Jared play on their own. Instead of just watching them and talking to them, Pete and Jessica turn to face one another on the couch and briefly speak.

During the discussion the parents finally talk about part IV and how remarkable it is that they are able to speak on their own. The therapist explores what it is that made it possible.

In session 8 the change is even more marked. The parents do not resort to any threats; they simply turn to one another on the couch and became engrossed in a quiet discussion among themselves. In the second half, with the therapist, they are able to reflect on what they have accomplished that session.

Comment

In addition to parents learning to set clear but flexible limits, the added value of part IV in RFP is that it provides parents with a contained framework to begin exploring or exercising their reflective function with one another, before the therapist returns to work with them. In this way, it also addresses the coparenting relationship.

Follow-up

The family returns for one last follow-up session, where they give feedback on their experience and complete a second LFP. During the feedback the parents note a number of positive shifts in their family, while recognizing there is still plenty of room for further improvement. Early in the feedback Jessica describes how the children are more willing to share the same space with one another at home now, and that there is much less bickering between them.

The parents also report that they are finally able to have dinner together and talk, no longer needing to "divide and conquer" with each parent managing one of the children.

Finally, the parents note that they are now able to set limits around their time in the master bedroom. This part of the discussion ends with an acknowledgment that the couple still hopes for even more alone time, and the possibility of a date night is explored.

Post-treatment LFP

The follow-up LFP was done on the same day as the feedback session with the parents. Our initial impression of the interactions was that there was a dramatic shift. First, the family remains seated at the table for the duration of the LFP, with Jared standing on his chair only a couple of times, but never leaving the setting. Both parents are able to set clear limits. The parents no longer use a timer to determine when they should transition through the parts, but rather they negotiate these with one another.

In part I Pete is able to engage the children in some "puppet" play with the socks, and although it never actually leads to any true story, he is far more active than in the pre-treatment LFP.

Similarly, Jessica is calmer than in the first LFP. At one point Kayla throws her sock puppet on the floor. Rather than allowing the children to go get it, Jessica and Kayla work together to retrieve the sock without leaving their seats. On Kayla's suggestion, they tie the spoons together using the remaining socks and make a very long stick with which they are able to drag the sock over and retrieve it from the floor. Jared continues playing on his own, sharing a narrative with his mother about what he is doing, while she continues to work with Kayla on making the stick.

In part III, the family never quite plays together as one, although at a certain point they do all put the socks on their hands and hold their spatulas.

In part IV, the parents mostly attend to keeping the children at the table, but they do manage to have a few moments of conversation where they remark on the improvements compared to their first LFP. Near the very end of the session the children both bang their toys on the table, not truly sharing this moment of mischief with one another, but certainly making their parents' discussion inaudible. The parents end the LFP at this point.

Coding

The coding of the play shows a significant improvement in the family alliance, although the family is still considered in the clinical zone. The improvements noted by the coders are in a number of domains. The difference in the parents' styles of interacting is much less marked. The father's affective presence, although still coded as "low mood," shows a couple of brief moments where he is able to share some playfulness with the children or with his wife. Jessica is still noted to be "overdone" in terms of her affect, but it is mostly in reference to her strong reaction to Kayla's solution to the lost sock.

The coparenting style still falls in the child-at-center range. The affective connection between the parents is still "poor," but the parents are better coordinated, especially in their ability to set limits. As for the children, in the pre-treatment LFP they are clearly oppositional; however, now, they still test the limits on a few occasions, but much less so. In families with child-at-center coparenting, the children are in a role-reversed position. Pre-treatment this is seen in their misbehavior and opposition that guide all of the family's interactions as the parents simply react to the children. Post-treatment the children are still role-reversed but less so. Furthermore, they are more likely to use animation or caretaking strategies (e.g., figuring out how to retrieve the sock), which seem more adaptive.

The coders conclude by noting that the parents have done remarkable work towards drawing clear intergenerational boundaries – for example, the limit setting – and that the children have in turn responded well to them. The concern around the parents' problematic connection is tempered by a hope that they can now create a space for themselves and will in turn develop further in this area as well. Finally, the sense is that there is potential for the children's multiperson communication to also be set on a more adaptive trajectory with the shifts that have been accomplished.

Comment

In knowing the family background, both on the pre- and post-treatment LFPs, some of the discordance in the parents' affect, and the disconnect between them, may be understood by the father's ongoing struggles with low mood. Similarly, the disengagement between Kayla and her brother may also be understood in light of Kayla's struggles with anxiety (at the end of the treatment she was referred again for treatment of her anxiety).

The post-treatment LFP reinforced the findings from the feedback session with the parents, but also added a reality check. While the family and the clinicians described great improvements in a number of areas that were to a large degree reflected in the final LFP, there were clearly still areas for this family to further progress.

Conclusion

When first introduced by Fraiberg, Adelson, and Shapiro (1975), the idea of bringing the infant into the room was a novel one. Later treatments began to look at the infant not only as a catalyst to the parent's treatment but also as part of the treatment equation. The focus of dyadic treatments has often been on improving parental attunement and shifting infant attachment towards greater security. While treatments have emerged from more behavioral approaches, such as Parent-Child Interaction Therapy (Eyberg et al., 2001), more directive video-feedback, such as Interaction Guidance (Rusconi-Serpa, Sancho-Rossignol, & McDonough, 2009), and more psychodynamic approaches, such as WWW, these treatments have all been geared to the dyad.

The LTP offered a way to look at the family as a whole, with the coparenting couple influencing the infant, just as the infant in turn influenced the parents. The Developmental Systems Consultation, Trial Interventions, and Longitudinal Developmental Consultations all provide an approach to working with whole families in a consultation model as well as in ongoing treatment (see chapters 10 and 11). These approaches, as noted earlier, are more directive than RFP.

In Developmental Systems Consultations or even in Longitudinal Developmental Consultations, families come in at a key moment in their child's development. The clinician must seize this one opportunity to intervene. He might use Trial Interventions, small maneuvers like shifting the parents' orientations towards one another at the time of an LTP, to facilitate change in the family. The remainder of the intervention then happens at the video-feedback. The consultant preselects video clips that demonstrate the family's resources and difficulties, and opens up discussions around these with the family. Because we see families on a weekly basis in RFP, the pace can be different in how we intervene.

In following the parents' lead, we lose the opportunity to show parents our observations, or to even focus on their strengths. Too often, however, parents are not ready to hear what we have to show them or tell them, returning week after week reenacting the same patterns that brought them to see us in the first place. By adopting the stance of following the family's lead, and what stood out most to them, we wait for them to bring their observations to us, and to work on what they are ready to see.

In RFP, we have opted to capitalize on the power of video, unlike in WWW. This allows families the dual experience of living their interactions and then reviewing them at arm's length (Fivaz-Depeursinge, Corboz-Warnery, & Keren, 2004; Rusconi-Serpa et al., 2009). Other clinicians who use the LTP and video-feedback have noted more rapid change and improved therapeutic alliances with families (see chapter 13) compared to when video-feedback is not part of the treatment. In RFP we typically contract for eight sessions, which is much briefer than other treatments we were previously using.

RFP has now been used with over 20 families. We assess their progress with pre- and post-treatment LTP assessments. The age range is from 6 month-old infants and their parents up to 9 year-olds and their families. RFP has now been used in families headed by same sex parents and in cases of children with medically complex histories. It has also been adapted for single parents concerned about difficulties in the sibling relationship. The hope is to begin looking more rigorously at some of the data we have been collecting on this group. For the moment, we are encouraged by the results we are seeing clinically and the feedback we are receiving both verbally as well as on standardized measures.

Notes

1 Names and identifying information have been altered to protect subject and patient confidentiality.
2 For simplicity, we refer here to "child," although often there are siblings present.

References

Clark, R., Tluczek, A., & Gallagher, K. C. (2004). *Assessment of parent-child early relational disturbances.* New York: Oxford University Press.

Duncan, L. G., Coatsworth, J. D., & Greenberg, M. T. (2009). A model of mindful parenting: Implications for parent-child relationships and prevention research. *Clinical Child and Family Psychology Review, 12,* 255–270.

Eyberg, S. M., Funderburk, B., Hembree-Kigin, T., McNeil, C., Querido, J., & Hood, K. (2001). Long-term effectiveness of parent-child interaction therapy: A two-year follow-up. *Child and Family Behavior Therapy, 23,* 1–20.

Fivaz-Depeursinge, E., Corboz-Warnery, A., & Keren, M. (2004). The primary triangle: Treating infants in their families. In A. J. Sameroff, S. C. McDonough, & K. B. Rosenblum (Eds.), *Treating parent-infant relationship problems: Strategies for intervention* (pp. 123–151). New York: Guilford Press.

Fonagy, P., Steele, M., Steele, H., & Moran, G. S., & Higgit, A. C. (1991). The capacity for understanding mental states: The reflective self in parent and child and its significance for security of attachment. *Infant Mental Health Journal. 12(3),* 201–218.

Fraiberg, S., Adelson, E., & Shapiro, V. (1975). Ghosts in the nursery. *Journal of American Academic Child Psychiatry, 14,* 387–421.

Lopes, F., & Favez, N. (2012). *Parental and interparental mentalization and links with family interactions: Preliminary results.* Paper presented at the World Association of Infant Mental Health, Cape Town.

Marcu, I. (2013). *Parental insightfulness regarding the child's inner world: Its contribution to the family alliance in families with toddlers.* Dissertation, University of Haifa.

Meins, E., Ferneyhough, C., Wainwright, R., Clark-Carter, D., Das Gupta, M., Fradley, E., & Tuckey, M. (2003). Pathways to understanding mind: Construct validity and predictive validity of maternal mind-mindedness. *Child Development, 74,* 1194–1121.

Muir, E. (1992). Watching, waiting, and wondering: Applying psychoanalytic principles to mother-infant intervention. *Infant Mental Health Journal, 13*(4), 319–328.

Muir, E., Lojkasek, M., & Cohen, N. J. (1999). *Watch, Wait and Wonder: A manual describing a dyadic infant-led approach to problems in infancy and early childhood.* Ontario: Hincks-Dellcrest Institute.

Philipp, D. (2012). Reflective Family Play: A brief family therapy model for the infant and preschool population. *Infant Mental Health Journal, 33*(6), 599–608.

Philipp, D., & Hayos, C. (2013). Le Reflective Family Play: Un traitement de la famille entière centré sur l'attachement et le système familial. In N. Favez, F. Frascarolo-Moutinot & H. Tissot (Eds.), *Naître et grandir au sein de la triade* (pp. 227–250). Brussels: De Boeck.

Rusconi-Serpa, S., Sancho-Rossignol, A., & McDonough, S. (2009). Video-feedback in parent-infant treatments. *Child and Adolescent Psychiatric Clinics of North America, 18*(3), 735–751.

Slade, A. (2008). Mentalization as a frame for parent work in child psychotherapy. In E. Jurist, A. Slade, & S. Bergner (Eds.), *Mind to mind: Infant research, neuroscience and psychoanalysis* (pp. 307–334). New York: Other Press.

Chapter 13

Clinical applications of the LTP at other sites

As we have noted throughout this book, the original goal of Lausanne Trilogue Play (LTP) was to be of use in work with clinically challenging families in the infant and preschool population. Prior to the development of this model there was no formal assessment tool for two-parent families in this age group, nor interventions aimed at the entire family. In chapters 10 and 11 we described the clinical applications of the LTP paradigm that have now been developed at the Centre for Studies of the Family (Centre d'Etude de la Famille – CEF), part of the University of Lausanne Institute for Psychotherapy. In chapter 12 we presented Reflective Family Play (Philipp, 2012; Philipp & Hayos, 2013), a brief family therapy model that combines elements of LTP and video-feedback with the attachment-based treatment, Watch, Wait, and Wonder (Muir, 1992; Muir, Lojkasek, & Cohen, 1999). For this last chapter on clinical applications, we present a general overview of a broad array of contexts and applications where the LTP has been applied at several centers throughout the world.

While the common thread across sites is the use of the LTP for either assessment or as a tool in the treatment of families, the nature of the therapy can vary, from adaptations of dyadic treatments (one parent with one child) to traditional brief systemic family therapies. As this is meant as merely an overview of the work at these other sites, we will focus on key clinical differences and points of similarity.

When and where to use the LTP

Disconnect between what parents describe and how the child presents in the clinic

Often when we first meet families in the clinic, there is a notable gap between what the parents describe as the problem and what is seen in the initial interview. School reports may not corroborate the parents' description of their child's behavior either. For many of these families, the presenting problem may be seen only in the context of the whole family. Furthermore, it might require putting them through a more structured task, such as the LTP, in order for the symptoms to come to light and for the parents to feel heard.

For example, at the Geha Infant Mental Health Unit at Tel Aviv University Medical School, Keren, Dollberg, Kosteff, Danino, and Feldman (2010) have been using the LTP as part of their assessments for symptomatic children aged 0–3 years. In this setting, they first see referred infants and their parents for a family intake. The clinician reviews the history with the parents and also observes the behaviors of the parents, the infant, and their interaction. For some of these families the presenting problem is not evident from simple observation of an unstructured parent-infant interaction. In these instances the families are asked to do an LTP, and it is here that the presenting concerns may become much more evident.

Comment

This disconnect between presentation and report should be familiar to clinicians working with young children. Even if the LTP is not a standard part of a clinician's assessment, it may be very useful to add it in such situations where the history does not match what we are seeing.

In parts I and II of the LTP each parent has a turn playing actively with the child,[1] while the other one remains in the context, but "simply present." This allows us to see the resources and difficulties of each parent in these two different roles, as well as how the child responds to the different role expectations. In part III they play together as a family. As we have seen in this section of the book, many clinical families may struggle with what it means to play together. For some this may mean the parents take turns playing with the children in this part because they cannot coordinate to play together. In families with more than one child, it might mean the parents divide the children and each play with one or more, still not playing together as a family. Finally, in part IV the parents are supposed to talk among themselves. Again, many clinical families struggle with this part. Some struggle because of conflict between the parents. Other parents may struggle with the idea of setting limits on their children and creating an appropriate "intergenerational boundary" (Minuchin, 1974) between themselves and the children. By asking families to go through all of these parts, and navigate all of the transitions it requires, problems not previously evident may well emerge.

In-home settings

Hedenbro, a clinical psychologist, has adapted the setup for the LTP in order to use it clinically during home consultations in Sweden (Hedenbro, 1997). Families are asked to do an LTP and it is taped using just one camera with the aid of a mirror placed behind the child. In this way, Hedenbro is able to capture all three faces; the camera captures a direct image of the child, and a mirror image of the parents. Obviously in this setting it is not possible to leave the room, as there is no one-way mirror through which the family can signal to the therapist that they have completed the task. Rather, Hedenbro remains in the room with the family, and stands behind the camera. The family still signals her when they have completed all four parts of the play.

McHale, Fivaz-Depeursinge, Dickstein, Robertson, and Daley have also used the one-camera approach for research purposes. McHale's team also went into the homes of young families and filmed LTPs with the aid of a mirror. They succeeded in recording the multiple gaze shifts of the infant characteristic of triangular communication at 3–4 months of age (for a picture of the setting see McHale, Fivaz-Depeursinge, Dickstein, Robertson, & Daley, 2008).

Comment

This model of staying in the room with the family is useful for any clinical setting where there is no one-way mirror, not just for home visits.

Extending the LTP to older children

Colleagues in Italy have adapted the LTP as well as the coding system, for the purposes of assessing clinical families beyond the infant and preschool years and well into adolescence (Malagoli Togliatti, Mazzoni, Lubrano Lavadera, & Franci, 2013). They are now able to assess families up to when the children are 17 years old. The task is adapted to be age-appropriate, taking into consideration the verbal skills of older children and teens.

To understand their work better, recall that at the CEF, when children are older, they are brought in to do a number of LTP-related tasks, including the Lausanne Narrative Play (LNP). For the LNP, they are asked to sit around a table and play out a story using dolls in the same four parts of the LTP. First one parent plays out the story with the child, while the other parent is simply present. Then the parents switch roles and the second parent continues the story with the child. In the third part, the whole family completes the story, and then in the fourth part the parents talk, while the child is present, and playing on their own.

The Italian group has chosen to use this same idea of the story, but with children 11 years and up. They provide them with pencil and paper to write it out rather than dolls. In families with children 5–10 years old, the consultants provide Lego and ask families simply to build something together with their child, again following the four parts.

Comment

The richness of the narrative in these older children is incorporated into the coding scheme.

Blending the LTP with other modalities

Family systems therapy

In Italy the same colleagues are also applying the LTP with their family therapy cases. Families are invited in to do an LTP at the third session of treatment. Subsequent family sessions are enriched with video clips from the LTP that are chosen by the clinician to share key moments of strength and difficulty. A second LTP is then done at the end of treatment.

Watch, Wait, and Wonder

In chapter 12 we presented Reflective Family Play as a model that combines elements of the LTP with Watch, Wait, and Wonder (WWW) an attachment-based dyadic approach of treatment. The basic structure of the LTP is used in the first half of each session, but, as in WWW, families are free to move about the play space and parents are asked to follow their child's lead when it is their turn to play. In the second half of each session, the therapist follows the parents as they discuss their observations of the play. Video clips are selected through the course of this discussion to enhance the observation process.

Interaction guidance

Similarly, Hedenbro has combined Interaction Guidance (Aarts, 2000; McDonough, 1993) with a family systems framework using the LTP. In standard Interaction Guidance parent-child dyads are asked to play together for about 10 minutes. The interaction is videotaped and clips are selected by the clinician to review with the parent from week to week. It is a short-term dyadic therapy, and, like in other forms of video-feedback treatments, the clinician always begins with the parent's strengths and then shows them clips where they struggled.

In her work with two-parent families, Hedenbro videotapes an LTP. She then chooses excerpts from all four parts of that LTP to use in ongoing Interaction Guidance sessions with the two parents, incorporating family therapy concepts into this treatment.

Child custody and access

Assessment

In the case of separation and divorce Malagoli and colleagues have also made valuable inroads in the Italian legal system, using the LTP to support decisions around coparenting post-divorce (Malagoli Togliatti, Lubrano Lavadera, & di Benedetto, 2011). The degree to which a couple can work together or coordinate as parents after they separate has a significant effect on a number of outcome measures for the child or children involved (McHale & Carter, 2012). In addition to simply determining the custody and access arrangement, part of any assessment of separating and divorcing families should also look at the current level of family functioning, and in particular the couple's ability to work together in the children's best interest – in other words, how they coparent.

In Rome, family court judges are now able to request an expert opinion, which includes an LTP, to assess family coordination and in particular coparenting.[2]

Families are seen by a consultant and asked to participate in an LTP or LFP, depending on the number of children involved. The family is seated at a table and given a tub of Lego. They are instructed to play in the four parts. In the case of an LFP, the children are treated as a unit, so each parent takes a turn at playing with both children, while the other is simply present in parts I and II. In part III they play together as a family, and in part IV the parents are supposed to talk with one another while the children manage on their own, but are still seated at the table.

The play session is coded and a report is provided for the courts. In a typical assessment of a two-child family, the clinician would address a number of questions. How well was the family able to cooperate in play together? Were the parents competing with one another for the children's attention, particularly in part III, or did they split the children, each playing exclusively with one child but never playing together as a foursome? Did one parent self-exclude, especially in the part where they were supposed to be simply present? Perhaps they did the exact opposite, intruding on the play of the other parent, competing for the children's attention rather than actively observing? Or perhaps they waffled between the two extremes, intruding at times and withdrawing at other times.

Similarly they will look at the child's behaviors. Does the child take on the parenting role, deciding when to have the transitions? Is the child triangulated with one parent against the other? Does the child try to decrease the conflict between the parents?

In part IV, still very much in the throws of their battle, many separating and divorcing couples will engage in some sort of sparring with one another. In response, the children may engage in a variety of behaviors. They may become increasingly rambunctious or even fight with one another. The siblings may try to divide the parents, each drawing one of the parents into an interaction. Alternatively, they may leave the table and wander about the room; withdraw into what they are playing; or request to leave the room. One sibling, often the eldest, but not always, may take on the role of directing the play in order to free the parents up to argue. The possibilities are numerous, and poignant for the observer.

Finally, the findings from the LTP are compared to other sources of data in the assessment process. Often one or both parents may be so entrenched in the conflict that they see their situation as more problematic than it appears on the LTP. In these situations, the family's resources can also be pointed out to the parents.

Clinical intervention

In the video-feedback, once again, the clinician selects clips from all four parts of the LTP to demonstrate the family's strengths as well as areas of concern. The initial hope is that the parents will be able to observe for themselves the impact of their conflict on the children, and that these observations can then be explored and alternative responses considered. Often, however, the clinician needs to prompt observations. In the most extreme cases the parents remain entrenched in their battle and it is impossible for them to explore the role they play. In this way the consultant gets a sense of next steps:

- If the family alliance is coded as "cooperative" (or "stressed")
  - no further intervention is needed and it is hoped they will settle or mediate.
- If the alliance is coded as "collusive" – there are areas of concern, but also an openness to work on improving –
  - further intervention is recommended, targeting coparenting through video-feedback sessions.
- If the alliance is coded as "disorganized" and rigidity and hostility predominate
  - the clinician may recommend supervised transfers between the parents in order to mitigate the children's exposure to the conflict.

Comment

So often the focus with separating and divorcing families is on custody and access, involving individual parenting assessments. This process can be quite costly, and regardless of the outcome, most separated couples will still need to find ways to work together as coparents. Clinicians and child protection agencies, as well as child advocacy groups, must also consider the impact of problematic coparenting and ways to intervene at this level, given the degree of risk to children exposed to parental conflict (McHale & Carter, 2012).

Working with non-traditional families and the LTP

In a number of locations now, the LTP has been used clinically to look at other sorts of non-traditional families. Salvatore d'Amore looked at the LTP in non-referred families with same-sex parents. Not surprisingly, the findings were that the distribution of alliances was the same as in heterosexual couples (D'Amore, Simonelli, & Miscioscia, 2013). In Toronto, at the Hincks-Dellcrest Centre, we see a number of families headed by same-sex couples and have included the LTP or LFP (Lausanne Family Play for families with two or more children) in the assessment.

Adoptive and families struggling with infertility

With a certain subgroup of adoptive families, as well as some couples who have struggled with infertility (Cairo, Darwiche, Tissot, Favez, Germond, Guex, & Despland 2012; Darwiche, Maillard, Tissot, Corboz-Warnery, & Guex, 2010), many clinicians are now familiar with the "over-indulged child" with parents uncomfortable with setting limits on this long-sought-after child (Darwiche, Favez, Guex, Germond, & Despland, 2013). During the LTP, these parents particularly struggle with managing parts III and IV.

Comment

Certain parents coming in for clinical assessment will see part IV as intolerable to their child and perhaps even fear that the child will experience it as punitive. They may try to do part IV, but sabotage it through their nonverbal behavior. They may continue to turn to the child and talk to them as we saw in some of the cases presented earlier in this section of the book. Others may even "forget" to do part IV, and will need to be asked to do it after the fact. In the latter case, this "forgetting" may need to be explored as part of the therapeutic alliance. By "forgetting" the couple is perhaps also sending a message to the consultant that they do not care for this last part of the LTP. But often it is symptomatic of not being able to set a boundary and the feelings that come with this inability.

Late adoption

In the case of late adoption, often struggles have to do with a biological or environmental predisposition in the child leading to the concerning behaviors. In these cases, the assessment of the family alliance in the LTP may actually be unremarkable, since much of the difficulty resides in something that happened during the pregnancy, such as exposure to drugs or alcohol, or to a disordered attachment due to chaotic care prior to adoption.

In other families, there may be a process of realigning the family alliances as new children are brought into the family. There can be a variety of outcomes depending on a number of factors such as: the age of the child at adoption, what has transpired prior to the adoption in terms of the degree of stability or chaos, and what other children there are in the household.

Comment

Just as we have pointed out that sometimes the clinical picture painted by the parents does not match with what we see at intake and so an LTP is warranted, the inverse is also true. Families can have "good enough" LTPs, and therefore multiple forms of assessment are key to our understanding of them.

Findings in clinical populations

Now let's discuss some of the clinical observations as well as preliminary findings from pilot projects at some of these other clinical settings.

Higher distribution of problematic LTPs in clinical populations

Most sites that are using the LTP as part of their assessment for young families note a higher proportion of problematic LTPs in this population. This was first noted at the CEF (Frascarolo, Gertsch-Bettens, Fivaz-Depeursinge, & Corboz-Warnery, 1997); however, it has been observed at a number of other sites now.

Keren has found that the majority of referred families do in fact have problematic LTPs (Keren, 2010). More recently, Hervé and colleagues assessed a population of 34 families coming for treatment in an outpatient service in a small urban setting in France. They found that 65% of these families had dysfunctional LTPs prior to starting treatment (Hervé, Lavanchy Scaiola, Favez, & Maury, 2013). Furthermore, Mazzoni and Lubrano Lavadera (2013) in Rome have found correlations between problems in coparenting coordination on the LTP and the presence of symptoms in the presenting child.

Comment

It is important to bear in mind that families present at a clinic for a variety of reasons. Our aim is not to place the onus of pathology on the coparents as causing all of the problems we see. The infant makes his own contribution to the family alliance, and at times a child may have psychiatric or developmental difficulties that have pushed an "almost good enough" family towards problematic interactions. At times is can be a question of goodness of fit.

Difficulties with latter half of the LTP

In section II of this book we described how when parents are poorly coordinated, they tend to engage in excluding coparenting in parts I and II of the LTP (see chapter 7). In the second half of the LTP, most of these same parents adopt different coparenting styles: competitive coparenting (chapter 9), and child-at-center coparenting (chapter 8). Some of these parents also engage at times in cohesive coparenting (section I of this book).

In parallel, clinicians using the LTP for their work with referred families have now noted that the second half often appears the most problematic. The focus of clinical consultations with video-feedback is often centered on how the family plays together in part III, or how the couple carves out their space for part IV. At the Hincks-Dellcrest difficulties with part III or IV is one of the indications for choosing couple's therapy or a family-level intervention such as Reflective Family Play, as opposed to a dyadic approach (Philipp, 2012).

Mazzoni and Lubrano Lavadera (2013) have been looking at outcomes of family therapies using the LTP. One preliminary result coming from this research is that clinical families do indeed have far more difficulty with the fourth part of the LTP in particular, when the task is for them to communicate adult to adult. They have noted this to be especially the case in families where the identified patient's presenting problem is behavioral or anxiety. They hypothesize that parents presenting to a clinic may have greater difficulty creating a clear boundary between the parental subsystem and the child subsystem. The idea of boundaries and subsystems is from Minuchin's work in Structural Family Therapy (1974). In order for a family to function optimally, the parents need to give the children a clear sense that they are working together as a team to make decisions for the family and are consulting with one another. Part IV of the LTP pushes the parents most to do this task; if the boundary is not clearly defined children can and will intrude, but more concerning is when the parents turn to the children, blame the children, or in some other way co-opt them into problematic positions (see chapter 9).

Comment

For some families part IV can be quite stressful. They may need to contend with a distressed child who is making his unhappiness very visible. What we are looking for is not a rigid boundary, where they ignore the child entirely and let his needs go unmet. Rather, we are interested in how the parents work together and support one another in setting a clear boundary that is flexible enough for them to be sensitive to their child's needs when appropriate.

Fostering the alliance and hastening change

Early on in dyadic work with infants, Zelenko and Benham (2000) noted that incorporating video-feedback notably improved the therapeutic alliance. Similarly, a number of clinicians have now noted a positive impact on the therapeutic alliance if an LTP with video-feedback is done relatively early in treatment. For example, Keren describes a case report (2010) where the LTP was done as part of the assessment and then reviewed as part of the treatment. They noted a significant improvement in the presenting problems and in a shorter time frame. In more traditional psychodynamic treatments, improvement typically was seen after 12 sessions at their site; however, in this case report, using the LTP and video-feedback, improvement was noted after five sessions.

The LTP video-feedback sessions were also seen as bolstering the therapeutic alliance between the parents and the therapist. At the end of treatment the parents also endorsed greater confidence in their parenting. They asked to do the LTP again at the end of the treatment "to see ourselves again, now that we feel better at parenting." Many centers now routinely repeat the LTP at the end of treatment to see the changes over the course of therapy.

Mazzoni and Lubrano Lavadera (2013) note greater compliance in the families that undergo an LTP. In other words, families in their clinic who participate in an LTP consultation and subsequent video-feedback are more likely to follow through with treatment than those who have more traditional systemic family therapy without the LTP.

Clearly more research is needed to confirm these clinical reports, but Mazzoni and Lubrano Lavadera's findings are certainly consistent with the reports.

Comment

How can we understand these observations, given what we have learned about the LTP? Something about being able to observe the interactions on video is likely critical in improving compliance, hastening change, and strengthening the therapeutic alliance. As we discussed in chapter 11 on video-feedback, while some parents first express concern over being filmed, video can be a very powerful tool in treatment. It allows both the clinician and the family to re-experience an interaction and slowly break it down to understand it better (Rusconi-Serpa, Sancho-Rossignol, & McDonough, 2009). In LTPs with clinical families a lot can be going on at the same time, and in the moment, it can feel quite chaotic even for the observer. During video-feedback sessions the family and the clinician can work together to come to a new understanding of the family and the relationships between its members.

In terms of the therapeutic alliance specifically, having the moment-to-moment video clips allows the therapist to reinforce the parents' strengths in a very clear and concrete way that then frees them up to speak about some of their vulnerabilities. We saw this occur in several of the cases discussed in this last section of the book. Parents also often express a sense of relief that the clinicians were able to "see the problem" in the context of the LTP. While clinical applications of the LTP have been around for quite some time now, these questions remain to be better understood with future clinical research on process and outcomes.

Outcome studies

We have discussed some of the work of Mazzoni and Lubrano Lavadera looking at outcomes for families using the LTP. Hervé et al. (2013) recently did an exploratory study looking at the LTPs of clinical families before and after a brief psychodynamic treatment. The population was a heterogeneous group, like one would typically see in an infant and preschool clinic, with an array of presenting problems. Length of treatment also varied, with a mean length of three sessions. As was already noted, the majority of families, 65%, had dysfunctional LTPs at the outset. One of the goals of the study was to explore change in the family alliance as a result of treatment. Even though the treatment was not specifically geared towards the family system, it was thought that by altering one aspect of the system, a change might result in the whole system. In fact, there was overall improvement in the presenting symptoms of the children. Maternal symptoms also improved. Finally, 38.5% of the families showed improvement in their post-treatment LTP scores as compared to their pre-treatment scores. Interestingly, 31% of the families actually showed a decline in their scores post-treatment. The authors hypothesize that for these families, while many of the presenting symptoms had improved, the family's way of interacting had been destabilized – at least for the short term. It would be interesting to do a follow-up on these families 6 months post-treatment. With certain treatments, even brief dynamic treatments, some of the positive findings were not evident until more time had passed (Cohen, Lojkasek, Muir, Muir, & Parker, 2002), and a new equilibrium presumably could be established. It is difficult to comment further on these findings, given the heterogeneity of the treatments offered and that the average number of treatment sessions was only three.

Conclusion

We have very briefly reviewed some of the exciting work that is being done at other sites, applying what we know of the LTP paradigm to a variety of clinical settings. We encourage other clinicians to consider some of these applications in their own work. It is our hope to further develop the network of those of us using the LTP and its applications in our practice with young families. Collaborations across sites will also allow us to look more rigorously at treatment outcomes for some of the innovations we already have presented here.

Notes

1 We refer to "child"; however, there may be siblings and they should always be included in clinical evaluations, even if they are not the identified patient.
2 This is not done in instances where there has been substantiated domestic violence or abuse.

References

Aarts, M. (2000). *Aarts productions.* Marte Meo: Basic Manual.

Cairo, S., Darwiche, J., Tissot, H., Favez, N., Germond, M., Guex, P., & Despland, J.-N. (2012). Family interactions in IVF families: Change over the transition to parenthood. *Journal of Reproductive and Infant Psychology, 30*(1), 5–20.

Cohen, N. J., Lojkasek, M., Muir, E., Muir, R., & Parker, C. J. (2002). Six-month follow-up of two mother-infant psychotherapies: Convergence of therapeutic outcomes. *Infant Mental Health Journal, 23*(4), 361–380.

D'Amore, S., Simonelli, A., & Miscioscia, M. (2013). Les alliances coparentales dans les familles lesboparentales. In N. Favez, F. Frascarolo-Moutinot, & H. Tissot (Eds.), *Naître et grandir au sein de la triade: Le développement de l'alliance familiale.* Brussels: De Boeck.

Darwiche, J., Favez, N., Guex, P., Germond, M., & Despland, J. N. (2013). Alliance familiale entre père, mère et leur bébé conçu par fécondation in vitro. In N. Favez, F. Frascarolo-Moutinot, & H. Tissot (Eds.), *Naître et grandir au sein de la triade: Le développement de l'alliance familiale* (pp. 245–301). Brussels: De Boeck.

Darwiche, J., Maillard, F., Tissot, H., Corboz-Warnery, A., & Guex, P. (2010). Familles issues de la médecine de la procréation: De la grossesse aux interactions entre père, mère et bébé. In I. S. D'Amore (Ed.), *Les nouvelles familles* (pp. 281–301). Brussels: De Boeck.

Frascarolo, F., Gertsch-Bettens, C., Fivaz-Depeursinge, E., & Corboz-Warnery, A. (1997). Configurations corporelles et engagement visuel dans la triade père-mère-bébé. *Neuropsychiatrie de l'Enfance et de l'Adolescence, 45,* 233–242.

Hedenbro, M. (1997). Interaction, the key to life: Seeing possibilities of children through videopictures. *Signal,* October–December, 9–15.

Hervé, M. J., Lavanchy Scaiola, C., Favez, N., & Maury, M. (2013). Alliance familiale dans les troubles fonctionnels et du comportement du nourrisson: Évaluation avant et après une intervention thérapeutique. Une étude exploratoire. In N. Favez, F. Frascarolo-Moutinot, & H. Tissot (Eds.), *Naître et grandir au sein de la triade: Le développement de l'alliance familiale.* (pp. 177–192) Brussels: De Boeck.

Keren, M. (2010). *Using the Lausanne Triadic Play in an infant mental health unit*. Paper presented at the World Association for Infant Mental Health, 12th World Congress, Leipzig, Germany.

Keren, M., Dollberg, D., Kosteff, T., Danino, K., & Feldman, R. (2010). Family functioning and interactive patterns in the context of infant psychopathology. *Journal of Family Psychology, 24*(5), 597–604.

Malagoli Togliatti, M., Lubrano Lavadera, A., & di Benedetto, R. (2011). How couples reorganized themselves following divorce: Adjustment, co-parenting and family alliance. *Life Span and Disability, XIV*(1), 55–74.

Malagoli Togliatti, M., Mazzoni, S., Lubrano Lavadera, A., & Franci, M. (2013). Nouvelles Directions en Thérapie Familiale. In P. Ferrari & O. Bonnot. (Eds.), *Traité européen de Psychiatrie et de Psychopathologie de l'enfant et de l'adolescent* (pp. 761–768). Paris: Lavoisier.

Mazzoni, S., & Lubrano Lavadera, A. (2013). Le Jeu Trilogique de Lausanne (LTP) en clinique: Application dans le contexte d'interventions de soutien à la relation parents-enfants. In N. Favez, F. Frascarolo-Moutinot, & H. Tissot (Eds.), *Naître et grandir au sein de la triade: Le développement de l'alliance familiale* (pp. 193–210). Brussels: De Boeck.

McDonough, S. C. (1993). Interaction guidance: Understanding and treating early infant-caregiver relationship disorders. In C. Zeanah (Ed.), *Handbook of infant mental health* (pp. 414–426). New York: Guilford Press.

McHale, J., & Carter, D. (2012). Applications of focused coparenting consultation with unmarried and divorced families. *Independent Practitioner, 32*(3), 106–110.

McHale, J., Fivaz-Depeursinge, E., Dickstein, S., Robertson, J., & Daley, M. (2008). New evidence for the social embeddedness of infant's early triangular capacities. *Family Process* (47), 445–463.

Minuchin, S. (1974). *Families & family therapy*. Boston: Harvard University Press.

Muir, E. (1992). Watching, waiting, and wondering: Applying psychoanalytic principles to mother-infant intervention. *Infant Mental Health Journal, 13*(4), 319–328.

Muir, E., Lojkasek, M., & Cohen, N. J. (1999). *Watch, Wait and Wonder: A manual describing a dyadic infant-led approach to problems in infancy and early childhood*. Ontario: Hincks-Dellcrest Institute.

Philipp, D. (2012). Reflective Family Play: A brief family therapy model for the infant and preschool population. *Infant Mental Health Journal, 33*(6), 599–608.

Philipp, D., & Hayos, C. (2013). Le Reflective Family Play: Un traitement de la famille entière centré sur l'attachement et le système familial. In N. Favez, F. Frascarolo-Moutinot, & H. Tissot (Eds.), *Naître et grandir au sein de la triade: Le développement de l'alliance familiale* (pp. 227–248). Brussels: De Boeck.

Rusconi-Serpa, S., Sancho-Rossignol, A., & McDonough, S. (2009). Video-feedback in parent-infant treatments. *Child and Adolescent Psychiatric Clinics of North America, 18*(3), 735–751.

Zelenko, M., & Benham, A. (2000). Videotaping as a therapeutic tool in psychodynamic infant-parent therapy. *Infant Mental Health Journal, 21*(3), 192–203.

Where we are and where do we go from here?

At the heart of this book are the infant and the couple and the ways in which parents work together to facilitate their child's capacity to emotionally connect with both of them at the same time. Remember the sequence of Lucas, 9 months old and playing "the sneezing game" with his two parents, in chapter 3? His parents are seated facing him and have finally got his attention. He looks back and forth at them with anticipation. They pause a moment longer and then they both sneeze together. The baby laughs. He looks up at his father and then at his mother, anticipating the next round. The parents go on . . . the excitation rises with each turn, until they all break into joint laughter.

On viewing this sequence, Daniel Stern noted that the parents' signals are different. The father's sharper movements and low voice contrast with the mother's smoother movements and higher voice, yet they are in rhythm and in tune with one another. These differences make the interaction much richer, but the synchronization and the coordination of the parents, together with the baby's response, form an overarching "dynamic form" or Gestalt of a three-way interaction, beginning with a well marked staccato, then a pause, then the sneezing explosion. It is experienced in the minds of all three, both parents, and seemingly the infant as well (Stern, 2008). It is a lovely example of what Stern referred to with us as triangular or collective intersubjective communication.

The Lausanne Trilogue Play situation (LTP) has allowed us to systematically observe infants playing with their parents, sharing these moments of intersubjectivity, in the four possible configurations of a triad (Corboz-Warnery, Fivaz-Depeursinge, Guertsch-Bettens, & Favez, 1993). It has opened up a breadth of opportunities for us in understanding infants in everyday life as well as in clinical contexts. But it has also put into question a number of theoretical underpinnings to our understanding of infant and child development and leaves us wanting to consider more ways that we can look at the baby and the couple. In closing, the next question to consider is, given what we know about infants, their parents, and the siblings that join their families, where do we go from here as researchers, and as clinicians?

Developmental theory and infant triangular communication

Triangular communication: An integral part of developmental theory

In this book, we have devoted section I to a detailed description of the typical development of triangular communication, not only because this was uncharted territory, but also because we feel that the greater our understanding is of typical development, the more we as researchers and clinicians stand to gain. In fact, we recommend that observations of typical families and their infants be a more integral part of training. Without this perspective, we risk losing a sense of what is typical or normal, to the point of having unrealistic expectations based on observations of psychopathology alone (Stern, 1985).

Our propositions for a developmental theory integrating triangular communication are in need of experimental as well as clinical testing, but are based on the following:

Triangular communication paves the way from primary to secondary intersubjectivity. In classical developmental theory, it is the merging of dyadic parent-infant interactions with infant-object interactions that lead to "triadic" or person-person-object interactions. These "triadic" interactions were considered the marker of secondary intersubjectivity (Carpenter, Nagell, & Tomasello, 1998). We suggest in addition that early triangular, person-person-person interactions pave the way from primary to secondary intersubjectivity by introducing a person as the third pole of attention right from the outset. Very recent data further supports this proposition. Tremblay and colleagues have found evidence of triangular communication, in particular in the form of shifting gaze and affect, amongst newborns (mean age of 59 hours) interacting with their two parents (Tremblay, Rovira, Lemonnier, & Sorin, submitted). The fact that this third pole is social provides the infant with easier access to three-way or three-pole interactions (Nadel & Tremblay-Leveau, 1999). Obviously, this hypothesis demands a careful and imaginative program of research (Nahum, 2010; Stern, 2010).

Derailed triangular communication and non-cohesive coparenting. In section II we explored how sensitive the infant's capacity for triangular communication is to the quality of the parents' relationship. About a third of the infants in our longitudinal study of non-referred families were at a disadvantage in terms of their triangular communication in conjunction with problematic coparenting; so too are the infants in the clinical families described in section III. Given how different these outcomes can be, it underscores the need for coparenting and infant triangular communication to be part of the study of infant development.

Non-cohesive coparenting, family coalitions, and the prenatal context. Our results on infant triangular communication and the various coparenting contexts in which it develops (McHale, 2007) show remarkable convergence with Salvatore Minuchin's structural model on family coalitions (S. Minuchin, 1974; see also sections II and III of this book). In addition, in chapter 6 we discussed how the prenatal coparenting alliance seems to predict the trajectory for the family alliance (or coalitions) once the child is born, as well as the child's behavior, emotion regulation, and theory of mind. Elaborating on Patricia Minuchin's push for greater collaboration between family therapists and those working in developmental theory (P. Minuchin, 1985), we propose further investigation into the prenatal coparenting alliance as a factor in later child development.

The LTP paradigm

Observing infant-parent triangular interactions: Which setting for which goal?

The infant's capacity for triangular communication might not have come to light without the strict physical setting of the LTP (chapter 1). It is designed to create optimal conditions for three-way communication with an infant. All parties have each other in view, although at times it is only peripheral. This strict setup has also allowed us to film the interactions for detailed and systematic observation of the nonverbal behavior of all participants.

A *trade-off.* When we ask families to remain seated in the LTP setting, we recognize that we also lose some data about the family. What would their interactions look like if they were free to move about the room? In particular, fathers will sometimes tell us that they do not tend to play with their children in this way, and that they prefer to be more physical, even with their very young infants. We have been inspired by some of the research on the role of fathers' rough-and-tumble play in mediating development of exploration behavior in children (Paquette, 2004). Although methodologically challenging, it would be interesting to capture more of the rough-and-tumble contribution of fathers in an LTP model, and to observe the role mothers play in facilitating, impeding, or perhaps containing this more aggressive play.

One complementary task that has given us some information about this facet of family interactions is the Lausanne Picnic Game (PNG), which we presented in chapter 5. Others have modified the format of the LTP and allowed families to move about freely during it. With the family no longer seated in a triangle there is clearly a richness of information that can be gleaned. For example, do the family members even bother to keep one another in view to communicate nonverbally with one another? Under these conditions, however, it makes coding their three-way interaction and the infant's triangular communication much trickier or even impossible. For some clinicians in particular, however, allowing families to move about in the setting, at the expense of systematic observation, will allow them to begin using the LTP to observe more spontaneous interactions.

At this point in the development of the model, if we are to use the LTP for assessment purposes, and in particular the infant's triangular communication, then fixed seating positions and preferably two cameras are still the ideal (some have used one camera, filming the infant straight on, with the parents in profile). Where at all possible, we would encourage both the structure of the LTP as well as a second, less structured assessment tool if we want to capture both of these sides of family interactions.

The LTP paradigm as a double perspective

The LTP was never intended as an end unto itself. It has always been intimately associated with the video-feedback sessions we offer all families, not just those that are clinically referred. We see the LTP and video-feedback as an opportunity for parents and children to directly experience how they communicate as a family. During the LTP itself, we get a window into the "practicing family" (Reiss, 1989) or the enacting family (Fivaz-Depeursinge & Corboz-Warnery, 1999). During video-feedback, families gain a second perspective of the same experience by seeing themselves in video and reflecting about it (Bateson, 1979; Rusconi-Serpa, Sancho-Rossignol, & McDonough, 2009).

As we discussed in the chapters on video-feedback (10 and 11), it is a complex and delicate matter. Identifying resources is often far more difficult than detecting problems, particularly with clinical families (Fivaz-Depeursinge, Fivaz, & Kaufmann, 1982). There is much potential for shame when we ask families to observe themselves on video alongside "experts" in family dynamics. A good enough alliance between the consultant and the family is key. Adequate training is essential, and our hope is that as we continue to expand the network of centers doing this kind of work, training opportunities for new researchers and clinicians interested in incorporating the LTP in their work will grow as well.

Complementary triadic paradigms

As we were developing the LTP, other triadic paradigms complemented our views on the infant's capacity for triangular communication. Infants have been observed interacting with two strangers (Tremblay & Rovira, 2007), in a group of three infants together in a room, in Selby and Bradley's "infant trios" paradigm (2003), and with their mother while she was playing with a life-like doll (Hart, Carrington, Tronick, & Carroll, 2004). In all of these different situations, we have convergent evidence of the infant's ability to manage multiperson communication, and a more nuanced understanding of it as well. For example, with the three infants paradigm, we see a model for understanding earliest peer relationships. The mother-baby-doll paradigm elicits evidence of jealousy.

We have also described how we modified the still face paradigm (chapter 2) by asking one parent to pose a still face to the 4 month-old infant. McHale and colleagues modified the paradigm a little differently, asking both parents to pose the still face and then observing the coparents manage the repair of the relationship afterwards (McHale, Fivaz-Depeursinge, Dickstein, Robertson, & Daley, 2008).

Potential for new LTP tasks

The LTP was originally developed to better understand infant triangular communication and family interactions in two-parent households. The aim was to shift our thinking away from a strictly dyadic view of the infant's world. There are clearly other multiperson contexts within which an infant may be raised and for which new variants can and should be developed.

Non-traditional families. Many young mothers (and fathers) are raising their infant with their own parents as co-caregivers, creating a grandparent-parent/child-child/grandchild triad. McHale and colleagues have made some inroads with this group, finding that, just as with any other two-parent household, cooperation is key (Baker, McHale, Stozier, & Cecil, 2010; McHale, 2013). Some single parents have more than one child, and we still have much to learn about triangular communication when the context is parent-child-child (Dunn & Munn, 1988). McHale has cogently argued that in most families, even if the parents do not live together, other adults take the function of coparents. Even if couples are living together, for economic and cultural reasons, many families live with multiple generations all together in the same household. This scenario provides many opportunities for the infant to learn multiperson communication, but complicating the task of defining coparenting. Finally, there are many couples who have found themselves expecting a child, and have no intention of cohabitating. McHale's group has been exploring ways of understanding these families and how to facilitate their coparenting as well (McHale & Irace, 2011).

Postpartum psychosis. In an observational study of 13 families where the mother was hospitalized due to a postpartum psychosis, we found that both parents typically engaged in highly unpredictable and problematic behaviors with very little cohesiveness in their coparenting. The infants themselves were also atypical in their styles of engagement. They tended to maintain a hypervigilant stance, and any evidence of triangular behavior was typically in the service of monitoring the parents' erratic behavior, and not about actually sharing affects with them (Philipp, Fivaz-Depeursinge, Favez, & Corboz-Warnery, 2009). While a few centers in addition to ours have been working with coparents and their infants during and immediately after acute hospitalizations, we would propose that family assessments be a routine part of discharge planning and preventive health care in this high-risk population.

Newer technologies. Our Italian colleagues have adapted the prenatal LTP using ultrasound (Ammaniti, Mazzoni, & Menozzi, 2010). They bring expectant couples in to view their infant's ultrasound video and ask them to go through the same four parts of the LTP interacting with the images. This innovation speaks to other opportunities to consider how technology is now shaping our families. With the demands of work now pulling many parents far away from the rest of the family, sometimes living in different cities during the week, staying connected through the Internet has become commonplace. Even on a day-to-day basis, increasingly we see infants interacting with devices, sometimes to speak with one parent who is at work while the other is present. These are all as yet unexplored opportunities to understand the evolution of multiperson communication and the family.

Video-feedback in other settings

In all of the complementary or new paradigms mentioned earlier, we can see the potential for video-feedback. For example, when using the still face paradigm, with the dyad (Papousek, Schieche, & Wurmser, 2008) or adapted for two parents, in our studies (see chapter 2), we share it in a video-feedback session. It is an opportunity to explore how the family manages a controlled but stressful situation. The parents see how the infant coped with this challenging situation, making various bids to regain their attention. By showing these behaviors to the parents, on the video and with some distance from the actual stress, we stand to improve the parents' sensitivity to their infant's cues. The repair in the family relationship after the still face is also invaluable for parents to watch. They see how they worked together, or did not, to soothe their infant and move on to play again. We highly recommend this practice in research as well as in clinical practice.

Giving back to the infant a sense of agency after stress. We have discussed with others the idea of manipulating triadic paradigms to give the infant a sense of agency (Hélène Tremblay, personal communication), and to once again look at this in video-feedback with parents. For instance, what if rather than abruptly ending the still face after the prescribed 2 minutes, we instead signaled parents to end the still face after the infant made a certain number of bids to try to change the context (charm, fuss, triangular bid), and then validate those bids and resume normal interaction? In a sense this is what happens in part IV of the LTP with very responsive parents. The infant tries to regain their attention through a variety of maneuvers, and eventually they respond to one such maneuver, giving the infant a sense of agency. These scenarios also mirror real life. At times infants need to make multiple attempts to capture their parents' attention.

The infant gaining entrance into therapeutic conversations. We end this section on other triadic paradigms with a bridge to further clinical intervention. We know from Legerstee's work (Legerstee, Ellenbogen, Nienhuis, & Marsh, 2010) that an infant confronted with her mother talking to a stranger will try various tactics to try to gain entrance into that conversation, similar to what happens in part IV of the LTP when the infant tries to gain entrance into the parents' discussion.

This scenario is akin to the infant in a more traditional dyadic treatment, included in the room, but not necessarily included in the conversation. Hervé and colleagues found that having the infant included by the therapist as an equal partner in the triad (therapist-mother-baby) improved treatment outcomes (Hervé, Andreu, & Maury, 1998). As we have seen in chapter 12, the inclusion of the baby is a central feature of Reflective Family Play, and not simply during the play part. The infant will at times try and succeed at gaining entrance into the conversation between the therapist and parents (Philipp, 2012).

The LTP paradigm and clinical intervention

Early triadic and dyadic communication as models of therapeutic communication

Let us return to Lucas and the sneezing game and how we have come to see that the infant can perceive these moments of three-way intersubjective connection. Various authors have written about these experiences. Beebe and Lachmann (1994) referred to them as "heightened affective moments" that stand out for us in a disproportionate way, compared to other positive or negative moments we have shared with others. Lyons-Ruth has discussed "knowing how to be together" (Lyons-Ruth, 1998), and Stern (2004) referred to the "*now moment*" – a moment where partners reach a new or greater level of complexity in their "implicit relational knowing."

From the vantage point of systems theory, moments of dyadic or triangular affect sharing constitute an "emergent phenomenon" (Fivaz, 1989). In triadic play, these are the signature moments of success, like Lucas and his parents laughing together about the sneezing. Whether experienced at the dyadic, triadic, or multiperson level, these very real experiences of connection that we all can identify with have a close tie to therapeutic action.

The Boston Change Process Study group (Lyons-Ruth, 1998) described a type of present moment that also occurs in therapeutic interactions between clinicians and patients called "*moments of meeting.*" As with the infant and preschool population, these moments of intersubjective communion are more often than not experienced on a pre-verbal level, in the form of shared affective signals – for example, joint smiles, gazes, or even tears. The Boston Change Process Study Group viewed these moments as part of the "nonspecific factors" that account for so much of the improvement in patients, regardless of therapeutic modality. While they were speaking primarily of interactions between one therapist and one adult patient, we see the parallel phenomenon in our work with young families, both in dyadic interventions (Beebe & Lachmann, 2002) and in family interventions (Fivaz-Depeursinge et al., 1982).

The infant's triangular communication and other perspectives

Triangular communication and the Oedipus triangle

It may seem odd for some that we have come this far in a book about the infant and the primary triangle and have almost completely avoided talking about the Oedipus triangle (Freud, 1909). For others Freud's theories about psychosexual development may hold less sway. Regardless of one's theoretical framework, it is still worth considering how our understanding of early triangular capacity relates or changes our thinking about this earlier formulation.

Within the psychoanalytic world the field of trauma research has changed how many think about the Oedipus complex, questioning its use as a theory of pathogenesis when traumatic events and other environmental factors seem more likely causes (Lachmann, 2010). Others influenced by developmental and systems theories have pushed for revision of the Oedipus complex as well. They stress the role of the family system in shaping development over drives and fantasies arising from the child's mind (Emde & Oppenheim, 1995). They also have pointed out what we have been discussing in this book – that the triangular interactions of the infant and young child precede the arrival of the Oedipus complex (Lichtenberg, 2008).

Yet we are all familiar with behavior in many young children suggestive of a yearning for closeness with the opposite gender parent while pushing away the same gender one. What is missing when we over-focus on this one version of the family triangle, however, is the context of the full system of triangular dynamics, and how the coparents manage when confronted with this behavior. Do they somehow encourage it and exaggerate the split in the context of poor intergenerational boundaries (see section II, Lausanne Narrative Play), or do they accept it as a way in which their child is beginning to test his place in the family and in his gender?

The child participates in many triangular interactions in the family. Even during this "Oedipal phase" we have seen numerous times, in chapter 5, when he shares his experience equally in one of those "now moments" we have been discussing. At other times he will be closer with the same gender parent, and of course other configurations will occur when we add siblings to the equation. Being able to master these other contexts of the triangular system is of equal value to the Oedipal triangle and warrant our attention clinically as well.

Triangular communication, family systems, and attachment theory

At the outset of our studies, we expected to find links between attachment and the family alliance. Interestingly, our results on family alliances and mother-toddler attachment security as measured in the strange situation (Ainsworth, Blehar, Waters, & Wall, 1978) showed no significant links (Frascarolo & Favez, 1999). In particular there was no correlation between problematic alliances and insecure or disorganized attachment.

Byng-Hall (1995) has proposed a family-level attachment, or a network of relationships that family members can then use as a secure base. While there currently is no measure for family-level attachment, we know that things can look different at the family level than at the dyadic level. Perhaps a child might be secure in the context of his two dyadic relationships with each of his parents, but faced with the instability of his parents' marital relationship, his family-level attachment system is activated and triggers a problematic behavior that would not otherwise be seen.

The final point of intersection between attachment and family systems theory is one we have been discussing throughout – that of the interplay between the child's need for sensitive, attuned parenting, and the parents' need to create clear but flexible intergenerational boundaries as described by Minuchin (Minuchin, Nichols, & Lee, 2006). We see both of these at times competing needs as critical for optimal family functioning. Moreover, recent data suggests a link between the two. When both parents are insightful about their infant's mental state (Marcu, 2013), or have the capacity to mentalize each other's mental states (Lopes & Favez, 2012), then family functioning as measured on the LTP is also stronger. These findings support the clinical work we are doing both in LTP-based consultations and in Reflective Family Play (Philipp, 2012; Philipp & Hayos, 2013), where the goal is to improve reflective function as well as coparenting and the family system.

Methodological recommendations

Before we close, there are a few recommendations for future research that we would like to touch upon as areas where we could add to our understanding of families. First we are acutely aware that many things happen in families when they are not all together. A case in point is "covert coparenting," where one parent may undermine or disparage his coparent in her absence. McHale has used a questionnaire format to look at this with families (McHale, 1997). We encourage others to consider how one might capture and study other subsets of family interactions that impact on overall functioning.

Second, just as we are recommending structured and less structured methods of observing the family clinically, a number of authors (McHale, Kuersten-Hogan, Lauretti, & Rasmussen, 2000) and Favez et al. (2012) have also shown the value of using multi-method studies to better understand family dynamics. These would include structured and more free-form observation tasks, but also questionnaires, and interviews about the family members' representations.

Finally, in order to support the intervention models that have developed from the LTP paradigm, we need empirical studies exploring their methods and efficacy. These are long-term enterprises, but there are already several in progress. We encourage clinical researchers and practitioners to join this journey as the more we are able to collaborate in this endeavor the sooner we find better ways of helping young families.

In closing

The developments that have emerged since the publication of the *Primary Triangle* in 1999 are promising from the perspective of both research and clinical work. This added layer of context enriches our understanding of the infant and of the whole family. In our view, one of the advantages is that at the same time as it has provided us with a system for evaluating interactions, the LTP is also malleable enough to be used in different contexts, family configurations, and ages. In the future, perhaps others will use it to explore the infant's contribution and his parents' coparenting in tasks other than play – for example, attachment at the family level, limit setting, feeding interactions, sleep, and teaching, to name but a few. There remain so many more avenues to explore in terms of the resources and struggles of the baby and the couple.

References

Ainsworth, M. D. S., Blehar, M. C., Waters, E., & Wall, S. (1978). *Patterns of attachment: A psychological study of the strange situation.* Hillsdale, NJ: Lawrence Erlbaum Associates.

Ammaniti, M., Mazzoni, S., & Menozzi, F. (2010). Ecografia in gravidanza: Studio della co-genitorialità. *Infanzia e Adolescenza, 3,* 151–157.

Baker, J., McHale, J., Stozier, A., & Cecil, D. (2010). The nature of mother-grandmother coparenting alliances in families with incarcerated mothers: A pilot study. *Family Process, 49*(2), 165–184.

Bateson, G. (1979). *Mind and nature.* Toronto: Bantam Books.

Beebe, B., & Lachmann, F. (1994). Representation and internalization in infancy: Three principles of salience. *Psychoanalytic Psychology, 11,* 127–165.

Beebe, B., & Lachmann, F. (2002). *Infant research and adult treatment: Co-constructing interactions.* Hillsdale, NJ: Analytic Press.

Byng-Hall, J. (1995). *Rewriting family scripts: Improvisation and systems change.* New York: Guilford Press.

Carpenter, M., Nagell, K., & Tomasello, M. (1998). Social cognition, joint attention and communicative competence from 9 to 15 months of age. *Monographs of the Society for Research in Child Development, 63*(4).

Corboz-Warnery, A., Fivaz-Depeursinge, E., Guertsch-Bettens, C., & Favez, N. (1993). Systemic analysis of father mother baby interactions: The Lausanne Triadic Play. *Infant Mental Health Journal, 14*(4), 298–316.

Dunn, J., & Munn, P. (1988). *Relationships within families.* Oxford: Oxford Science.

Emde, R. N., & Oppenheim, D. (1995). Shame, guilt, and the Oedipal drama: Developmental considerations concerning morality and the referencing of others. In J. P. Tangney & K. W. Fischer (Eds.), *Self-conscious emotions: The psychology of shame, guilt, embarrassment, and pride* (pp. 413–436). New York: Guilford.

Favez, N., Lopes, F., Bernard, M., Frascarolo, F., Lavanchy Scaiola, C., Corboz-Warnery, A., & Fivaz-Depeursinge, E. (2012). The development of family alliance from pregnancy to toddlerhood and child outcomes at 5 years. *Family Process, 51,* 542–556.

Fivaz, R. (1989). *L'ordre et la volupté.* Lausanne: Presses Polytechniques Romandes.

Fivaz-Depeursinge, E., & Corboz-Warnery, A. (1999). *The primary triangle: A developmental systems view of fathers, mothers and infants.* New York: Basic Books.

Fivaz-Depeursinge, E., Fivaz, R., & Kaufmann, L. (1982). Encadrement du développement, le point de vue systémique: Fonctions pédagogique, parentale, thérapeutique. *Cahiers Critiques de Thérapie Familiale et de Pratiques de Réseaux* (4–5), 63–74.

Frascarolo, F., & Favez, N. (1999). Comment et à qui s'attache le jeune enfant? *Le carnet Psy,* October, 39–40.

Freud, S. (1909). Analysis of a phobia in a five-year old boy. In J. Strachey et al. (Eds.), *The standard edition of the complete psychological works of Sigmund Freud* (Vol. 10, pp. 3–149). London: Hogarth and the Institute of Psychoanalysis.

Hart, S., Carrington, H., Tronick, E., & Carroll, S. (2004). When infants lose exclusive maternal attention: Is it jealousy? *Infancy, 6*(1), 57–78.

Hervé, M., Andreu, M., & Maury, M. (1998). *Infant's contributions during triadic mother-infant-therapist consultations.* Paper presented at International Society for the Study of Behavioral Development, Bern.

Lachmann, F. (2010). Addendum: Afterthoughts on Littel Hans and the universality of the Oedipus complex. *Psychoanalytic Inquiry, 30*(6), 557–562.

Legerstee, M., Ellenbogen, B., Nienhuis, T., & Marsh, H. (2010). Social bonds, triadic relationships and goals: Preconditions for the emergence of human jealousy. In S. Hart & M. Legerstee (Eds.), *Handbook of jealousy: Theory, research and multidisciplinary approaches* (pp. 163–191). Malden, MA: Wiley-Blackwell.

Lichtenberg, J. (2008). *Sensuality and sexuality across the divide of shame.* Hillsdale: Analytic Press.

Lopes, F., & Favez, N. (2012). *Parental and interparental mentalization and links with family interactions: Preliminary results.* Paper presented at World Association for Infant Mental Health, Cape Town.

Lyons-Ruth, K. (1998). Implicit relational knowing: Its role in development and psychoanalytic treatment. *Infant Mental Health Journal, 19*(3), 282–289.

Marcu, I. (2013). *Parental insightfulness regarding the child's inner world: Its contribution to the family alliance in families with toddlers.* Dissertation, University of Haifa.

McHale, J. (1997). Overt and covert coparenting processes in the family. *Family Process, 36,* 183–201.

McHale, J. (2007). When infants grow up in multiperson relationship systems. *Infant-Mental Health Journal, 28*(4), 370–392.

McHale, J. (2013). Le coparentage comme construit universel caractérisant diverses formes familiales: Avancées et perspectives. In N. Favez, F. Frascarolo & H. Tissot (Eds.), *Naître et grandir au sein de la triade: Le développement de l'alliance familiale* (pp. 251–268). Brussels: De Boeck.

McHale, J., Fivaz-Depeursinge, E., Dickstein, S., Robertson, J., & & Daley, M. (2008). New evidence for the social embeddedness of infant's early triangular capacities. *Family Process, 47,* 445–463.

McHale, J., & Irace, K. (2011). Coparenting and diverse family systems. In J. McHale & K. Lindhal (Eds.), *Coparenting: A conceptual and clinical examination of family systems* (pp. 15–37). Washington, DC: American Psychological Association Press.

McHale, J., Kuersten-Hogan, R., Lauretti, A., & Rasmussen, J. L. (2000). Parental reports of coparenting and observed coparenting behavior during the toddler period. *Journal of Family Psychology, 14*(2), 220–236.

Minuchin, P. (1985). Families and individual development: Provocations from the field of family therapy. *Child Development, 56,* 289–302.

Minuchin, S. (1974). *Families & family therapy.* Boston: Harvard University Press.

Minuchin, S., Nichols, M. P., & Lee, W. Y. (2006). *Assessing families and couples: From symptom to system.* Boston: Allyn & Bacon.

Nadel, J., & Tremblay-Leveau, H. (1999). Early perception of social contingencies and interpersonal intentionality: Dyadic and triadic paradigms. In P. Rochat (Ed.), *Early social cognition: Understanding others in the first months of life* (pp. 189–212). Mahwah, NJ: Erlbaum.

Nahum, J. (2010). Prefiguring and refiguring triangular interpersonal relationships: Commentary on paper by Elisabeth Fivaz-Depeursinge, Chloé Lavanchy-Scaiola, & Nicolas Favez. *Psychoanalytic Dialogues, 20*(2), 141–150.

Papousek, M., Schieche, M., & Wurmser, H. (Eds.). (2008). *Disorders of behavioral and emotional regulation in the first years of life: Early risks and intervention in the developing parent-infant relationship.* Washington, DC: Zero to Three.

Paquette, D. (2004). Theorizing the father-child relationship: Mechanisms and developmental outcomes. *Human Development, 47,* 193–219.

Philipp, D. (2012). Reflective Family Play: A brief family therapy model for the infant and preschool population. *Infant Mental Health Journal, 33*(6), 599–608.

Philipp, D., Fivaz-Depeursinge, E., Favez, N., & Corboz-Warnery, A. (2009). Young infants' triangular communication with their parents in the context of maternal postpartum breakdown: Case studies. *Infant Mental Health Journal, 30,* 341–365.

Philipp, D., & Hayos, C. (2013). Le Reflective Family Play: un traitement de la famille entière centré sur l'attachement et le système familial. In N. Favez, F. Frascarolo-Moutinot & H. Tissot (Eds.), *Naître et grandir au sein de la triade* (pp. 227–250). Bruxelles: De Boeck.

Reiss, D. (1989). The represented and practicing family: Contrasting visions of family continuity. In A. J. Sameroff & R. N. Emde (Eds.), *Relationship disturbances in early childhood* (pp. 191–220). New York: Basic Books.

Rusconi-Serpa, S., Sancho-Rossignol, A., & McDonough, S. (2009). Video-feedback in parent-infant treatments. *Child and Adolescent Psychiatric Clinics of North America, 18*(3), 735–751.

Selby, J. M., & Bradley, B. S. (2003). Infants in groups: A paradigm for the study of early social experience. *Human Development, 46,* 197–221.

Stern, D. (1985). *The interpersonal world of the infant.* New York: Basic Books.

Stern, D. (2004). *The present moment in psychotherapy and everyday life.* New York: W.W. Norton.

Stern, D. (2008). *The issue of internal representations in dyads and triads. Discussion of Fivaz-Depeursinge: "The infancy of triangular communication in the family."* Paper presented at the Conference on Gestalt Therapy, Rome.

Stern, D. (2010). Forward to Fivaz-Depeursinge, Lavanchy-Scaiola, & Favez paper. *Psychoanalytic Dialogues, 20*(2), 121–124.

Tremblay, H., & Rovira, K. (2007). Joint visual attention and social triangular engagement at 3 and 6 months. *Infant Behavior and Development, 30,* 366–379.

Tremblay, H., Rovira, K., Lemonnier, L., & Sorin, A-L. (submitted). *Neonates' triangular communication abilities.*

Index